A MARVELOUS SOLITUDE

The Bernard Berenson Lectures on the Italian Renaissance
Sponsored by Villa I Tatti
The Harvard University Center for Italian Renaissance Studies
Florence, Italy

A Marvelous Solitude

The Art of Reading in Early Modern Europe

LINA BOLZONI

Translated by Sylvia Greenup

HARVARD UNIVERSITY PRESS
*Cambridge, Massachusetts,
and London, England*
2023

Copyright © 2023 by the President and Fellows of Harvard College
All rights reserved
Printed in the United States of America

FIRST PRINTING

First published in Italian as *Una meravigliosa solitudine : l'arte di leggere nell'Europa moderna*: Berenson Lectures 2012, Villa I Tatti, Firenze, The Harvard University Center for Italian Renaissance Studies, by Giulio Einaudi editore, Torino, 2019.

Library of Congress Cataloging-in-Publication Data
Names: Bolzoni, Lina, author. | Greenup, Sylvia, translator.
Title: A marvelous solitude : the art of reading in early modern Europe / Lina Bolzoni ; translated by Sylvia Greenup.
Other titles: Meravigliosa solitudine. English
Description: Cambridge, Massachusetts ; London, England : Harvard University Press, 2023. | Series: The Bernard Berenson Lectures on the Italian Renaissance | Includes bibliographical references and index.
Identifiers: LCCN 2023003427 | ISBN 9780674660236 (cloth)
Subjects: LCSH: Books and reading—Europe—History. | Books and reading—Psychological aspects. | Literature—History and criticism.
Classification: LCC Z1003.5.E9 B6516 2023 | DDC 028/.9094—dc23/eng/20230417
LC record available at https://lccn.loc.gov/2023003427

Contents

	List of Illustrations	*vii*
	Introduction	*1*
1	Petrarch and the Magical Space of the Library	*13*
2	The Text as a Body and the Resurrection of the Ancients	*35*
3	Portraits, or The Desire to See the Author	*64*
4	Reading, Writing, and the Construction of the Self	*129*
5	Machiavelli's Letter to Vettori	*143*
6	Montaigne's Tower	*161*
7	Tasso and the Dangers of Reading	*179*
	Epilogue: Ruskin, Proust, and the "Miracle of Reading"	*193*
	Notes	*201*
	Index	*243*

List of Illustrations

Introduction

Figure I.1 Teodoro Wolf Ferrari, advertisement poster for the Olivetti M1 typewriter, 1912.
Figure I.2 Bronzino, *Portrait of Laura Battiferri.*
Figure I.3 Anonymous artist, sixteenth century, *Portrait of Sir Thomas Bodley.*

Chapter 1

Figure 1.1 Anonymous artist, Portrait of Petrarch at his desk.
Figure 1.2 Francesco Petrarca, *De remediis utriusque fortunae.*

Chapter 2

Figure 2.1 Roman girl discovered under the Via Appia in Roma in 1485, in Bartolomeo Fonzio, *Liber monumentorum Romanae urbis et aliorum locorum.*
Figure 2.2 Giovanni Boccaccio, *Genealogie deorum gentilium.*
Figure 2.3 A genealogical tree, in Giovanni Boccaccio, *Genealogie deorum gentilium.*
Figure 2.4 Poggio Bracciolini, Florence, translation of Xenophon's *Cyropaedia.*
Figure 2.5 The burning of Jerome of Prague, in John Foxe, *The Book of Martyrs.*

Chapter 3

Figure 3.1 Angelo Decembrio, *De Politia literaria,* frontispiece.
Figure 3.2 Justus van Ghent (or Pedro Berruguete), *Portrait of Federico da Montefeltro with His Son Guidubaldo.*
Figure 3.3 Piero della Francesca, Portrait of Federico da Montefeltro and Battista Sforza.

List of Illustrations

Figure 3.4 Piero della Francesca, triumphal scenes on the back of the portraits of Federico da Montefeltro and Battista Sforza.
Figure 3.5 The wood inlays in the Studiolo di Urbino, Palazzo Ducale.
Figure 3.6 The portraits of illustrious men in the Studiolo di Urbino, Palazzo Ducale.
Figure 3.7 Justus van Ghent, *Gregory the Great*.
Figure 3.8 Justus van Ghent, *Pope Pius II*.
Figure 3.9 Justus van Ghent and Pedro Berruguete, *Pope Sixtus IV*.
Figure 3.10 Justus van Ghent, *St. Ambrose*.
Figure 3.11 Justus van Ghent and Pedro Berruguete, *Augustine*.
Figure 3.12 Justus van Ghent and Pedro Berruguete, *Cardinal Bessarion*.
Figure 3.13 Justus van Ghent and Pedro Berruguete, *St. Jerome*.
Figure 3.14 Justus van Ghent, *Duns Scotus*.
Figure 3.15 Justus van Ghent and Pedro Berruguete, *Saint Thomas Aquinas*.
Figure 3.16 Justus van Ghent and Pedro Berruguete, *Albertus Magnus*.
Figure 3.17 Justus van Ghent, *Cicero*.
Figure 3.18 Justus van Ghent and Pedro Berruguete, *Ptolemy*.
Figure 3.19 Justus van Ghent, *Euclid*.
Figure 3.20 Justus van Ghent, *Moses*.
Figure 3.21 Justus van Ghent and Pedro Berruguete, *Plato*.
Figure 3.22 Justus van Ghent and Pedro Berruguete, *Seneca*.
Figure 3.23 Justus van Ghent and Pedro Berruguete, *Solon*.
Figure 3.24 Justus van Ghent, *Bartolo da Sassoferrato*.
Figure 3.25 Justus van Ghent and Pedro Berruguete, *Aristotle*.
Figure 3.26 Justus van Ghent, *Solomon*.
Figure 3.27 Justus van Ghent, *Homer*.
Figure 3.28 Justus van Ghent e Pedro Berruguete, *Virgil*.
Figure 3.29 Justus van Ghent and Pedro Berruguete, *Vittorino da Feltre*.
Figure 3.30 Justus van Ghent and Pedro Berruguete, *Peter Abanus*.
Figure 3.31 Justus van Ghent, *Hippocrates*.
Figure 3.32 Justus van Ghent and Pedro Berruguete, *Dante*.
Figure 3.33 Justus van Ghent, *Boetius*.
Figure 3.34 Justus van Ghent and Pedro Berruguete, *Francesco Petrarca*.
Figure 3.35 Albrecht Dürer, *Portrait of Erasmus*.
Figure 3.36 Quentin Matsys, *Portrait of Erasmus*.
Figure 3.37 Quentin Matsys, *Portrait of Peter Gilles*.
Figure 3.38 Thomas More, Peter Gilles, and Raphael Hythlodaeus in Gilles's garden, in Thomas More, *Utopia*.
Figure 3.39 Raphael Hythlodaeus shows Peter Gilles and Thomas More the island of Utopia, in Thomas More, *Utopia*.

List of Illustrations

Figure 3.40 Portrait of Ariosto and motto *pro bono malum* in Ludovico Ariosto, *Orlando Furioso*.
Figure 3.41 A ewe suckling a wolf cub, in Ludovico Ariosto, *Orlando Furioso*.

Chapter 4

Figure 4.1 *Gorgo dell'artificio*, in Giulio Camillo, *Trattato delle materie*.

Chapter 6

Figure 6.1 Montaigne's tower, Dordogne, Saint Michel de Montaigne.
Figure 6.2 Montaigne's tower, inscriptions on the beams.

Chapter 7

Figure 7.1 Parmigianino, *Portrait of a Man Reading a Book*.

Introduction

> A book is like a garden that can be carried in a sleeve, . . . a being that speaks on behalf of the dead and acts as an interpreter for the living, a friend who will not go to bed before you yourself have fallen asleep.
> —Al Jâdiz, Arab sage of the ninth century

Books can cause insanity. Petrarch had not read *Don Quixote,* but he was already fully aware that this might happen, for he had made books—whether books to be read or books to be written—into one of the great loves of his life.[1] It was a passion he recounted and described in meticulous detail, so much so that it became an important component in the construction of his own image, his own myth.

Should we believe that Petrarch and, like him, so many others we shall encounter in the following pages as they relate their experiences as readers were people from a world that has disappeared forever? In this world, reading is a shared experience but at the same time something absolutely intimate and personal; it is a journey where, in meeting the other, one recognizes (and redesigns) one's own self—a life-giving experience that offers hospitality to an unknown guest and, for this very reason, is at once fascinating and dangerous.[2] It is a voyage to the outermost bounds of time and space, where myriad virtual worlds are delineated and reality stretches out into the infinitely possible. One feels the need to ask this question because we live in a world where technological transformations are taking place at a speed quite unknown in the past.[3] Possibilities are opening up that not even science fiction had imagined, and differences between generations and within the same generation are exacerbated as never before. This is something we can experience every day, but a few dates will help us to grasp the speed of this change. Writing, the first great revolution in means of communication, dates back to about 4000 BC; Egyptian hieroglyphics appeared somewhere about 3200 BC, while alphabetic writing was not adopted until 1000 BC. About the third century AD, the codex replaced the scroll, thus creating the kind of "book" that has lasted up to the present day. The great adventure of mobile type printing started about the middle of the fifteenth century. The revolutions of our own time began in the last decades of the twentieth century: the word "internet" dates from 1974; the "web" originated in 1991 in the CERN laboratories and became widespread in the 1990s; 1998 saw the start of Google—and that was just the beginning.

We can ask ourselves whether what happened in the past will happen once again: perhaps the new technologies will not bring about a radical break with the past but will lead rather to new forms of coexistence and continuity. The multiple creative forms of orality have not ceased to exist even in the age of printing, and manuscripts are produced even while printed books are circulated and sold. This question should be asked because it is now clear that the new instruments of communication are not just objects, not just instruments as such: they have a profound impact on the individual using them (or being used by them), to the extent that they transform expectations, abilities, and emotions and consequently affect the brain itself, which is subjected to a pace of life quite unthinkable in the past.[4] Indeed some people have decreed the end of the book itself as well as the end of, or a profound crisis in, reading, at least in the forms hitherto known.

Because of the far-reaching transformations of the present moment but also perhaps as a reaction to the dangers that are emerging, I became interested in the idea of retracing the great myths that the Renaissance constructed about reading. I wished to look more closely at the way writers represented themselves as readers in the centuries that saw the birth of the modern world in Europe. In particular, I have chosen to focus on a powerful and enduring theme: reading as a dialogue with books, an encounter with the authors who gave life to them. Since these authors often belong to the past, our theme may be usefully renamed "reading as a dialogue with the dead," a form of lay resurrection or a necromantic rite, to use an image dear to Thomas Greene.[5]

It is this set of ideas that led me to take Petrarch as my starting point. Every beginning must of course be an arbitrary choice, and indeed Petrarch's views on reading had strong connections with the classical world, as well as with medieval monastic experiences and naturally with Dante, the great

Introduction

unacknowledged interlocutor. Dante presents us with another way of engaging in dialogue with the dead. Virgil is, of course, his guide, but Dante dialogues with the great men of antiquity in Limbo, in the world beyond the grave, whereas Petrarch dialogues with them in his library in Vaucluse and does so on equal terms, even to the point of reproaching them for their weaknesses and errors. Or, at least, that is how the two poets represent themselves; that is how they construct the scenario in which they position themselves.

My point of departure will be an image that has enjoyed a certain popularity on the web, the *Portrait of Laura Battiferri with Her iPad, after Agnolo Bronzino,* by Mike Licht.[6] This is part of a "gallery of works featuring technology and iconic modern objects juxtaposed with classic works of art." In some respects, this juxtaposition brings to mind Teodoro Wolf Ferrari's 1912 poster depicting Dante as he points to the M1, the first Italian typewriter produced by Olivetti, which had been presented the previous year at the Turin Universal Exhibition (see Figure I.1). When the instruments of communication change, their association with memories from the past may create not only a sense of estrangement but also an aura effect that is reflected onto the present and in some ways legitimizes and ennobles it. If Dante had been alive in 1912, it is suggested, he would have written the *Divine Comedy* by hitting the keys of an Olivetti typewriter; if Laura Battiferri were alive today, she would be holding not a manuscript but an iPad. However, besides this anachronistic play, what is intriguing is the choice of this particular portrait by Bronzino (see Figure I.2), all the more so if we examine it more closely, bearing in mind its original context and the rich cluster of words and images from which it sprang and to which it gave life.[7]

Depicted in the portrait is a woman poet, called Laura, just like the woman loved by Petrarch. Her profile, however, reminds us of Dante's face, as fixed by tradition. She is therefore at once object and subject of poetry, a kind of hermaphrodite. Laura is, moreover, represented as a reader: the book she is holding in her long, slender fingers is open at two sonnets by Petrarch (LXIV and CCXL), which are, however, not consecutive in the *Canzoniere*. It is therefore an anthology, a reading path arranged by Laura herself or by someone else for her. Both inside and around this sixteenth-century portrait, there exists a world of words: we can see the poems Laura is reading, but we are also reminded of those poems she herself wrote. Furthermore, this portrait occasioned an exchange of eulogies in verse between Laura and Bronzino, a painter who

Figure I.1. Teodoro Wolf Ferrari, advertisment poster for the Olivetti M1 typewriter, 1912. *Archivi Alinari, Florence.*

was not averse to writing poetry himself and was in his turn to be a source of inspiration for other poets belonging to the circle of his Florentine friends. This portrait and its modern reworking in the age of the internet may therefore introduce some of the themes we shall try to develop: the relationship between reading and writing; how writers' self-representation as readers contributes to their "self fashioning,"[8] to the way in which they construct their own identity for themselves and for others; the possibility that all around the act of reading—and around the reader-writer—a community of friends, of interpreter-readers, may come into being; the role that the portrait, in its various forms, may play in celebrating the pleasant and sometimes dangerous rites of reading.

Introduction

Figure I.2. Bronzino, *Portrait of Laura Battiferri,* oil on wood, 87.5×70 cm, ca. 1555–1560, Palazzo Vecchio, Florence. *Archivi Alinari, Florence.*

We, in our turn, will offer hospitality to the authors: from Petrarch and Boccaccio to the humanists, to Machiavelli, Erasmus, Montaigne, and Tasso. We shall listen to what they tell us about their own experiences as readers; we shall observe—for example, in the case of the Studiolo of Federico da Montefeltro—how they construct around the library and their own selves an extraordinary theatrical machine aimed at self-promotion, a stage where first-rate actors give outstanding performances. We shall close, with a leap over the centuries, by examining an unexpected return of our topos of reading in the writings of Ruskin and Proust.

The aim of this book is to allow ourselves to be enchanted by the myth of reading created by the authors it discusses, to elicit elements that are certainly fascinating but perhaps also true. Admittedly, not only nowadays but also in the centuries we are surveying, it is abundantly clear just how illusory was one of the central threads of this myth, namely, the idea that the text was a kind of *speculum animi,* that the word was a transparent means of access to the inner life (that of the other and, therefore, as if in a mirror, of one's own). In retracing this experience, I have deliberately ignored or bypassed—left suspended in a sense—many of the components of modern criticism and literary theory, from formalism to structuralism, from the idea of the death of the author to the concept of the autonomy of the text, of its character as an artificial linguistic and rhetorical construct.

There are also other questions that will not be examined, even if they are related to our theme, such as the social history of reading, or the different modes of reading: reading aloud to an audience of listeners, reading in a low voice, for oneself, or silent reading, which is the most common form nowadays. It is true, on the other hand, that it is precisely reading aloud that gives, as it were, a body to the theme we are exploring, because it restores a voice to the book, allowing it to speak out and create a community around a text. Some excellent examples of this have been provided by Alberto Manguel.[9]

We shall not be dealing with the passion of book collecting, nor shall we venture into that domain of uncertain contours, where the passion for books and for book collecting turns into an obsession called "bibliomania." The *Encyclopédie* devoted two entries to this phenomenon, and a penitent bibliomaniac, Louis Bollioud-Mermet, described this obsession with a suspect precision of detail that revealed perhaps what remained of his former love.[10] We shall only mention that Walter Benjamin showed no interest at all in marking out the boundary line between book collecting and bibliomania when, in a celebrated 1931 essay, he furnished a description of himself as he took his books from the boxes where they had been confined for two years. He retraces in memory where and when each book came into his possession: "I am not exaggerating when I say that to a true collector the acquisition of an old book is its rebirth." Thus, Benjamin explains, in old age we may still experience the childhood pleasure that consists in the faith that existence may be made anew: "For a collector—and I mean a real collector, a collector as he ought to be—ownership is the most intimate relationship that he can have to objects. Not that they come alive in him; it is he who lives in them."[11]

Introduction

The world of reading is a fascinating galaxy, and I shall leave the reader with the task, and hopefully also the pleasure, of finding in this book a stimulus to further explore questions that I have only touched on and that may open up new perspectives. I should point out that in our history, there are no women. In the centuries I have examined, I have not been able to find—though I hope others will—any texts in which women are depicted as engaging in a dialogue on an equal basis with the authors they are reading.[12] Certainly, further research can be carried out so as to enrich the already considerable body of critical work that has brought to light the female presence in literary production. There are, in any case, evident reasons to explain the difficulty I have encountered. It is well known that over the centuries women's access to culture has been viewed with profound distrust; the teaching of reading and the various forms of knowledge was dealt out sparingly, depending on social status and the diverse circumstances that made it necessary to allow such weak but dangerously sensual creatures to gain access to books. There is a text that might appear grotesque and paradoxical if it were not a serious and faithful interpreter of what must have been at the time shared feelings and that offered a kind of compendium of the perils that awaited women who read. The first months of 1801 saw the publication in France of the *Bill of Law Forbidding Women to Learn to Read*. After an extensive catalogue of considerations regarding the damage caused in public and domestic life by women who know how to read, the articles of the law are then deduced "rationally." For example, Article XII reads, "Reason demands that the only books belonging to wives shall be their husbands, living books, where night and day they may learn to read their destiny." Article XLVII lays down, "Reason demands that henceforth permission to be writers, intellectuals or artists shall be granted exclusively to courtesans." Article LXIV states, "Reason demands that women who persist in writing books shall not be allowed to have children," and Article XVI states something that is "obvious": "Reason demands that women shall abstain from astronomy: let them count the eggs down in the yard, not the stars in the firmament!"[13] It is significant that the author, Sylvain Maréchal, had taken part in the French Revolution and had contributed together with François Noël Babeuf, Filippo Buonarroti, and Augustin Darthé to the writing of *The Manifesto of the Equals* (1796), in which was proclaimed the need for radical social equality. Women were clearly left on the sidelines even in Utopia.

Actually, that bill of law was also a reaction to a changing reality. The voices of women, also as protagonists in the experience of reading, were destined to be heard louder and louder, albeit amid a thousand difficulties. There springs to mind *A Room of One's Own,* which Virginia Woolf wrote in 1929 and in which the question of what and how women read (or do not read) and write (or do not write) is addressed in a style that is at once stimulating, polemical, and original. A few years earlier, in 1926, in an essay based on a talk given at a girls' school in Kent, Woolf had urged women readers to become friends—accomplices even—of the author whose book they were reading so that they could subsequently become judges; she concluded with a splendid eulogy of reading as pure pleasure: "I have sometimes dreamt, at least, that when the Day of Judgment dawns and the great conquerors and lawyers and statesmen come to receive their rewards—their crowns, their laurels, their names carved indelibly upon imperishable marble—the Almighty will turn to Peter and will say, not without a certain envy when he sees us coming with our books under our arms, 'Look, these need no reward. We have nothing to give them here. They have loved reading.'"[14]

What ideas or attitudes from the centuries that saw the birth of the modern world are still relevant nowadays? It is noteworthy that the texts we meet, devoted as they are to engaging in a dialogue with books, adopt those forms that are themselves the most dialogical, the letter and the dialogue, as if to reflect their theme in the form itself, to enact in their turn a ritual to which they are giving life. This tradition, as we shall see, also constitutes a reply to the criticism made in Plato's *Phaedrus* (274b–275b) against the written word, which, since it neither speaks nor replies, is essentially lifeless. The texts examined in this book therefore adopt those forms that are closest to orality, namely, the dialogue or that substitute for an oral exchange between friends, which is the letter. At the same time, their overall tendency is to incorporate the text into life, to make reading a vital experience, to create a theater of the mind animated by the presence of the authors. Something similar was taught by mnemonic techniques, which sought in particular to re-create in a person's inner life moments and characters from the Bible as if they were present, next to and together with the person who was reading or meditating.[15]

The theme of a dialogue with books may strike us as distant and extraneous when it becomes some sort of magic rite, conjuring up a lost world in which the secrets of beauty are deposited. In other respects, however, it

Introduction

may sound familiar. We have learned that if the reader needs books, books also need readers, as George Steiner has written, for it is precisely through the encounter with readers, be they male or female, that the book takes on life—in fact comes back to life—through all the various ways in which it enters into a dialogue with them, interacting with their imagination and their passions.[16] In this light, the critic-reader is no longer someone in possession of the true interpretation of the text, the external "scientific" observer who dissects and reveals its artistry, its hidden structures; rather, they are someone who in turn is willing to be closely involved in this experience. Thus, a new approach gives new life to some of the metaphors we will encounter as we look through the ancient texts: friendship, for example, or the journey. The friendship created in the dialogue with the text may become a mark of an ethics of reading that entails respect for the other, the recognition of their otherness, something that in fact happens with a friend;[17] the journey may become the image of the freedom experienced by the reader, who is no longer a shadow produced by the book but a shadow that takes on life and solidity, so much so that they can break down the order established by the book and venture freely into the spaces of the text like a poacher in pursuit of their prey, free to take possession of whatever they need.[18]

Equally persistent and metamorphic is the magic of the library, its capacity to transport one into another world and to create at the same time a profound and secret bond with the self of the person who has created it. At the end of the sixteenth century, for example, the library became a portrait of the soul, as we learn from the words accompanying the portrait of Sir Thomas Bodley, who founded the Bodleian Library in Oxford in 1598 (see Figure I.3):

Thomae Bodlaei quicquid mortale Tabella
ingentemque animam Bibliotheca refert.

(This image portrays the mortal Thomas Bodley, but the library his vast soul)[19]

The library thus becomes a secret self-portrait and perhaps part of the narrative game of mirrors. An example of this is the library belonging to Captain Nemo, which is the first room into which he introduces his prisoner guests: "If every library is autobiographical—writes Alberto Manguel—that

Figure I.3. Anonymous artist, sixteenth century, *Portrait of Sir Thomas Bodley*, Bodleian Library, Oxford. *Bodleian Library, Oxford.*

of Captain Nemo reveals something of the hidden identity of its reader," someone who loves liberty and is terrorized by the world of the Earth's surface, by the society of men."[20]

Peter Kien, the protagonist of Elias Canetti's *Autodafé*, has devoted his entire life to studying Chinese and creating a large library.[21] At a certain point, his housekeeper, whom he has unwisely married, kicks him out of the house. She is, however, unable to separate him from his books, because he has stored them in his memory and gradually replaces them mentally in the rooms of a hotel where he has sought lodgings. Peter Kien has not only constructed his library but actually become his library: he has made it into

Introduction

protective armor against the pulsating and dangerous disorder of reality, and at the same time, he has brought back onto the twentieth-century scene an ancient typology, that of the man-library. Pliny the Elder and Seneca the Elder cited examples of this; Petrarch was fascinated by it; Pico della Mirandola was in a sense its embodiment. At the end of the sixteenth century, Filippo Gesualdo exalted the superiority of the library of the memory, freed as it was from any hindrance, capable of making knowledge immediately visible and enabling man to return to the Edenic state.[22] Would he have recognized any of these characteristics in the virtual world of today?

"I have provided a library (which by the way could furnish the surest and completest biography of myself)," wrote Bernard Berenson in May 1956, in the document where he outlines the future of I Tatti, the villa in the Florentine hills, which, together with the library, the collection of works of art, and the gardens, he entrusted to the University of Harvard so that it might become a center where scholars from different countries could devote themselves to the study of the civilization of the Renaissance.[23] Part of the research for this book was carried out at Villa I Tatti, where I had the opportunity to discuss its results with the international community of scholars that was there at the time. This experience was both a privilege and a pleasure. At times, I must confess, it seemed to me that the old magic of the library, whose development I was studying, was still present, mirrored in that place and in my work.

This book is based on the "Berenson Lectures" that I gave in Villa I Tatti in October and November 2012. I wish to thank Lino Pertile, who asked me to deliver them, and the members of the public themselves, whose attention, questions, and observations offered a most valuable contribution to my work. In the autumn of 2017, I returned to Villa I Tatti at the invitation of its director, Alina Payne, to continue my research, and I once more found the amazing support that the community of I Tatti offers. In particular, I wish to express my gratitude to Alina for her friendship as well as for her attention and intellectual stimulus.

This book is indebted to many other people as well. Among these are my students of the Scuola Normale Superiore of Pisa; New York University; the IUSS (the University School of Advanced Studies) of Pavia; the participants in the conference of the Society of Italian Studies, organized by Martin McLaughlin and held in Oxford in 2015; and my friends, who patiently listened to me. Among them, I wish to thank Marc Fumaroli, Nadia Fusini, Nicola Gardini, Siri Hustvedt, Carlo Ossola, Sandra Pesante,

Giorgio Pinotti, David Quint, Jane Tylus, and Marco Vigevani. I remember with affectionate gratitude Ernesto Franco and Irene Babboni, who were with me throughout the writing of this book.

Over the period of time it has taken for the English edition of this book to be produced I have contracted debts of gratitude towards many people. Among these I should at least like to thank Sylvia Greenup, who translated with intelligence, punctiliousness and passion a text that presented not a few complexities; Alessandro Benassi, without whose help I would never have solved the many difficulties presented by the acquisition of the necessary image rights; and finally, Emily Silk and Thomas Gruber, whose support and enthusiasm throughout have been much appreciated.

1

Petrarch and the Magical Space of the Library

1. "I Can Never Satisfy My Hunger for Books"

Petrarch took great care in constructing an image of himself as a reader, which is further proof of his ability to rework tradition in new ways (see Figure 1.1).[1] His work might also be regarded as a unique analysis of the different kinds of pleasure that reading affords, a record of the subtle variety of effects produced by the different ways in which it may be practiced.[2] I use the term "pleasure" because Petrarch had no qualms about infusing great physicality and emotion into the description of his relationship with books. "Feel free to give me all your books," he writes, for example, to Boccaccio on 28 May 1362, in a letter in which he describes himself as *librorum avidum* (greedy for books): "I am always avidly on the lookout for more. If you desire to get rid of the very instruments of literature by selling your books and are utterly determined to do so, I am grateful, by heaven, that you have offered them to me before anyone else since, as you say and I do not deny, I am so greedy for books."[3]

This profession was prompted by the words of Pietro da Siena, one of those preachers who achieved great success by stirring up great fear. Pietro had sent a terrible message to Petrarch and Boccaccio: Christ himself, he stated, had spoken to him, telling him that they must renounce literature and books and seek only spiritual goods if they wished to avoid eternal damnation. The message had shocked Boccaccio and left him deeply troubled, so Petrarch wrote to offer his friend reassurance and encourage him not to abandon the comfort of letters; nevertheless, should the need arise, he declared himself more than willing, as we have seen, to take all of Boccaccio's

Figure 1.1. Anonymous artist, portrait of Petrarch at his desk, fresco, Palazzo Liviano, Sala dei Giganti, Padua. *Archivi Alinari, Florence.*

books. Reading was for Petrarch a passionate love affair that one could not forswear, not even when threatened with all the torments of Hell.

The way such a passion unfolds and the forms it assumes are minutely described, starting with the unique pleasures reading affords: "I can never satisfy my hunger for books," Petrarch explains to Giovanni dell' Incisa, probably around 1346, "and perhaps I already own more than I should; but with books it is just the same as with other things: the more we obtain what we have been looking for, the more our greed is stimulated. In fact, there is something special about books. Gold, silver, precious stones, purple robes, palaces of marble, well-tended fields, paintings, palfreys with all their trappings, and all other such things give a silent and superficial pleasure; books instead please inwardly; they speak with us and confer with us, they attach themselves to us, that is, with a lively and penetrating familiarity."[4] The pleasure of reading is, Petrarch feels, more intimate and more intense than the satisfaction afforded by other worldly goods: its joy, which gets to the marrow itself, is the joy of a conversation, its pleasure stemming from the dialogue a book sets up with its reader. What is particularly relevant here is the way Petrarch rearticulates the theme of speaking books, so that this becomes a focal point in his portrayal of himself as a reader-writer; in doing so, he also performs the task of importing the models of orality and interpersonal exchange into the heart of modern book culture, into the very core of burgeoning humanism. We may see this strategy as implicitly answering the accusations leveled by Plato's *Phaedrus* against the written text (274b–275b), branded as an artificial repository of memory, fixed and undialogical. In the tradition that Petrarch crucially contributes to establishing, the book speaks, dialogues with its reader, because it is seen as something alive, because it carries within it the soul of its author.

An important key to understanding this idea is provided by a metaphor illustrating the relationship between a book and its author that appears in the famous letter Petrarch addressed to Boccaccio in 1359.[5] Here the poet recalls their first meeting, which took place in 1350, when Petrarch was on his way to Rome. "I cannot forget," he says, "the time when, as I was hastening across Italy in midwinter, you not only sent me affectionate greetings, which are like footsteps of the spirit, but came personally in haste to meet me, on the heels of your admirable poem, motivated by your great desire to see a man whom you had yet to meet. You thus revealed to me, whom you had determined to love, first the face of your talent and later that of your person."[6] The rather self-satisfied game of correspondences that emerges from Petrarch's words, only partly reproduced by the translation, pivots on the idea of the text as the face (*vultum*) of the soul. We see here a reworking of the topos of the book as a mirror, duly recorded by Curtius in his archive of European literary memory.[7] Petrarch breathes new life into this idea by suggesting there exists a reciprocal relationship between inside and outside, between the text and the body. The text makes visible what lies hidden inwardly, and, through this unveiling, the act of reading almost becomes a physical encounter; it allows the person reading to summon up the person read, to see, as it were, the contours of the other's soul in their mind's eye. This unveiling recurs in the dedicatory epistle of the *Letters on Family Matters,* in which Petrarch entrusts the man he calls his Socrates (Ludwig van Kempen) with an unfinished work: "That other work I have been polishing with great care, though not a Phidian Minerva, as Cicero asserts, but a true portrait and likeness such as it is of my talent if ever I shall be able to give it the last touches, that work, I say, when it reaches you, you may set up without concern at the summit of whatever stronghold you please."[8] Here the poet plays with the figurative dimension implicit in the metaphor of the text as a portrait of the soul, allowing it to emerge through the references to Phidias's statue of the goddess of wisdom, taken from Cicero's *De oratore* (II, 17, 73), in which the great orator is compared to the artist. While the negative construction ("though not") pays due tribute to the *topos modestiae,* what follows forcefully reaffirms Petrarch's belief in his own value, and, significantly, it does so by rhetorically deploying the spatial dimension implied in the image of the portrait. This makes it possible to "set it up at the top of any citadel you please."

2. The Scars from Reading

> Ramusio's tome has for many a day
> From the height of my bookshelves
> Been eyeing me up and down,
> Snoring at night like a pig.
> And when it awakens it wants
> To jump upon my back
> To pounce upon me.
> Even to break a bone.
> The tome has it in for me,
> Bares its teeth and sighs,
> Curses and wails,

> Because I have not sold it in Japan
> Nor yet to the library in Argenta.
>
> (Roberto Roversi, *Libri e contro il tarlo inimico*)[9]

The almost physical pleasure that Petrarch describes as being produced by reading has important links, as Andrea Torre has shown, with the practice of *lege memoriter,* a method of reading aimed at imprinting texts in the memory and transforming them into a living and essential part not only of the reader's mind but also of their body.[10] An age-old metaphor compared reading to a form of eating—rumination; in a letter to Boccaccio, Petrarch takes up this idea and infuses it with new strength as he dwells on the possibility that books may penetrate to our very marrow:

> I have read what is said in Virgil, Horace, Boethius and Cicero not once but countless times, nor was my reading rushed but leisurely, pondering them as I went with all the powers of my intellect; I ate in the morning what I would digest in the evening, I swallowed as a boy what I would ruminate upon as an older man. I have thoroughly absorbed these writings, implanting them not only in my memory but in my marrow, and they have so become one with my mind that were I never to read them for the remainder of my life, they would cling to me, having taken root in the innermost recesses of my mind.[11]

This way of reading involves a differentiated positioning of texts within the spaces of our memory: those authors that Petrarch has read rapidly, such as Ennius and Plautus, have been "laid aside as common property in an open place, in the very atrium, so to speak, of [his] memory," while those dearer to him have been allowed to seep into his hidden and innermost recesses.[12] This process, however, as he confesses to Boccaccio, is not without its risks, as this long intimacy results in a blurring of the lines of authorship and bears some of the hallmarks of obsession: "besieged by the mass of such writings, I may forget whose they are and whether they are mine or not."[13] We see here the dark side, as it were, of reading *medullitus:* the confines of awareness begin slowly to crumble, and one may fall into the error of using the poetic forms of others as if they were one's own, without modifying them as required by the rules of imitation. Petrarch in fact uses this reasoning to excuse his rather slavish evocation of Virgil's manner, arguing that this type of reading may produce an inner datum that is permanent and irremovable: for many years, he writes in his *Invectiva in medicum* (*Invective against a Physician*), he has devoted himself to reading sacred texts and no longer feeds on the poets; nevertheless, "they are so deeply ingrained in my mind that I could not eradicate them even if I wanted."[14]

Metaphors are therefore a risky business: they tend to cross the borders assigned to them and take on a life of their own. This is what happens with the notations used to fix in the memory certain passages from books that have been read, those "hooks" whose use is recommended by Augustine in the *Secretum* and that also serve as a remedy against slovenly curiosity and the slothful melancholy that accompanies it: "And if something is the result of attentive reading, then make clear notes alongside the useful passages (as I said earlier), as if to hold them hooked onto the memory when they might otherwise escape. Fortified in this way you will be able to stand firm not only against other passions but also against the dejection which, like a noxious cloud, kills the seeds of virtue and all the fruits of the intelligence."[15]

The metaphor of the "hooks" evokes two different levels of reality: the glosses written in the margins of books (a practice that Petrarch carried out throughout his life and that greatly adds to the fascination of the codices in his library) but also the traces left by memory in our inner life, where our soul abides. It was in this sense that Cicero had used the metaphor: such was the force of Pericles's words, said the writers of Old Comedy, that they stuck like darts in the minds of those who heard them.[16] But, as Cardinal Gianfranco Ravasi—whom I should like to thank for this suggestion—has pointed out, a passage from Ecclesiastes (XII, 10–11) is also relevant in this context: "The teacher searched to find the right words, and what he wrote was upright and true. The words of the wise are like goads. Their collected sayings are like firmly embedded nails."

In this case too, we see that metaphors in Petrarch may become dangerously solid: the marks or hooks of memory may even leave a physical trace, violent and bloody, on the body itself. This is what happened with the codex of Cicero's letters that fell onto his foot, as we see theatrically recounted in an epistle to Neri Morando da Forlì (*Fam.*, XXI, 10).[17] Writing to a friend who has health problems, he frames this episode as a tale of unrequited love, a cruel prank almost. Having since boyhood "always loved and cherished [Cicero]," he explains, "I have an enormous volume of his letters that with my own hand I transcribed some time ago while in bad health" (these were the letters of Cicero to Atticus, which Petrarch discovered in 1345 in the Capitular Library in Verona). "So as to have the volume always close at hand, I usually kept it in the doorway to my library resting on the doorpost. As I entered the room, thinking of something else as I often do, it so happened that a fold in my garment inadvertently caught the book; when it fell, it struck me lightly on the leg a little above the heel. I picked it up and jokingly said: 'What's this, my Cicero? Why do you strike me?'"[18] But the scene is repeated: the codex, which, in homage to its greatness, had been placed higher up, falls again and again onto the already wounded foot. Petrarch decides to pay little attention to the incident until the wound becomes infected and his unfortunate appendix swells. The letter closes with these words: "My beloved Cicero has now wounded my leg as he once did my heart."[19]

In this narrative, the codex containing Cicero's letters starts to breathe with a sort of diabolical vitality: the codex *becomes* its author and hurts the very man who had brought it back to life by transcribing it by hand and had given it a privileged place in his library, in his favorite reading material, and also in his writing, for Petrarch wrote the *Familiares,* the collection of letters on familiar matters, in the image and likeness of Cicero's *Familiares.*[20] Thus, as Andrea Torre has argued, the metaphor of the hooks of memory, closely linked to the image of the nails, the mark on the page that penetrates the surface, acquires here a physical consistency: the wound, the scar, marks the body through the vivid memory of the act of reading: "My Cicero thus made an indelible note on my memory and on my body with a scar that never disappeared. I would never have forgotten him in any case, but, so as to make absolutely sure this would never happen, he took necessary precautions, both within and without my body."[21] This is Petrarch's comment on the same episode in another letter, this time addressed to Boccaccio. Clearly, he has transformed the accident into a myth: at the threshold dividing body and psyche, *extra* and *intus,* the wound enshrines the strength of memory and the impossibility of forgetting; it is the true sign of the efficacy and profoundness of reading. Next to the more general Latin word *nota* (mark) is placed the more heavily charged *stigma,* which would appear to refer to the stigmata of St. Francis of Assisi.[22] Thus the memory of an extraordinary religious experience is deployed to reinforce the enactment of the compenetration between Petrarch and Cicero, between the reader and the author he loves most.

3. "I Brought with Me Your Cicero"

In the image of reading as a dialogue, in addition to a theatrical component, there is an illusionistic effect of refraction and multiplication. One very interesting example of this may be found in the preface to the *Secretum*, a work that also contains a wealth of reflections on the ethics of reading and on how different reading practices entail different forms of memory building.[23] Petrarch writes that the dialogue that took place between himself and Augustine is deeply engraved in his memory; but he has also set it down in writing, not in pursuit of personal glory, "but so that I may savour by reading as often as I wish those delights that I once savoured in discussion."[24] Reading thus doubles the pleasure of the dialogue. It is not, however, simply the literary fiction of its form that determines the dialogic nature of the *Secretum;* the text itself is the outcome of Petrarch's close dialogue not only with Augustine's works but also with the different *ways* of reading and interpreting the classical texts that form the common background of both Augustine and Petrarch. In other words, the image of the dialogue displays a powerful tendency to represent not merely the simple experience of reading but rather the intense and meaningful relationship that is set up between reading and writing.

Because books offer a faithful image of their author's soul, they carry the author within them so vividly that they become the instruments of an actual evocation. This is a component of metaphorical invention often deployed by Petrarch. It emerges importantly in a 1352 letter to Lapo da Castiglionchio the Elder, in which, to quote Paola Vecchi Galli's felicitous formulation, "an unexpected catalogue of phantasmal presences evoked by reading, a host of ancient authors materializes next to Cicero, Petrarch's favorite Latin guest:[25]

> As is my custom, I recently withdrew to my transalpine Helicon in order to escape the pressures of that detestable city. I brought with me your Cicero, who, astonished by the novelty of the place, confessed that he was never surrounded, to use his words, by icier waters in his Arpinium than he was with me at the source of the Sorgue.... This is why your Cicero seemed delighted and gladly remained with me. We spent ten thoroughly peaceful and tranquil days there together.... My guest was surrounded by countless illustrious and distinguished men who, aside from the Greeks, included our Romans, Brutus, Atticus,

Herennius. . . . There was his brother, Quintus Cicero . . . ; his son, Marcus Cicero . . . , the orator Hortensius, Epicurus.[26]

The numerous company that follows Cicero—and with him Petrarch—is made up of those authors with whom Cicero dialogues in his works: the model of reading-writing as a dialogue once again produces in this passage an illusionistic, and strongly theatrical, effect. It is as if a crowd of ghostly presences flowed out of the pages of the manuscripts Petrarch had brought with him to Vaucluse. He adopted similar tones in a 1366 letter to Boccaccio, in which he rejoiced on receiving the Latin translation of Homer by Leonzio Pilato, who had died in 1364: "I close by telling you that your Homer, now in Latin, has finally reached me—which renews my love for the sender and my memory, my sighs for the translator; it has filled me and all those who inhabit this library, be they Greek or Latin, with wonderful joy and delight."[27]

These book-friends inhabit the library and joyfully welcome the new arrivals. An important role is played in this narrative by the *site* of reading—and Vaucluse is precisely that safe haven, far from the madding urban crowd, which may by analogy be superimposed on other sites of antiquity that served a similar function, such as Cicero's villa in Arpinum. It is also the site of the polemical separation from the modern Babylon: the 1352 letter to Lapo originally contained a long passage against Avignon that would later be relocated in letter V of his *Sine nomine* epistles.[28] In its final redaction, although the polemic is given a more limited textual space, remaining essentially in the background, it loses none of its strength: we find it, for example, in a passage full of nostalgia for the happy period in Vaucluse and the company of Cicero, now no more than a distant memory, a paradise that clashes vividly with the Babylonian, infernal scenario in which Petrarch now finds himself: "for soon the Babylonian claw was again hurled at me and I find myself once more drawn unwillingly into the hell from which I now write this letter to you."[29] The same polemic is found in his valediction to his friend: "Farewell, O you who are so fortunate as not to have seen this Western Babylon."[30]

Vaucluse is therefore the privileged place where time is compressed, or rather coils in on itself so that men from different times may meet and live together. It is in Vaucluse that Petrarch, at different moments, celebrates this species of necromantic ritual that reading entails for him.[31] There is one text in which the peculiar pleasures afforded by his library are exalted against an especially dramatic backdrop: in the verse epistle to Giacomo Colonna, generally dated to 1338 on the basis of internal chronology (he had been in Vaucluse for a year, and he had been in love with Laura for ten years).[32] Petrarch's reconstruction of the various stages of his life is not always, however, reliable, as he enjoyed playing with time so as to set up correspondences and symbolical connections that would create an ideal self-portrait.[33] Here the refuge sought by the poet in the wild and solitary landscape of Vaucluse and in his dialogue with books is depicted as a flight from the perils of an amorous obsession. Laura is a beautiful and insidious ghost, whom it is almost impossible to escape: "Never did helmsman sailing through the night fear so much a rock, as I fear her face and her soul-stirring words and her golden hair and her snow-white bejeweled neck, her lissome arms, and her eyes, beautiful even in death."[34] What does Petrarch mean when he says that Laura's eyes are beautiful even in death? Does he wish to say that they are beautiful even if they give death or that they would be beautiful even if Laura were dead? Or does he simply mean that they are beautiful even now that Laura is dead? The latter interpretation, however, would suggest a dating of the letter to 1348 or later.[35] All that we can say with certainty is that the topos we are examining appears in the letter after a vivid and almost horror-charged description of the persecution Petrarch suffers at the hands of the ghostly figure of his love:

> Often, O wonder! In the dead of night,
> Passing my thrice-barred door, she seeks me out,
> Sure of my slavery: I cannot move,
> And suddenly through all my veins my blood
> Gathers to guard the citadel of my heart.
> If one should enter with a lantern then,
> And see me where I lie, he would behold
> My face pale with the fear that fills my breast.
> . . . .
> . . . leaving my house—
> My house of fear—I seek the woods and the hills,
> Casting my glance around, lest she, pursuing
> Prevent my wandering steps.
>   —when I think
> To be alone in pathless forest shades,
> I see the face I fear, upon the bushes

> Or on an oaken trunk; or from the stream
> She rises; flashes on me from a cloud
> Or from clear sky; or issues from a rock,
> Compelling me, dismayed to hold my step.[36]

Thus his library and the practice of reading become an essential part of Petrarch's life and come to coincide with the creation of a separate space-time dimension where he seeks refuge as he is tormented and besieged by the erotic ghost of Laura:

> The country folk
> Marvel that I despise those rare delights
> That seem to them supreme. They do not know
> My joy: my company of secret friends.
> They come to me from every century
> And every land, illustrious in speech,
> In mind, and in the arts of war and peace.
> Only a corner in my house they ask;
> They heed my every summons: at my call
> They are with me, ever welcome while they stay,
> Ready to go, if I wish, and to return.
> Now these now those I question, and they answer,
> Abundantly. Sometimes they sing for me;
> Some tell me of the mysteries of nature;
> Some give me council for my life and death;
> Some tell of high emprise, bringing to mind
> Ages long past; some with their jesting words
> Dispell my sadness, and I smile again:
> Some teach me to endure, to have no longing,
> To know myself. Masters they are of peace,
> Of war, of tillage, and of eloquence,
> And travel o'er the sea. When I am bowed
> With sorrow, they restore me; when I meet
> With Fortune's favour, they restrain my pride,
> Reminding me that the days of life are fleeting.[37]

Petrarch's library is described as the place where pleasures unknown to all others are pursued, where friends are met and entertained whom no one else can know or see. It becomes the magical site par excellence, where time and space contract (some "secret friends" who "come to [him] from every century / And every land" are welcomed). The exaltation of the encyclopedic knowledge that the library contains (all the various genres and the different types of books are listed) goes hand in hand with a highlighting of the paucity of the physical space: Vaucluse and once again, as in a game of Chinese boxes, the little room where the books are kept ("the humblest shelter is for them a mansion"). These book-friends are able not only to furnish all that is needed in the various fields of knowledge but also to provide psychological comfort and moral instruction; they have one important advantage over flesh-and-blood friends: they are entirely subjected to the needs of their host, always ready and eager to answer his many questions. Here the theme of the dialogue with books is expressed through the use of different verbs that correspond, as Loredana Chines has argued, to the different genres and functions of the books in the poet's collection: "*respondent* thus seems to be deployed in connection with theological and philosophical texts, which answer men's questions and speculative investigations; *canunt* is the verb used in connection with epic poetry, which deals with the great deeds of gods and men; while *loquuntur* describes human narration, the earth-bound word which tells the story of ordinary men and their world."[38] To take refuge in one's library, to converse with one's books, is, after all, as we have seen, an efficacious remedy against the anguish inflicted by the ghost of love, which continuously tempts and besieges "the citadel of the heart."

Vaucluse and the library are celebrated in a similar way in a passage from a letter to Zanobi da Strada, which seems datable to 1353. The library is the place where one can seek solace from the misery of exile, the ideal fatherland where the tormenting present may be swept away:

> As I said, I am at the source of the Sorgue.... Meanwhile here I have established my Rome, my Athens, and my spiritual fatherland; here I gather all the friends I now have or did have, not only those who have proved themselves through intimate contact and who have lived with me, but also those who died many centuries ago, known to me only through their writings, wherein I marvel at their accomplishments and their spirits or at their customs and lives or at their eloquence and genius. I gather them from every land and every age in this narrow valley, conversing with them more willingly than with those who think

they are alive because they see traces of their stale breath in the frosty air. I thus wander free and unconcerned, alone with such companions; I am where I wish to be. As much as possible, I remain alone with myself.[39]

Yet again Vaucluse is the place chosen to function as a library; here the mind re-creates an ideal homeland where the significant sites of antiquity (in this case Athens and Rome) come together. Petrarch describes the unification of different times and places that he achieves here in almost magical, alchemical terms ("I gather them, from every land and every age in this narrow valley"), and once more it is the smallness, indeed the modesty, of the place that renders even more evident the extraordinary character of the operation. The superiority of mental friends created through books compared with physical people is reaffirmed quite harshly, with an aside on bad breath that accentuates the poet's aristocratic detachment. As a bulwark against the limits and grossness of the contemporary world, Petrarch seeks to build an ideal community that may be formed outside the limits of space and time and peopled by his chosen interlocutors. The dialogue with books, as we shall see in greater detail later, is also nurtured through a sense of being unsuited to one's times, a feeling, almost, of extraneousness and alienation.

Let us look now at a passage from *De vita solitaria* in which Petrarch celebrates two central aspects of his dialogue with books: the unique pleasures this exchange yields and the complete availability of his interlocutors, that is, their authors:

> I also look for various kinds of books that are, because of who they were written by and the subjects they cover, pleasant and regular companions. These books are ready to be seen in public or go back into the drawer at your command, and are always willing to be silent or to speak, to stay at home or accompany you into the woods, to travel, to spend time in the country, to chat, joke, encourage, comfort, advise, reprimand or take care of you; to teach you the secrets of things, impress on you the memory of great deeds and the rules of moral living, contempt for death, the need for moderation in good fortune, strength in adversity; to instruct you to be imperturbable and constant. They are learned, joyful, helpful and eloquent companions: with them there is no tedium, no expense, no complaints, no murmurs, no envy, no deceit. And while they offer so many advantages, they are satisfied with

the smallest room in your house and a modest robe, they require no drink or food; indeed it is they who offer their guests invaluable spiritual riches, vast abodes for the soul, sumptuous clothes, pleasant banquets and the sweetest of viands.[40]

When compared with the previously quoted passage from the letter to Giacomo Colonna, this passage shows an artificial crescendo of effects: not only, Petrarch argues, are books friends without flaws, who content themselves with little or nothing and show an infinite willingness to submit to his will, but it is they themselves—and this is a significant reversal—who furnish infinite wealth and splendid abodes and host rich banquets. This is an idea that Federico da Montefeltro evoked in the inscription he placed above his library.[41]

Books, then, by means of the dialogue established through reading, summon friends to join Petrarch in a community that is timeless and ideal. They allow him to speak with the dead. Petrarch returned to this idea in March 1371 in a letter to Lombardo della Seta, in which his by-now-familiar phrasing introduces an intriguing variation.[42] Della Seta had told Petrarch that there were some people who had made him an object of ridicule for having said that he enjoyed the company of the dead and conversed with them, far away from the troubles and turmoil of the city.[43] Petrarch first rehearses his favorite themes, saying that he enjoys the tombs and company of the dead:

> The ignorant laugh at this; but the wise, if there are any, would praise it; for from those whom they call alive you can learn hardly anything good, either in word or example. On the contrary, you can hardly learn anything evil from the dead, but many good things every day, inasmuch as the former are most annoying, while the latter are always affable and modest. Although they may have been difficult and stubborn while they lived on earth (something that it is nearly beyond our frailty to avoid altogether), still, in their conversations which they wrote down and left behind, the flower and fruit of their intellect is undiluted and abounding in much that is honest, useful and enjoyable, whereas from our contemporaries, whether living (to say it more truthfully, breathing) or dead (more correctly, dead and buried), nothing good appears, not even a hope of it. Who, therefore, is so blind and so stupid as to prefer to be among them?[44]

About twenty years after his letter to Zanobi da Strada, the poet reasserts his aristocratic detachment from those of his contemporaries who believe they are alive merely because they breathe. His description of the authors of the books with whom he dialogues now becomes more clearly defined and realistic: the ghost one encounters through reading is *better* that the real person; the book remains the mirror of the soul, but it is a mirror that selects the best, that refines the image we see in it, cleansing it of all traces of mundane existence, revealing only the undiluted "flower and fruit of their intellect."

In Petrarch's wide-ranging reworking of the classical topos of reading as a dialogue, he develops a highly fascinating myth, and one that was destined to last. One component of this myth deploys the language of magic to enact what could be termed a necromantic evocation of the great literary figures of the past, subjecting them to his needs and forcing them to inhabit his own time and space. Proof that this reading is correct comes from an unexpected source. Let us look at a 1352 letter (*Fam.*, XIII, 6) in which Petrarch complains that poetry has been profaned and prostituted. Among the examples he quotes for the benefit of his friend Francesco Nelli, to whom the letter is addressed, there is one that concerns him closely: he has always been, he says, entirely hostile to divination and magic, and yet he has been accused of being a necromancer—proof of this being his friendship with Virgil. Petrarch advises his friend to join him in his indignation and amusement.[45] We, on the other hand, must be grateful to his accuser: with the single-minded dedication to consequential reasoning typical of the censor, he gave a body to the ghosts and made them clearly visible. To do so, he merely literalized the metaphors lying at the heart of the myth we are exploring.

4. Exile from the Present and the Pact with the Reader

Petrarch's library and the dialogue with books that the poet may enjoy there create, as we have seen in his writings, an ideal time and space that is nourished both by the need to escape the cruel ghosts of love and by a certain disdain for the present, a sense of foreignness from the world around him— or at least a desire to present himself as such. This is a crucial component in the myth of exile that Petrarch sets out to build: his having been born in exile becomes the emblematic sign of his *feeling exiled* from his own time.[46] A valuable testimony of this may be found in that ideal self-portrait that is the—unfinished—letter to posterity: "I have dwelt single-mindedly on learning about antiquity, among other things because this age has always displeased me, so that, unless love for my dear ones pulled me the other way, I always wished to have been born in any other age whatever, and to forget this one, seeming always to graft myself in my mind onto other ages."[47]

In Petrarch's *Rerum memorandarum libri* (Book of things to be remembered), he describes himself as at the cusp between two peoples (the ancients and the moderns, the latter in hopeless decline and devoted to vain matters): "being able to turn my gaze both backward and forward I have decided to pass on to posterity this complaint, which has not come down to me from our forebears."[48] The works of the great authors of the past with whom he communes help, when viewed from this perspective, to build a memory that is alternative to a present he wishes to forget, and at the same time, they seem more alive, more real, than the people who surround him, who inhabit the same physical world as himself. In exile from the present, Petrarch seeks the means to escape from it and thus calls on the men of the past, and those of the future, to engage in the same kind of dialogue with his own work as that which he himself conducts with the classics. The unfinished letter to posterity had originally been meant to close the book of the *Seniles,* in a sort of ideal correspondence with the last book of the *Familiares,* which contains letters addressed to the great authors of the past. Indeed it is here, in the last book of the *Familiares,* that the theme of reading as dialogue is doubled, as it were, and attains its absolute modernity: Petrarch is transformed from reader into interlocutor, reverses the roles, and speaks with the great writers of the past from a position of complete equality. One only needs to quote a passage from his letter to Seneca, written in 1348: "I enjoy speaking with you, O illustrious men, in whom every age has been wanting, about whom our own age has permitted ignorance and total oblivion. For my part, I daily listen to your words with more attention than one would believe, and perhaps I shall not be thought impertinent in wishing to be heard by you."[49] On the assumption that they are equals, Petrarch also criticizes his beloved Cicero and asks Seneca how he could ever have served such a cruel prince as Nero.[50] The dialogue with the classics has achieved maturity and through this very transition celebrates one of the founding myths of classicism itself: the idea that an eternal monument may be erected that will rise above the confines of time.

The letter addressed to present friends, but also to the ancients and to posterity, thus becomes an indispensable tool with which to break through the barriers of time, so that the letter becomes, and is embodied as, a real person: "valete amici, valete epistole" (Farewell, dear friends. Farewell, dear letters) are the closing words of the last book of the *Seniles,* the letters of his old age.[51]

The acts of reading and writing thus amount to experiencing a precocious form of immortality; through them, we read in *De vita solitaria,* "we are always reminded that we are mortals, albeit mortals to whom immortality has been ensured. We are free to wander in our souls through all time and across all places, stopping here and there to speak with all the illustrious men of the past."[52] These, Petrarch explains, are the fruits born of a solitary life. The freedom to transcend spatial and chronological barriers is linked here to the duty of remembering: to read the works of the ancients, to preserve their names and their works from the shadows of oblivion, is the foremost duty of gratitude. The pact between the reader and the writer is in its turn a guarantee of immortality: "But who can doubt that the literary work through which our own name or that of others is consecrated, through which the images of famous men are carved in a substance that ensures eternity far more than bronze or marble, can develop in any other place with greater ease and freedom than in solitude?"[53] The dialogue with past writers seems here to look to the future: he who celebrates its rites within the retreat and solitude of his library and reproposes it through his writing expects in his turn that his future readers will ensure that both he and his works are kept alive, that they may speak, from beyond time and death. Petrarch says so clearly in a letter to Giovanni Colonna: "Just as I am grateful to all those authors I have read who afford me this opportunity to test myself with appropriate examples, so do I hope that those who read me will be grateful."[54]

We can see, then, why the model of reading as dialogue implies a particularly demanding pact with the reader—from those who peruse his works, Petrarch requires total dedication: "I wish my reader, whoever he may be, to consider me alone, and not his daughter's marriage, nor a night with his lady friend, nor the wiles of his enemy, not his security or his home, not his land or his money. Even as he reads me, I want him to be with me."[55] The time given over to reading must be entirely free of any other preoccupations: Petrarch demands this in a tone wavering between that of a jealous lover and someone who feels he has suffered an injustice: "I refuse to have him simultaneously carry on his business and study; I refuse to allow him to learn without labor what I wrote with labor."[56] The magic of reading therefore obeys its own rules: it requires a specific effort, which corresponds to that of the writer; it recompenses, and in a certain sense, it both justifies and is justified by this effort. It requires both freedom and open-mindedness: the pleasure of reading may not be bought—not even popes or kings have access to any shortcut.

There is one work by Petrarch that would appear to achieve mediation between the vast wealth of the library and the need to have at one's disposal, as if distilled through an alembic, the treasures and the teachings we may need when the occasion arises: this is *De remediis utriusque fortunae* (Remedies for fortunes fair and foul), a vast work of the poet's maturity that engaged him in different phases between 1354 and 1366 (see Figure 1.2).[57] The preface to Book I offers a desolate vision of human life, which Petrarch portrays as frail and restless, fraught with anguish precisely on account of those qualities that distinguish human from beast—self-awareness, the ability to remember the past and to consider the future. Respite from this state of affairs may be found in conversation with the great men of the past that is attained through reading; this Petrarch evokes in emotionally vivid terms: "How much we owe to the brilliant and famous authors hundreds of years before our time, who still live and dwell with us, and talk to us with divine intellect in their great books."[58] It is they, Petrarch goes on to argue, who guide us through the stormy waters of our life. He does not wish to discourage Azzo da Correggio, the dedicatee of this work, from consulting the more demanding works of the philosophers in his war against Fortune but wishes rather to help him with "ready-made" weapons: "right now, you should be furnished with short and precise statements, as if with a handy coat of mail without a chink, protecting you against all assaults and sudden attacks from this side or that."[59] A little later, the image of weaponry intertwines with that of medicinal remedies: "If anything can be gained or expected from my work, consider first of all that you will no longer have to consult a whole library whenever you suspect the presence and imminent thrust of the enemy, since now you have *ad manum*—within easy reach—as they say, and before your eyes in all places and at all times, a quick remedy for every trouble or hurtful good, and for either Fortune, compounded by a helpful hand: a potent antidote against a double disease, as it were, packed in a little box."[60] This work was there-

Figure 1.2. Francesco Petrarca, *De remediis utriusque fortunae*, miniature, 1432, ms. Lat.10209, ca.5v, Bibliothèque Nationale, Paris. *Bibliothèque Nationale de France.*

fore engendered by an orderly arrangement of the material Petrarch had garnered from his readings: short, effective quotations are set out, like remedies in an imaginary pharmacy (or armory) to address the vicissitudes of fortune, whether good or bad. The reader would thus find collected together all the loci that Petrarch had carefully selected from the wild and disorderly forest of his library and fixed in his memory and in this book. Memory, *inventio,* and moral choice appear to be inextricably linked from the point of view of both the author and the reader. The *De remediis* could be thought of as a simple route, a shortcut almost, toward that dialogue with the great writers of the past; it is a pact that ties the writer inextricably to the reader.

5. The Dangers of the Library and the Sweet Words of the Ancients

Nevertheless, even at the heart of *De remediis,* the seed of doubt is sown, and risks loom on the horizon. The library, an indiscriminate love of multitudes of books, and the desire to possess them may hide certain dangers. In the chapter devoted to this subject, "De librorum copia," Joy's refrain celebrates the happiness that comes with the possession of many books, but Reason counters this argument by reworking a theme dear to Seneca: it condemns those who adorn their houses with books merely out of ostentation and vanity and delude themselves into thinking they truly own them only because they are there, decorating the walls of their homes rather that the rooms of their soul.[61] The vast libraries of antiquity, including that of Alexandria, appear to the eyes of Reason as a form of literary lust, destined either to be relegated to the sphere of pure appearances or to produce an incurable frustration in those who have a true thirst for knowledge, a Tantalus-like torment in which memory is forever oppressed by quantity and the thirst for knowledge remains unquenched forever. Most importantly, there are books that drive you insane: "Libri quosdam ad scientiam, quosdam ad insaniam deduxere" (books have led some to knowledge and some to madness); they are a potent and dangerous nourishment that should be administered with discernment.[62]

Petrarch, however, evidently believes that he can defend himself against such risks and is a safely permeable reader, capable of dialoguing with books, to the extent that for him not only books but also the library containing them are alive. In one memorable passage, written on 5 January 1353 from Avignon, Petrarch likens his library to a daughter he has adopted—"I feel the need for a guardian for my library, which is my adopted daughter"—paying tribute to the man who had long kept watch over his books and had recently died, an illiterate local peasant who loved them dearly and would clasp them to his breast because they made him feel wiser and happier.[63]

Similarly, one may achieve a calm and peaceful acceptance of that veritable invasion of the inner life that stems from the ingrained memories of our most beloved and most voraciously devoured authors. We have seen how, in a letter to Boccaccio, Petrarch described himself as "besieged by the mass of such writings" to the point that "I may forget whose they are and whether they are mine or others'."[64] But in a letter to Tommaso da Messina written between 1333 and 1337, Petrarch takes issue with the nominalists, inveighing against the empty exercise of dialectics, while at the same time pointing out the correct manner in which the new (and old) honey of letters may be produced, thereby overcoming the frustration that may derive from seeking absolute originality: "Believe me, it is possible to know something without noisy quarrels. It is not noise that makes the learned man, but contemplation. Therefore, unless we are determined to appear rather than to be, we will enjoy not the applause of the foolish multitude but rather truth and silence. And we shall be happy at the soft sound brought to us sometimes by words of genuine writers. Thus the fields will resound not with sharp noise but with a soft humming."[65] The "soft humming of the bees" flying from flower to flower is the music accompanying a species of writing that knowingly accepts the legacy of memory deposited by the ancients within our soul. Thus the voices of the ancients mingle with that of Petrarch, who reads his works out aloud and derives comfort from their music:

> Everyone may judge as they please, but as regards myself, I truly cannot express the comfort that I receive in solitude from certain known and familiar words that it is my custom not only to nurture within my heart but also to speak out loud when I wish to awaken my slumbering soul. The sweetness I experience when I turn the pages of books written by myself and by others, the respite this reading affords to my soul, oppressed as it is by the heaviest and most bitter of burdens, cannot be described. And it is mostly my own writings that comfort me most, because they are the most suited to assuaging my ills, like those remedies that a sick doctor, who is well aware of the pain he suffers, might opportunely apply: nor would such a result be obtained if such salutary words did not flatter my ear, did not encourage me with their innate sweetness to read them over and over again, did not insinuate themselves into me, slowly but deeply penetrating me with their secret stings.[66]

The "I" welcomes and celebrates authors who are read and loved and takes comfort in their invasion of its inner life, as their words turn into the honey that seeps into its secret recesses and heals its ills. Reading aloud melds these different voices, makes the fruits of that ongoing dialogue something present and tangible, and celebrates reading and writing as inextricably bound together.

2

The Text as a Body and the Resurrection of the Ancients

1. Boccaccio and the Manuscript of Madonna Fiammetta

The young Boccaccio adopted the mask and the language of Madonna Fiammetta to recount a love affair that had known moments of great joy and intense pleasure but had come to an unhappy end. As was normal in the *congedo* of love poems, in which the poet addresses his own text and advises it on how to go about in the world, Fiammetta "makes an end by speaking to her book and enjoining it in what dress it must go forth, when, to whom, and against whom to be on guard."[1] What is noteworthy here is the way in which Fiammetta (and, through her, Boccaccio) is reflected in the manuscript, projecting into it her exact state of mind and almost her physical body and dress. The manuscript has supposedly come from her own hands ("written by my own hand and in many places damaged by my tears"); in this guise, Fiammetta advises it to present itself to "women in love":

> You should be glad to show yourself similar to my disposition which is so very unhappy that it clothes you in misery, as it does me.
>
> Therefore, do not concern yourself with any ornamentation such as other books are accustomed to have, namely, with elegant bindings, painted and adorned with various covers, with clean-cut pages, pretty miniatures, or grand titles; such things do not suit the grave lamentations you bear; leave these things to happy books, and with them the broad margins, the colourful inks, and the paper smoothed with pumice; it is fitting that you go where I am sending you discomposed, with your hair uncombed, stained and in full gloom, to awaken by

my misfortunes blessed pity in the minds of those women who will read you. If it happens that through you the signs of such pity show in their lovely faces, give immediate rewards for it as best you can.[2]

There is an exact correspondence between the "misera veste" (miserable clothes) worn by Fiammetta during this time of unhappiness and the clothing of misery that must be adopted by the manuscript, which must forgo any elegant miniatures or plush binding. Ovid is a powerful model here: not, however, the Ovid of the *Heroides,* the heroines who address their lovers by recounting their doomed love affairs, but rather the Ovid of *Tristia,* the poetry of exile, one possible explanation being that Fiammetta feels exiled from the happy bygone days when her love prospered. At the very beginning, Ovid addresses his "little book" as follows:

Little book, you will go without me—and I grudge it not—to the city, whither alas your master is not allowed to go! Go, but go unadorned, as becomes the book of an exile; in your misfortune wear the garb that befits these days of mine. You shall have no cover dyed with the juice of purple berries—no fit color is that for mourning; your title shall not be tinged by vermilion nor your paper with oil of cedar; and you shall wear no dark bosses upon your dark edges. Books of good omen should be decked with such things as these; 'tis my fate that you should bear in mind. Let no brittle pumice polish your two edges; I would have you appear with locks all rough and disordered. Be not ashamed of blots; he who sees them will feel that they were caused by my tears. Go, my book, and in my name greet the loved places: I will tread them at least with what foot I may.[3]

Ovid describes point by point, but only to negate them, all those details that characterized an elegant *volumen*. Boccaccio's memory of the Latin poet thus happily interacts with his love of manuscripts: the repeated negations gradually allow a sumptuous and exquisitely decorated book to appear through the filigree of the text—a book suited, it would seem, to represent a happy love affair. What is interesting here is that the text is, literally, embodied in the manuscript: if its words mirror the soul of their author (or in this case that of the female mask it is wearing), it is through its material support that it can reach its readers (and especially its female readers). The writer thus *becomes* the manuscript, which incarnates both his body and soul. Through Fiammetta's passionate words, Boccaccio created an image—the text and the manuscript as a living body, which in turn was identified with the body of its writer—that attained wide currency with the humanists. In order to nourish this dialogue with its readers, the body-text itself must be alive: this is a necessary condition if the dialogue in its turn is to take on a life of its own.

There is a passage in Boccaccio in which the dialogue with books is described with particular force and intensity. This is in the *Consolatory Epistle to Pino de' Rossi,* written probably in either 1361 or 1362 and addressed to a friend who had been exiled for political reasons.[4] This was a difficult moment also for Boccaccio: relegated to the margins of public life (no further political office came his way until 1365), he had made over his house in Florence to his half brother Iacopo, with whom relationships were strained, and had retired to Certaldo. Here, his sense of being an exile led him to see his own situation reflected in that of his friend; toward the end of the letter, he gives a description of his life, perhaps intending it as a possible path toward regaining some of his lost serenity. Much more easily than he had imagined possible, he explains, he has grown accustomed to a rougher existence ("and I have begun to like coarse clothes and simple country fare"), finding unexpected comfort in being at a distance from the deceptions and miseries of urban life. "The pleasure I feel in hearing the song of the nightingales and of other birds is as great as was my discomfort in listening to the incessant deceits and disloyalties of our fellow citizens; with my little books I may as often as I wish and with no impediment whatsoever, freely converse. And so that in a very few words I may properly describe to you the state of my mind, I will tell you that here, mortal as I am, I believe myself to be savoring and partaking of eternal life."[5] Against this Arcadian backdrop, conversation with books constitutes an Edenic alternative to the corrupt world of the city. It is a comfort that, as we have already seen in Chapter 1, would soon be threatened by the baleful visions of Pietro da Siena's preaching—a threat that Petrarch, himself an expert in the secret pleasures and comfort provided by books, would help to dispel.

2. Boccaccio and the Gods of the Ancients

To engage in a dialogue with a book, it has been argued, often means to converse with the dead; it is equivalent to carrying out what could be termed a necromantic ritual, a descent into Hades, where encounters not otherwise possible take place. But books are something more than simply the mirror of their authors' souls or the essential tools in this evocation; they have the power to take over a writer's life, become one with them, with their very body, not just with their *mores*. This is what takes place in the humanist texts in which dialogue with the ancients intertwines with the narrative of the rediscovery of manuscripts long forgotten in the libraries of monasteries. Philological passion and the triumph of discovery are nourished through a set of metaphors, quotations, and textual allusions that, taken together, point to at least two separate traditions: the descent to Hades recounted in *Aeneid* VI and the myth of Aesculapius, the god of medicine, who gathers up the torn fragments of Hippolytus's body and restores them to life in a new organism. It is a myth that, as Nicola Gardini has argued, mingles with that of Osiris, torn limb from limb by his jealous brother and then together again and brought back to life by his sister-bride, Isis. The fear of sickness and bodily decomposition articulated an anxiety about a present crisis, which was both expressed and symbolically remedied by piecing together a fragmented body.[6]

It is fascinating to observe how the humanists conjured up, around the subject of the rediscovery of codices and their own philological endeavors, a host of dismembered and recomposed bodies, coaxing them out from their memory of the classics and inviting them to oversee their work, to become emblems of that resurrection of the ancient world from which, as A. Bartlett Giamatti has written, they feel they have been exiled.[7] Philology and archaeology were closely entwined. The statues and the sarcophagi that were gradually being unearthed symbolized the physical rebirth of that ancient world of beauty. The discovery of a sarcophagus buried under the Appian Way in Rome in 1485 neatly epitomizes this image: it contained the undecayed body of a young girl, covered in fragrant bark and unguents (Figure 2.1). This body seemed almost to be still alive, people thronged to visit it, men of letters wrote about it, inventing fake stories that might give a name and an identity to this girl who had reemerged from antiquity under Roman skies. One inscription identified her as Tulliola, the daughter of Cicero, who had greatly mourned her death.[8]

Similar resurrectionist fantasies are threaded through a number of texts that enact, as it were, their relationship with the works of the authors of antiquity: here classical texts are read, dissected, and recomposed into new writing or rediscovered and restored, given a new lease of life. At various points in the 1360s and 1370s, Boccaccio was involved in the compilation of an

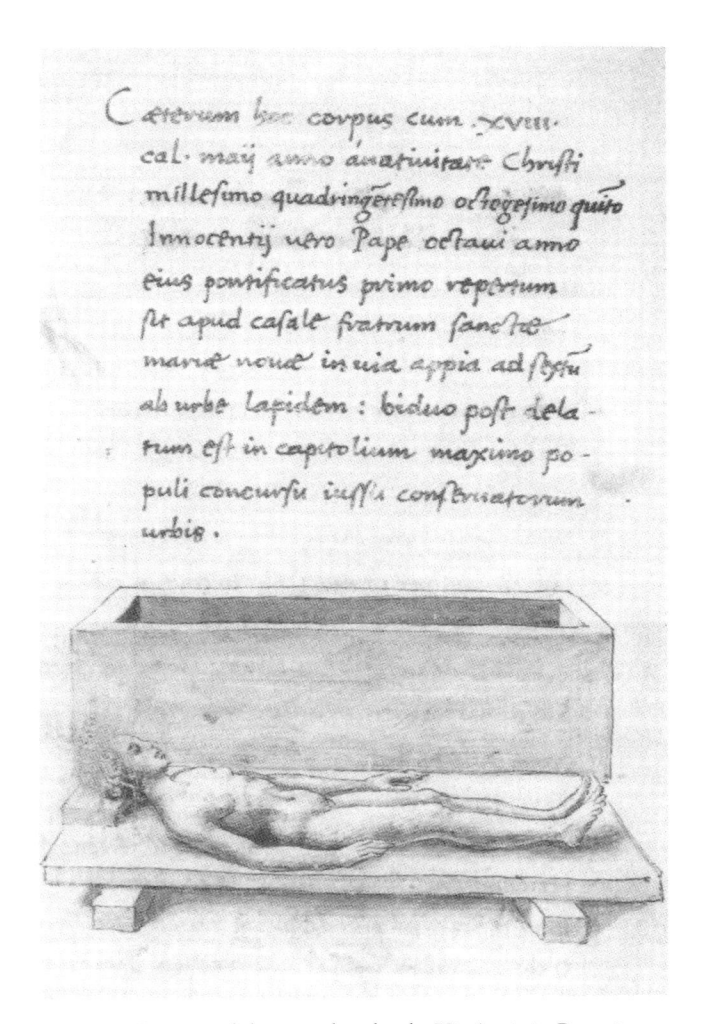

Figure 2.1. Roman girl discovered under the Via Appia in Rome in 1485, in Bartolomeo Fonzio, *Liber monumentorum Romanae urbis et aliorum locorum,* ms. Lat. misc. d.85, c.161v, end of the fifteenth century, Bodleian Library, Oxford. *Bodleian Library, Oxford.*

encyclopedic work in Latin, the *Genealogie deorum gentilium* (Figure 2.2); he had been asked to undertake this gargantuan task, he explains, by Hugh IV, King of Cyprus and Jerusalem. In the preface, Boccaccio converses with Donnino da Parma, one of the king's officials, recounting his hesitation in accepting the work and the difficulties encountered in the perilous voyage that he has had to undertake in order to accomplish his task. Here the metaphor of the journey is enriched and layered with various echoes

Figure 2.2. Giovanni Boccaccio, *Genealogie deorum gentilium,* ms. 100, c. IIr (1370–1406), University of Chicago Library, Chicago. *Hanna Holborn Gray Special Collections Research Center, University of Chicago Library.*

and themes, as Boccaccio describes how he will descend to the underworld and ascend into Heaven like a second Daedalus; he will collect an infinite number of books through which the relics of the pagans and such fragments of the ancient wreck as God will allow him to find may be wrought into a kind of whole: "Not otherwise than if I were collecting fragments along the vast shores of a huge shipwreck. . . . Even if they are ravaged and half-eaten by time . . . I will reduce them into a single corpus of a genealogy."[9] For such an arduous task, the help of God is needed, because, he explains, "I venture . . . to collect from here and there the huge corpus of gods and noble princes, torn from limb to limb, beaten, and reduced nearly to ashes, and to consolidate this corpus as if it were Hippolytus and I another Aesculapius."[10]

The Text as a Body

The operation Boccaccio performs is therefore predicated on his vast reading and on his ability to piece together these scattered fragments, injecting new life into them. Because of this, we find specific imagery clustering around textual areas concerned with the description of his work, which is likened to the task of those heroes who dared to pass the confines of our world and cross the gates of the underworld; he compares himself to Daedalus, who soared up to the heavens, to Aesculapius, who rebuilt and rebirthed a lacerated body—he even evokes Prometheus, who in bygone days was said to be able "to form men from mud."[11]

With his classical texts, Boccaccio works like a demiurge, coaxing them into a new shape, placing the scattered fragments within the orderly framework of family trees (see Figure 2.3), observing them from a distance, from the perspective of the revealed truth afforded by Christianity, and recreating them in his own image, or rather in the image of the world he inhabits.[12] The humanist writers were later to feel the lure of the same myths, but from a slightly different perspective.

3. Quintilian Dismembered and Reassembled

One figure in particular from classical antiquity may serve as a guide in the exploration of this strand of my theme: Quintilian, the great master of rhetoric who lived between 35 and 96 AD and was the author of the *Institutiones oratoriae,* a twelve-volume work that placed the teaching of eloquence at the center of a wider cultural and civic project. The *Institutiones* were already famous in the Middle Ages, but in a partial and seriously damaged form. We will see how this text-body gradually reappeared on the scene, first mutilated and then confined to a squalid prison, a classical Abbé Faria, as it were, discovered by Edmond Dantés in his cell, seminaked, his clothes all torn.[13] And we will witness how Quintilian was set free and returned to enjoy a full and healthy existence.

On 7 April 1350, Petrarch addressed to Quintilian one of his letters to the ancients in the last book of his *Letters on Familiar Matters.* Lapo di Castiglionchio, he writes, had given him an incomplete and battered manuscript of the *Institutiones:*[14] he sees it as a body lacerated and disfigured: "Your work came to my hands, but alas, mangled and mutilated. Knowing how time destroys all things, . . . seeing the dismembered limbs of a beautiful body, my mind was overcome by admiration and grief."[15] Somewhere,

Figure 2.3. A genealogical tree, in Giovanni Boccaccio, *Genealogie deorum gentilium*, miniature, cod. Pluteo 52.9, c.101r, 1365–1370, Biblioteca Medicea Laurenziana, Florence. *Reproduction used by permission of the Ministero della cultura, Florence. All rights reserved.*

The Text as a Body

Petrarch wrote to Quintilian, you must exist, unhurt and whole, and one day soon you might choose to come out of hiding and reveal yourself.[16] The author *becomes* both his work *and* the codex that contains this work; in turn, this lacerated codex *becomes* a human body that evokes other lacerated mythical bodies, described by the poets. As Giamatti points out, the manuscript of the *Institutiones* is *discerptus,* like the body of Orpheus in the fourth book of the Georgics (*Georg.*, IV, 522), ripped to shreds by the Bacchae and strewn across the countryside; it is *lacer* (lacerated) like Deiphobus, the Trojan prince who was horribly mutilated by his wife, Helen, and her former husband, Menelaus, on the night Troy was destroyed and who appears to Aeneas in Hades (*Aen.*, VI, 495).[17]

These passages in Petrarch may be seen as a sort of prophetic foreshadowing of the rediscovery of the complete text of Quintilian by Poggio Bracciolini in 1416 (Figure 2.4). Poggio served the Church during one of its darkest and most tormented of hours, first as apostolic scribe and later as apostolic secretary. He had been promoted by the Antipope John XXIII himself, who on 29 May 1415 was deposed by the Council of Constance. At such a difficult and dramatic time, when the future appeared uncertain and even the Curia was dissolved, Poggio decided to remain in Constance in order to pursue one of his favorite activities, hunting for ancient manuscripts. And it so happened that, between the end of June and early July 1416, in the dark basement of the monastery at St. Gall, he discovered a cache of ancient books, among which was a complete Quintilian. The unearthing of the *Institutiones* is recounted, or rather celebrated, in one of the most famous letters of the humanist period, addressed to Guarinus Veronensis and dated 15 December 1416. Poggio begins by praising Quintilian's rhetorical teaching and alluding to the sorry state of the codex through which it had been transmitted. Here, to an even greater extent than in Petrarch, the Virgilian echo of the descent to Hades becomes explicit, and the text-body of Quintilian is described through the horrendous apparition of Deiphobus:

> But among us Italians, he so far has been so fragmentary, so cut down, by the action of time I think, that the shape and style of the man has become unrecognizable. So far you have seen the man only thus:
> 'Whose face and limbs were one continued wound,
>   Dishonest, with lopp'd arms, the youth appears,
>   Spoil'd of his nose, and shorten'd of his ears.'[18]

Figure 2.4. Poggio Bracciolini, Florence, translation of Xenophon's *Cyropaedia,* ms. Strozzi 50, c.1r, fifteenth century, Biblioteca Medicea Laurenziana. *Reproduction used by permission of the Ministero della cultura, Florence. All rights reserved.*

But now finally, Poggio explains, the torment has ended: Quintilian has been recalled from exile and, indeed, restored to health from the sickness in which he lay, from death brought back to life, thanks to his recovery of the ancient manuscript in the monastery of St. Gall. The discovery of the codex is recounted as a personal encounter, a salvific act. The idea explored earlier whereby the codex becomes a body, becomes in fact the living suffering body of the writer himself, allows this evocation to take on vividly dramatic tones:

> By Heaven, if we had not brought help, he would surely have perished the very next day. There is no question that this glorious man, so elegant, so pure, so full of morals and of wit, could not much longer have endured the filth of that prison, the squalor of the place, and the savage cruelty of his keepers. He was sad and dressed in mourning, as people are when doomed to death; his beard was dirty and his hair

matted with dust, so that by his expression and appearance it was clear that he had been summoned to an undeserved punishment. He seemed to stretch out his hands and beg for the loyalty of the Roman people, to demand that he be saved from an unjust sentence, and to feel it a disgrace that he who once preserved the safety of the whole population by his influence and his eloquence could now not find one single advocate who would pity his misfortunes and take some trouble over his welfare and prevent his being dragged off to an undeserved punishment.[19]

The elegance of the text becomes the sign of the ancient elegance of its author, now trampled on and almost erased. And it is here, in the description of his miserable state, his draggled beard and his hair matted with dust ("squalentem barbam gerens et concretos pulvere crines"), that another Virgilian memory resurfaces, a reference that would have been easily recognizable by his humanist friends as they read this letter: Hector, with his draggled beard and blood-clotted hair ("squalentem barbam et concretos sanguine crinis"; *Aen.*, II, 277), who appears to Aeneas in a dream as Troy is burned and plundered. If it is Hector who entrusts Aeneas with the duty of founding a new Troy, it is Poggio who will save the prisoner from death and resurrect him in another space-time, that of the modern world. There is perhaps a Petrarchan memory also in the image of the incarcerated codex. In the chapter of *De remediis* that we have already briefly examined (see Chapter 1, section 5), titled "De librorum copia" (Many books), Joy, with blind obstinacy to the very end, extolls the happiness that stems from the possession of many beautiful books and is reprimanded by Reason as follows:

Joy: I keep many excellent books.

Reason: You keep many in chains. If, perchance, they could break away and speak, they would summon you to judgment for keeping a private prison.[20]

Another much more powerful and significant memory resurfaces, however, in this description of Quintilian as a prisoner, unjustly condemned to death and still richly endowed with the beauties of eloquence that had been his hallmark: as Stephen Greenblatt has shown, through the filigree of the text, we may detect an allusion to the fate of Jerome of Prague, the follower of

Figure 2.5. The burning of Jerome of Prague, in John Foxe, *The Book of Martyrs* (London: John Day, 1563). *Private collection.*

Jan Huss, sentenced to be burned at the stake for his heresy (Figure 2.5).[21] Poggio reevokes his figure and his tragic end in a magnificent letter written in the heat of the moment and addressed to Leonardo Bruni on 30 May 1416, on the very day Jerome was executed, as we read in the epigraph under the date, "on which Jerome suffered his sentence."[22] Poggio says that he does not know whether Jerome was a heretic, though his true thoughts break through the barrier of caution and manifest themselves quite clearly in the text.[23] That he was entirely fascinated by his character, by his extraordinary strength, is beyond all doubt. In his vivid description, we find elements that returned, a few months later, in his account of the discovery of Quintilian. Jerome is above all an incarnation of the eloquence of the ancients and something more besides: he represents faith in the power of eloquence, in the persuasive force the spoken word may exert: "I must confess that I never saw anyone who in pleading a cause, especially a cause on the issue of which his own life depended, approached nearer to that standard of ancient eloquence, which we so much admire. It was astonishing to witness with what choice of words, with what closeness of argument, with what confidence of countenance he replied to his adversaries."[24]

The Text as a Body

Poggio then reevokes Jerome's "impressive peroration" before his accusers, in which he denounced the injustice of not being listened to before but only asked to answer the charges against him: "What gross injustice is this! Exclaimed he, that though for the space of three hundred and forty days, which I have spent in filth and fetters, deprived of every comfort, in prisons situated at the most remote distances from each other, you have been continually listening to my adversaries and slanderers, you will not hear me for a single hour!"[25] The horror of the dungeon cell, the torment of the flesh that does not subdue the greatness of the soul, is a theme that is picked up again a little later, this time by Poggio speaking in the first person, in a turn of phrase that reminds us of the tormented and lacerated body of Quintilian, held prisoner "in a foul and gloomy dungeon" by his barbarous owners. Jerome, pleading in vain for a just hearing from the prelate who would condemn him to death ("He arose, and stretching out his hands, he said in a pathetic tone of voice, Fathers! To whom shall I have recourse for succor? Whose assistance shall I implore? Unto whom shall I appeal, in protection of my innocence?—Unto you?"),[26] almost comes to life again in the portrayal of Quintilian, at the end of the passage I have already quoted: "He seemed to stretch out his hands and beg for the loyalty of the Roman people, to demand that he be saved from an unjust sentence, and to feel it a disgrace that he who once preserved the safety of the whole population by his influence and his eloquence could now not find one single advocate who would pity his misfortunes and take some trouble over his welfare and prevent his being dragged off to an undeserved punishment."[27] Indeed, it is precisely the bitter memory of Jerome's tragic execution that explains this theatrical, dramatically charged representation of Quintilian, begging to be saved from an "undeserved punishment." On behalf of Jerome of Prague, that almost miraculous reincarnation of a great classical orator in the corrupt modern world of fifteenth-century Europe, Poggio, the refined Italian humanist, could do nothing, except admire him from afar and give a faithful account of him to his friends. A few months later, the memory of that tragic event is superimposed on that of the rediscovery of Quintilian: this time the diligence and good fortune of the philologist ensured that the destiny of this lacerated and imprisoned body should be entirely different.

Even before the physical recomposition of the text, it had already come back to life in the exchange of epistles that comment on Poggio's discovery. On 15 September 1416, Leonardo Bruni wrote to him: "For Quintilian, who was mangled and in pieces, will recover all his parts through you. I have seen the headings of the chapters; he is whole, while we used to have only the middle section and that incomplete. Oh wondrous treasure! Oh unexpected joy! Shall I see you, Marcus Fabius, whole and undamaged, and how much will you mean to me now? For I loved you even when you were cruelly deprived of your mouth, of your mouth and both your hands, when you were 'spoil'd of your nose and shorten'd of your ears.'"[28] Arguably, Virgil's Deiphobus, his amputated and mangled body, had now become a mnemonic image of the amputated and mangled Quintilian that circulated before Poggio's discovery. It also highlighted a specific code shared among a circle of humanist friends, the mark of a unique form of complicity. The manuscript granted them proximity with the breathing presence of its author and allowed them to see him whole. At the same time, it was as if Poggio, the man who had accomplished this, was somehow infected with the power of the author-text he had unearthed: "Just as Camillus was called a second founder of Rome after Romulus, who established the city, while Camillus restored it after it was lost, so you will deservedly be called the second author of all the works which were once lost and now returned to us by your integrity and diligence."[29] The man of letters who breathes new life into a text, who restores, as it were, the possibility of conversing with it, becomes a sort of double of its author ("secundus auctor").

Also worth analyzing in this context is the letter written to Poggio on 6 July 1417 by Francesco Barbaro, a young patrician from Venice, who had moved to Florence two years earlier and was destined to enjoy an important political career. Here, as noted by Giamatti, Quintilian is one of the numerous host of individually named Latin authors whom Poggio has unearthed, thereby inaugurating a new historical era of rebirth.[30] Like the Penates from Troy, the ancients, thanks to Poggio, have returned to Italy, back to Latium after a long absence. Barbaro redeploys the twin images of the prison and of the death sentence, his tone, this time decidedly anti-Germanic: "Indeed the Germans ought to be branded with shame for leaving celebrated men buried alive for so long. . . . If their burial occurred through thoughtlessness, what could be more careless? If it was through intent, what could be more cruel?"[31] The image of the sepulcher immediately evokes that of the resurrection, with Poggio depicted as a new Aesculapius:

> We accept Aesculapius as belonging among the gods because he called back Hippolytus, as well as others from the underworld, when he had reached the day fixed as the last of his life, and thus allowed him to die only some years later. If peoples, nations, and provinces have dedicated shrines to him, what might I think ought to be done for you, if that custom had not already been forgotten? You have revived so many illustrious men and such wise men, who were dead for eternity, through whose minds and teachings not only we but our descendants will be able to live well and honourably.[32]

Taking shape around Quintilian and his rediscovery we can see here the scaffolding, as it were, of a theater of memory. These texts are shot through with Virgilian echoes that are repeated and amplified: Deiphobus but also Hippolytus, torn to pieces and brought back to life by Aesculapius (*Aen.*, VII, 762–782). Hippolytus was called back "as well as others" from the underworld; thus Quintilian becomes one of a set of ancients brought back to light by Poggio from exile and death. Also, and more importantly, the rebirth of classical eloquence becomes in Barbaro's narrative the sign of a peaceful civil coexistence.

4. Poliziano, the Magic of the Library, and the Myth of Orpheus

Toward the end of the fifteenth century, some of the mythical characters we have encountered in the work of Petrarch, Boccaccio, and Bracciolini reappear on the scene.

In 1473, the young Poliziano (he was born in 1454), who had recently entered the Medici household as a protégé of Lorenzo, gave an early proof of his ability as a humanist and a poet by addressing a Latin elegy to a friend only a little older than himself, Bartolomeo Fonzio, also a poet and a philologist.[33] After declaring his intention of celebrating the greatness of the Medici, Poliziano recounts his daily routine, following a model that we have already encountered (in Petrarch and in Boccaccio's *Consolatory Epistle to Pino de' Rossi*) and that we will see exemplified yet again in Machiavelli's famous letter to Vettori. This is evidently a theme that thrives in the heart of quotidianity, that embodies and ennobles the mundane. Poliziano also used this opportunity to celebrate the Medici milieu, the flourishing cultural life he was now part of.

Poliziano tells of his mornings devoted to study, to the translation of Homer, to meetings with friends, and to his lessons with Marsilio Ficino. In the afternoons, he would go to the workshop of Vespasiano da Bisticci, the bookseller and copyist of humble origins who was later praised as the "princeps omnium librariorum" (the foremost of all booksellers) and made a significant contribution to the birth of the great humanist libraries.[34] Poliziano addresses him in the affectionate and admiring tone of a friend:

> And your library also receives me, Vespasiano, to whom both the Greek and Latin Muses owe as much as the land of Greece owes to the old man of Smyrna. For just as the god of Epidaurus used Cretan herbs to restore Androgeos to his father after his death, so too, Vespasiano, you restore to Latium the men whom the decay of antiquity has taken away. Thanks to you Greece now scorns the streams of Lethe, and the language of Romulus does not fear the Stygian god. Fortunate the one who can recall to the light of life so many of the dead monuments of ancient men! Fortunate the one who can rescue from the flames of the pyre the lost names of sacred poets![35]

The debt of gratitude that classical antiquity, both Greek and Latin, owes to Vespasiano is, Poliziano argues, comparable to that of Greece to Homer—whom, it should be observed, Poliziano himself was translating so that he might be ferried into the modern world. The library becomes here the ideal site where the miracle of Aesculapius ("the god of Epidaurus") is performed time and time again. There is, however, a slight variation from the tradition we have seen forming so far: it is no longer Hippolytus who is brought back to life but Androgeos, the son of Minos, following a version of the myth transmitted by Propertius (II, 2, 61–62). A whole world is resurrected in the library. A few years later, around 1481, as Bausi has justly observed,[36] Poliziano became more critical of modern codices, often incorrectly copied out and produced precisely by workshops such as that of Vespasiano: "The Duke of Urbino," he writes, "has bought a great quantity of books for twenty thousand ducats, and Cosimo spent almost as much on the Library of San Marco: I, however, esteem the Duke's library to be worth less than ten thousand, because the books are new and full of mistakes (corropti), while the library of San Marco, which is filled with ancient books with no mistakes (correptissimi) is, to me, worth more than Croesus's treasure."[37] The two great libraries that are mentioned here—the one belonging to the

The Text as a Body

Medici and the other created by Federico da Montefeltro—were among those to which Vespasiano da Bisticci had largely contributed; he had also furnished the Estense and the Aragonese libraries as well as that of Matthias Corvinus. Setting aside the philological reservations that Poliziano expressed a few years later, the verses just quoted may be read as magnificent praise of that unique site that is the library, where the patient work of resurrection seen in the texts we have examined finds its ultimate meaning—the site, therefore, where the myth of Aesculapius is ideally embodied. This myth, which incarnated men's hopes of staving off death, or at the very least of slowing down time, seems to ideally project itself over Poliziano's life, through the medium of the library. As we read in the verses immediately following, "I linger by him until the star of Cythera raises its torch to call forth for the bright stars. This is how I prolong the hours of the day as it slips away among the pleasant gifts of Hyantean chorus."[38] As Venus rises, she summons the light of the other stars; thus the young Poliziano, as he delays the moment he must leave his friend's library, basking in the gifts of the Muses, prolongs the hours of the dying day.

One of the teachers whom Poliziano encounters during the typical day he describes is, as we mentioned, Marsilio Ficino. Here (ll. 181–188) he is celebrated not only as a master of philosophy and medicine but also for his skill in healing through music the turmoil of the soul: he is seen as a sort of reincarnation of Orpheus, the poet-singer who could tame wild beasts and move the rocks of the mountains and the sea to hear his melodies. Through Ficino's translations of hermetic and Platonic texts, age-old wisdom came back to life in the present world. He loved to stage the Orphic hymns he had translated, accompanying himself with the music of his lyre, which, it was said, was decorated with a portrait of Orpheus himself.[39]

The lure of the myth of Orpheus continued to exert its fascination on Poliziano, though in different contexts and from different perspectives. He chose it, around 1480, for the theatrical fable he staged at the court of Mantua. He wrote it in haste—as he explains in the introduction—in less than two days at the request of Cardinal Francesco Gonzaga, and he would have wished to do as the ancient Spartans did, who did not allow any of their sons born weak or with a physical defect to remain alive: he would have wished that "the fable of Orpheus . . . should be immediately, as Orpheus himself had been, rent to pieces," but he was obliged to bow to the will of the his aristocratic friends who wished it to live.[40] The myth of Orpheus, or rather the ghost of his lacerated body, reverberates throughout

Poliziano's work, remodeling it in its own image and likeness. The imperfect state of the work is a sort of *mise en abyme* of its protagonist's fate, and at the same time the act of writing, and the volume that contains this writing, guarantees the reassemblage, or at least the preservation, of Orpheus's body.

If the myth of Aesculapius seemed to make its appearance here next to that of Orpheus, its presence became explicit later, at the start of the second *Centuria* of the *Miscellanea*. This is a work that brings together Poliziano's philological work; the first *Centuria*, published in 1489, had met with great success; he worked on the second *Centuria* in the last years of his life, between 1493 and 1494, at a time when he was under attack from Giorgio Merula, who was spreading rumors about him and accusing him both of plagiarism and gross philological mistakes. This is the beginning of the first chapter, "De divinatione":

> The second book of Cicero's *De deorum natura*, in all exemplars, both modern and ancient, is in a state no less pitiful than that of Hippolytus, torn limb from limb by frightened horses. The story goes that Aesculapius gathered and recomposed the scattered pieces of his dismembered body, giving them new life, but was then struck down by lightning by the envious gods.
>
> But no envy, no lightning will sway me from my attempt to bring back to life the father of the Roman language and philosophy, whose head and hands have once more been struck asunder by I know not what Antony.[41]

Cicero's murder at the hands of Marc Antony's assassins has repeated itself: history has mutilated the codices containing his works. The philological work of Poliziano symbolically restores life to Cicero and to his writings: in this work, the myth of Aesculapius is once again embodied, its miraculous power repeating itself, undeterred in this noble enterprise by the malice of his detractors, who become a degraded reincarnation of the malicious gods.

5. The Comfort of Reading

Let us now return to Poggio Bracciolini. We have seen what a crucial role he played in constructing the myth of the rebirth of the fragmented and dispersed bodies of the ancients. It should not surprise us therefore to see him also extolling the pleasures of the library, the space that enables the intimate dialogue with these authors to take place. The year was 1438: Poggio's relationship with the Curia had had its triumphs and disappointments; two years earlier, at the age of fifty-six, he had taken an eighteen-year-old wife by whom he would have six children; in 1438, he bought a country house, called la Valdarnina, as if to herald his return to Florence, which took place in 1453, when he received the office of chancellor.

At his villa Valdarnina, which he had built close to his native village of Terranuova, Poggio assembled his books and his collection of antiquities; here he spent all the free time he had when not working in the service of the Curia. It is intriguing to observe how in three letters he wrote to three different friends between the middle of September and the end of October 1438, the idea of the dialogue with books recurs, all similar but with variations, like a musical theme executed in different ways. "I have begun a small building," he wrote on 17 September 1438 to Pier Candido Decembrio, "to serve as a place for my studies, and so that my books may rest there when I am absent... I have escaped the plague by returning home, to my Penates and pleasantly spend my days there with my little books; they had murmured a little, complaining that I had been away so long. Therefore, now that I am back with them, I give them that little time that I have free from engagements."[42] We see books taking on a life of their own: they complain—albeit discreetly ("paulum")—about Poggio's absence: indeed, he had built his library so that they might rest there while he was away, and he cherished the time he spent with them ("me oblecto cum meis libellis"). Hovering in the background was the ravage wreaked by the plague, which the following year forced the Council of Basel to move from Ferrara to Florence, but here in his country seat, in the company of his books, Poggio worshiped his Penates, felt close to his origins, and found spiritual nourishment.

Poggio returned to this theme a few days later in his letter to Gerardo Landriani, Bishop of Lodi, one of the main protagonists of the Council and another ardent bibliophile: "Here I am in the country, employed in building and in my literary pursuits; my beloved books are gathered close around and rejoice at my return after all this time. And so that they may better tolerate my absence, I have built them a house, where they may with a certain ease reside."[43] Here the books-friends rejoice at his return, and the building of the library seems almost a gift to make up for his past and future absences. His affectionate tone is palpable: there is genuine joy in their meeting again, true suffering in separation. The happiness felt by these friends in their reunion is reciprocal, and in these letters, there lingers the echo of Cicero's letters to Varro, the friend whose presence he yearns for: "For you must know that since I came to the City, I have become reconciled with my old friends, in other words, with my books. And yet it was not because I was a little angry with them that I had put them away, but because they made me a little ashamed of myself. For it seemed to me that when, thanks to my utterly untrustworthy associates, I plunged into the seething cauldron of affairs, I had not quite obeyed their instructions. They forgive me, and invite me back to the old intimacy."[44] Almost a month later, on 26 October, Poggio wrote to Francesco de Lignamine and praised the pleasantness of conversing with his books, which marked the high point of his return home, his true fatherland, far from any *negotium* and especially from the world of the Curia, where men stooped and submitted like sheep, living a life that in fact resembled death: "There exists nothing sweeter or more agreeable, my dear Francesco, nothing worthier of a good and not uncouth man, than to be in his fatherland, among his Penates, among his books, and converse with those who in their writings have bequeathed to us the precepts for a proper way of life. No passion arises from them, no lust, no vice; rather, they teach us how to despise what is fleeting and fix our gaze on what is eternal."[45] The world of the library is a sort of Paradise, where vice and disorderly passion have no place, where everything speaks of eternity. Harsh reality, however, soon forces him out of this heaven— alas, Poggio comments, he must earn his living, and that prevents him from being always with his books. Poggio could certainly have counted on the understanding, even the complicity, of his interlocutor, who was also a member of the Pontifical Curia and a passionate book collector.[46] It is clear that dialogue with books was an essential component in this interchange between humanist friends, variously involved in public life; it was a common code, pointing to a real experience, described in terms of complicity, as a shared myth, but at the same time it constituted the dream of a possible escape. A very short time later, between 1439 and 1440, Bracciolini wrote the dialogue titled *De vera nobilitate,* in which he summons two friends, Lorenzo de' Medici and Niccolò Niccoli, to his *buen retiro;* he shows them the antiquities he has brought from Rome, and it is this collection of portraits and books that prompts their debate as to what constitutes true nobility, whether this is the nobility of blood, testified by a gallery of ancestors, or that of the soul, which is born of virtue and wisdom.[47]

Intriguingly, the theme we are examining also appears in a different and rather singular social context, that is, in the memoirs (*Ricordi*) of the Florentine Giovanni di Paolo Morelli (1371–1444). Morelli, the son of a wealthy wool merchant and moneylender, held important political offices in the city.[48] The text presents itself as a set of instructions to a young orphaned boy on how to remedy the terrible situation in which he has found himself, because, as Morelli observes, the "pupilli," that is those who have been left fatherless, are "robbed, cheated and betrayed by all, but mostly by [their] in-laws and neighbours." Therefore, so as not to "leave thus naked and abandoned the luckless young boy," he will teach him seven remedies suited to the seven misfortunes that may befall him; remedies "that he should take care to follow, if he wishes to grasp at any spark of hope that this thorny and cruel life may offer."[49] The reasons for such a harsh, pessimistic tone will become clearer later. Morelli is actually talking about himself, because it is he who was orphaned at the age of three and taught to work and study through a great deal of corporal punishment. He too, as he recognized in a bitter recollection of his own life that he claims the devil had inspired him to write, behaved with detached severity toward his oldest son, who died in his youth:

> Your first child was a son, so that his death would really break your heart. You saw him intelligent and healthy, so when you lost him you would suffer more; you loved him and yet you never made him happy in this love; you did not treat him as a son but as a stranger; you never gave him a moment's rest; you never looked on him kindly; you never kissed him once; you worked him to death in your shop, and thrashed him cruelly and often. And finally, when he was mortally ill, you didn't realize that he was on the brink of death.[50]

The "you" to whom the memoirs are addressed is therefore evidently also the mirror image of the "I" of Morelli himself. One of the seven remedies the orphan is advised to follow is to read and study the great writers of the past, such as Virgil, Boethius, and Seneca; this should be done habitually, for at least one hour a day. If such an exercise may appear exacting, Morelli assures his readers that its benefits will be felt in old age:

> You shall not prize so much wealth, children, status or any great or honorable preeminence, once you have knowledge and can repute yourself a man and not a beast.

> ... You shall have all the great men at your disposal: you can be with Virgil in your study as long as you want; he won't tell you no, but will answer your questions and will advise and teach you at no cost whatsoever; he shall take away your melancholy thought, and give you pleasure and consolation.[51]

As Petrarch had already argued, we are sure that books will be at our complete disposal and allow us complete freedom and control ("you shall have all the great men at your disposal"); moreover—the merchant observes—these services are entirely free. The theme of the pleasure of reading is intertwined here with that of a remedy against melancholy: reading becomes a therapy against boredom but also, as we read immediately afterward, the tool to achieve knowledge and elevate the soul so that it may be prepared to understand the teachings of religion: "You can be with Boethius, with Dante and the other poets, with Cicero, who will teach you perfect diction; with Aristotle, who will teach you philosophy. You shall know the reason for things, and every little thing shall give you the greatest pleasure. You shall be with the blessed prophets in the Holy Scripture, you shall read and study the Bible, you shall learn the great acts of those holy prophets, you shall be fully instructed in the faith and the advent of the Son of God, your soul shall have great consolation, great joy and great sweetness."[52] The recurrent theme of sweetness and pleasure seems to cluster around reading, making it an oasis of peace in "this thorny and cruel life," dominated by the harsh laws of economic interest and violence. What also stands out, in this work by a lay Florentine from the first half of the fifteenth century, is the author's belief that we should make it our business to read and study the Bible.[53]

As with the classics, what takes place is once again communion with a living presence: the holy prophets, Morelli assures his reader, will be with you. Was there, we may ask, in such advice, an echo of the preachers, as well as of those prayer manuals, such as the *Meditationes de vita Christi*, which taught their readers to re-create as vividly as possible in their minds and in their hearts scenes from the Bible so that they might interact with them? "When you hear something said or done by Christ—as one such manual advised—in the Gospels or in a sermon, or elsewhere, place yourself before the eyes of your mind and as you think it over become accustomed to Him, develop your familiarity with Him and be His servant."[54] The passage from Morelli recalls, as Eugenio Garin pointed out, a 1425 sermon by St. Bernardine of Siena.[55] Engaging in that direct dialogue with his audience to which so much of his popular success was due, Bernardine argues, "Should you not experience great pleasure if you saw or heard Jesus Christ preach? Indeed the greatest! And may not the same be said for St Paul, St Augustine, St Gregory, St Jerome, St Ambrose and the other Doctor Saints? Of course! Now go, read their books, whichever you like or esteem best; you will talk to them and they with you; they will hear you and you them, and your enjoyment will be great."[56]

Bernardine's particular skill lay in reworking, through a vigorously physical lens, the traditional images of hermeneutic reflection, such as those connected with the need to eat, to ruminate on the word of God, to seek the juice that lies hidden within the bark. Soon after the passage just quoted, Bernardine remarks on the greater sweetness afforded by the Scriptures compared to that of secular reading matter. "The Holy Scriptures hide within them the sweetness and the glory of Paradise. . . . Squeeze the Holy Scriptures, that is their glosses, and the more you read them and study them, the more sweetness they will yield, and the more gratifying will be the flavor of God you will taste."[57] Just one year earlier, in 1424, he had preached to his audience the need to savor the word of God "like the drunken man who almost devours his wine" and, through this practice of reading, to set free the God that lay as if entrapped in the letter of the word: "And then God will tell you: 'I was in prison and you freed me,' that is you made the effort to bring me out of the letter, that is from my word. And thus you did not take the prison with you but rather God you led from the prison."[58] Here, once again, is the image of the text as a prisoner awaiting his freedom, an image that carried the day in the humanist rediscovery of Quintilian. Certainly, the meaning here is radically different: what must be freed is the spirit of the word, but it is fascinating to see how the same images recur again and again, how this liberation is entrusted into the hands of the reader.

Between 1438 and 1441, Leon Battista Alberti wrote *Theogenius,* which once completed was dedicated to Lionello d'Este and sent to him on the occasion of his father's death. Written at a time of great suffering and difficulty, this dialogue in Italian seeks to suggest possible remedies and administer comfort. Theogenius, the wise man who lives alone at the top of a hill and spends his time reading and writing, receives a visit from Microtiro, to whom he recounts, as in a game of Chinese boxes, the speech given by the old sage Genipatro to Tichipedo, the powerful and arrogant youth (Alberti enjoyed playing with invented names). Genipatro was once rich and famous but now extolls poverty and solitude, and it is precisely here that we find the passage in which he celebrates the pleasures and the enchantment of reading:

> I am never less alone that when I find myself in solitude. I always have close to me men who are both extremely clever and beautifully eloquent, *and I can go to them in the evening and usefully employ most of the night reasoning with them;* so that if I take enjoyment from things that are funny and festive, then I find all the comic writers, Plautus and Terence, and those specializing in the ridiculous, such as Apuleius, Lucian and Martial, will furnish me with as much laughter as I want. If I wish to learn things that may be useful in the management of the household, and to preserve oneself without pain, I find many wise men, when asked, will tell me about agriculture, about the education of children, about managing and regulating the morals of a household, about friendships, and statecraft, all excellent and valuable things. Or, if I want to explore the causes and principles of the various effects I see caused by nature, if I want to distinguish truth from falsehood, good from evil; if I seek to know myself as well as the things that we do in order to recognize and revere, through them, our Father, the excellent and first teacher and creator of such wonders, there is no lack of the holiest of philosophers, by listening to whom I grow by the hour a more satisfied, wiser, and better man.[59]

The company of books is the true remedy for solitude: they stave off the evils that are attendant on frequent commerce with men and the moral degeneracy of politics: Theogenius had retired to the country when the "republic" had slid into "disaster and poverty."[60] As Genipatro had observed immediately before, "You cannot, within such a multitude, avoid being surrounded by pleaders, informers, assenters, sycophants, denigrators, by men who are lascivious or superficial, immodest, full of vices, and noxious, from whom hour after hour you hear or are subjected to hateful things that cannot but make you indignant."[61] The dialogue with books is therefore placed at the very heart of an alternative world, an oneiric and utopian space, where poverty and solitude paradoxically signify their opposite.[62] Martin McLaughlin has called attention to how the opening of the passage, "I am never less alone than when I find myself alone," echoes the beginning of Book III of Cicero's *De officiis,* where Cato's words to Scipio, "numquam se minus otiosum esse, quam cum otiosus, nec minus solum, quam cum solus esset," are reported.[63] Scipio's remedy for solitude, however, is not books but dialogue with himself. Cicero stresses that, while for Scipio *otium* and solitude were a choice, he himself was violently forced out of public life.[64] In this context, Alberti's echoing of Cicero's text is charged with particular intensity: the situation that his characters find themselves in is closer to that of Cicero than to that of Scipio, and their retreat to solitude is linked to the cruelty and petty baseness of public life. Therefore, dialogue with books marks a departure from the traditional model and assumes a particular relevance. As McLaughlin points out, we are presented with a valuable updated catalogue of what Alberti considered to be classics (with the comic writers in a very prominent position and the important new inclusion of Lucian). In doing so, the author outlines a sort of pattern for an ideal library, where books, as they did for Petrarch, offer not only knowledge but a moral guide.[65]

One particularly striking detail in this description, in which books are presented as living beings, is that the time of day marked out as most propitious for this conversation should be the evening, which immediately brings to mind the most renowned and fascinating example of the motif we are exploring: the letter sent by Niccolò Machiavelli to Francesco Vettori on 10 December 1513.

Nevertheless, it should be noted that Alberti's dialogue vigorously questions the thaumaturgical value of studying and conversing with books. Tichipedio says,

> Among the other things that cause unhappiness, my dear Teogonio, the most important one seems to me that you spend your nights awake wrestling with so many works and that you employ such assiduous effort on supremely useless things. Will you ever allow yourself to desist from turning your pages day and night, day after day? What sweet friendship do these books of yours offer that you spend your time with them and become pale, exhausted, consumed, poor, and sickly? . . . You seek immortality by being not fully alive while still living, through this obstinate study of yours.[66]

True, this speech is made by the morally deficient Tichipedo; nevertheless it constitutes a vigorous desecration of one of the cornerstones of the myth whose development I am trying to reconstruct: reading as a form of friendship and the world of books as a world endowed with life.

6. Bembo, Raphael, and the Lacerated Body of Rome

The myth of the lacerated and reassembled body gained, as we have seen, a central position in texts celebrating the rediscovery of Quintilian's *Institutiones;* more generally, its subterranean presence is perceivable in those humanist texts that lament the waning of the classical world and dream of its rebirth. To bring back to life the works of antiquity is the first and most obvious step to their rebirth into new literary forms through the practice of imitation. The myth of Aesculapius thus features in the background of both the rediscovery of codexes and the philological work that follows this rediscovery. Particularly noteworthy in this light is a set of powerful images that occurs in a short philological work by Pietro Bembo, *Dialogue on Virgil's Gnat and Terence's Comedies* (*De Vergilii Culice et Terentii fabulis liber*), or, to be more precise, in the framing dialogue that introduces the philological part proper.[67] The textual context is a journey to Rome, which Pietro did in fact make in 1502 in the company of Vincenzo Querini, though inspiration for the dialogue most certainly preceded it: Fedra (the classical pseudonym given to Tommaso Inghirami) is here recalling conversations that took place, probably between 1490 and 1493, between Pomponio Leto and Ermolao Barbaro, the Venetian ambassador who in 1491 became the patriarch of Aquileia. The two friends are filled with melancholy as they observe a decapitated bust lying in the grass and denounce the sorry state of the ruins, caused by the action of time and the neglect of their contemporaries. The bust that lies at their feet was perhaps the stone portrait of a great man, who wished to leave a memory of himself to posterity: if he could see himself in that state, he would indeed weep and beg to be restored. This, however, observes Pomponio, would be impossible: ancient Rome was full of statues of illustrious men, a stone population that was almost double that of the living: "so that it seemed that in Rome there lived a second people, made of stone."[68] The almost surreal image we are presented with must have been rather common: Bembo here seems particularly conscious of Alberti's use of it, but the same image snakes its way around the poems of Tebaldeo and is to be found also in Pomponio Gaurico.[69] If, Bembo continues, it seems impossible to reassemble the statues and the disfigured "corpses" of the ancient buildings, an even more urgent and arduous task is required: to bring back to life the texts of antiquity, so that we may hear the voice of their authors.[70] Many texts, he laments, are forever lost, and many have reached us "mutilated and shortened" either in the form of manuscripts or in careless printed editions.[71] If Terence, Horace, and Virgil could be resurrected, Pomponio wonders, "would [they] prefer me to look at their faces, or would they rather I listened to their words and speeches?"[72] As tradition decreed, we find the spoken word once more reaffirming its superiority: the true portrait of a writer lies in his work rather than in his statue. At the same time, however, it is fascinating to see how certain metaphors are threaded through and intertwined with the subject of restoring ancient ruins, reconstructing the *true* "face" of a text, and the production of new works. These metaphors are permeated by a powerful desire that the text should return to life. The reassemblage of scattered fragments and the idea of rebirth offer the lens through which to analyze the task that Leo X had entrusted to Raphael: to reconstruct the map of Imperial Rome.[73] When Raphael died, in the prime of his life, in 1520, among those who mourned his loss was his friend Castiglione, who immediately summoned up the myth of Aesculapius:

> Because he healed our broken bodies with the art of medicine, and recalled Hippolytus from the Stygian waters, the god of Epidaurus himself was dragged to the waves of the Styx: thus the price for life was death for the maker [of life]. You too, Raphael, have moved the jealousy of the gods, while restoring Rome, her whole corpse dilapidated, with your miraculous art, and recalling to life and pristine glory the remains of a city maimed by arms, fire and age: death's indignation was aroused by returning to life what had once been extinct, and of renewing once more, disdaining the way of all flesh, what the long days of time had slowly taken away. Thus you lie, alas, miserably taken away in the prime of life, and bring home to us: we owe ourselves and all that is ours to death.[74]

The reader who conjures up the writer so that he may dialogue with him, therefore, performs a ritual that is part of an overarching myth of rebirth, whose constitutive elements are the possibility of bringing back to life what no longer exists and recomposing that which—in ancient ruins as in time-worn manuscripts—is fragmentary and dispersed. In both cases, a ghost is being pursued, and the desire that fuels this pursuit feeds on a sense that something is lacking, that our relationship with the present is unsatisfying. It is the subtle action of this constellation of ideas that inflects the preface to Book III of Bembo's *Prose della volgar lingua* (Writings on the vulgar tongue), when, in his description of the ruins of Rome and the pilgrimage of artists from all over the world to study and imitate them, the hidden spring of literary memory evokes the ghost of Beatrice: "This city, which by its many and reverend relics left unto this day lying about, by the insults of the enemy nations and of time, who is himself no simple adversary, even more so than by her famous seven hills, above which she yet sits, she at once reveals herself as Rome to those who behold her; she sees coming toward her throughout the day a throng of artists from near and distant parts."[75] This city that "sé Roma essere subitamente dimostra a chi la mira" (at once reveals herself as Rome to those who behold her) here recalls the Beatrice of what is perhaps the most famous sonnet of the *Vita nova*, "Tanto gentile e tanto onesta pare." This allusion, which has hitherto escaped critical notice, is a memory so powerful and viscous that, once recognized, we are forced to look with new eyes on the description of the ruins of Rome, at the heart of which we now find the image of Beatrice.

> E par che sia una cosa venuta
> da cielo in terra a miracol mostrare.
> Mostrasi sì piacente a chi la mira,
> che dà per li occhi una dolcezza al core
> che 'ntender no la può chi no la prova.
>
> (She seems to be a creature come from Heaven
> To earth, to manifest a miracle.
> She appears so beautiful to those who see her,
> That she imparts, through the eyes, a sweetness to the heart,
> And he who has not felt this cannot understand.)[76]

The ability to behold ("mirare"), the particular quality of the gaze, is the essential requirement for the miracle to take place and for Heaven and Earth to communicate.[77] Thus the ruins of Rome become like "relics," parts of a body that is dead, but also fragments from which the ancient power and beauty may be released anew, traces that mark an irredeemable absence but can be revisited, interpreted, and reembodied in new forms. And there, hidden among the ruins of Rome, at the heart of the text that aims to show the path to be followed if new life is to be breathed into Italian poetry, is the ghost of Beatrice.

The recuperation of antiquity, the renaissance of the arts, and the rebirth of literature in the vulgar tongue are closely enmeshed. In particular, as we have seen, the dialogue written by the young Bembo, *De Virgilii culice,* re-proposes, albeit within the canonical hierarchy, a juxtaposition between the portrait of an author (in this case represented by statuary) and the text he has written. It was a long-lasting cultural debate; some of the significant moments in which it intertwines with the central theme of this book are discussed in Chapter 3.

3

Portraits, or The Desire to See the Author

1. The Portrait of the Soul and the Portrait of the Face

Pliny the Elder (*Naturalis historia,* XXXV, 151) gives one well-known account of the origin of the portrait. A young girl captures the image of her beloved, who is about to go abroad: on the wall, she draws in outline the shadow of his face cast by a lamp. Butades, her father, fills this contour with pressed clay, thus making the first portrait, the object of which was to comfort his daughter for the absence of her beloved. Desire is thus ingrained in the very origin of portraiture, which both makes its absent object present and highlights the very fact of its absence, of its distance; it is located on a threshold; it is a "sign tinged with reality."[1]

It is easy to understand why, as mentioned at the end of Chapter 2, the theme of the portrait crosses paths at regular intervals with the theme of this book. At the root of the magic of reading, the element that enables dialogue and indeed an almost personal encounter with an author, is precisely the capacity of the text to represent its writer's soul, to furnish a truthful portrait. According to an ancient hierarchical distinction, while an image can only represent a face and must therefore stop at the surface, the written word can faithfully reflect the soul of a writer. Between book and portrait, a complex game is played out, their relationship teeming with analogies but also reciprocal competition and negation.[2]

For example, between 56 and 55 BC, Cicero (*Epist. Fam.,* V, 12, 7) asked Lucceius to write a history of his life, from the conspiracy of Catiline to his return from exile: he praises Lucceius's extraordinary qualities as a writer and extolls the superior power and significance of the biography compared to the portrait: the noble Agesilaus, king of Sparta, he points out, "would never suffer any picture or statue of himself to be taken. The single treatise which Xenophon has written in praise of that renowned general is more to his glory, than all the pictures and statues of all the artists in the Universe."[3] Cicero was expressing what in all likelihood was a widespread and probably sincere conviction, even if it is here less immediately apparent because of the context in which it is expressed and by the flattering and insistent tone of the letter.

Seneca's position is more nuanced and intriguing. In his *Letters to Lucilius,* he compares the writings of the ancient authors to the portraits of the great men of the family, the ancestors, which were placed in the atrium of the house.

> Why shouldn't I keep images of great men beside me, to stir my mind to action, and even to celebrate their birthdays? Why shouldn't I address them by name each time, as a way to honor them? The same homage I render to my teachers, I also owe to the teachers of the human race, who are the source of so much good. If I see a consul or a praetor, I will honor their office in all the usual ways: I'll jump down from my horse; I'll uncover my head; I'll yield them the walkway. Well then! Am I to give anything but the most respectful welcome to Marcus Cato, the elder and the younger? To Laelius the Wise? To Socrates and Plato? To Zeno and Cleanthes? Truly I revere these men: when such great names are mentioned, I rise to my feet.[4]

The parallel between writing and portraits is staged through a colorful comparison with the honor and deference shown to the authorities one may encounter in a public place. Both become the object of a cult that keeps their memory alive: we mark the anniversary of the birth of great men, we symbolically stand up when their names are mentioned or when we find ourselves in the presence of the great works that inhabit the spaces of the soul. To liken this to the encounters one may have in everyday life, in the streets of the city, serves to construct an inner theater where the portraits and the writings of great men, indeed their very names, become alive and almost physically tangible.

This attitude is something very different from that which Seneca mocks in *De tranquillitate animi* (IX, 5–7), in a passage redeployed, as we have seen, by Petrarch (see Chapter 1, section 5), in which both books and the portraits of their authors are merely ornaments that decorate the space between the hot and cold baths in a rich man's house, the accoutrements of a social display that only thinly veils indifference and ignorance. Here Seneca hints, albeit with critical intent, at a custom (that of exhibiting portraits in libraries) that we will discuss at a later point. For the moment, I only wish to observe that, here too, Seneca establishes, between visual image and text, a hierarchy that exalts the latter above the former: "I am grateful to you for writing so often," he thanks Lucilius, "for you are showing me yourself, in the only way you can. It never fails: I receive your letter and right away we are together. If portraits of absent friends are a delight, refreshing our memory and easing the pain of separation with a kind of comfort, though false and empty, how much more delightful are letters, which bring us real traces, real news of an absent friend! For what is sweetest about seeing someone face to face is also to be found in a letter that bears the imprint of a friend's hand—a moment of recognition."[5] Following the ancient topos, the written form triumphs over the visual in its ability to convey the true and secret portrait of the absent person. The autographical letter, in particular, has the additional advantage of preserving and transmitting a physical trait, "the imprint of [his] hand": a notion that enjoyed a long history of popularity, unfolding through different formulations, right down to the particularly eloquent example of a short treatise by Camillo Baldi, a professor at the University of Bologna, titled *Come da una lettera missiva si conoscano la natura e qualità dello scrittore* (How from an epistle one may know the nature and quality of its writer; 1622).[6] In this essay, stylistic analysis, the traditional method used to reconstruct the soul of the writer by examining his writing, its "nature and quality," is flanked by graphology and physiognomy. More will be said of the latter further on, but it should be noted here that a modern version of physiognomy, promoted by Lavater, may have been one of the factors that stimulated Goethe's fascination with autographs, of which he possessed a vast collection. In a letter to Jacobi, he waxes lyrical over his passion for this type of written document: "This visual experience is indispensable for me, because great men become present through their handwriting."[7] The autograph here clearly contributes to the magic of reading.

2. Portraits in Libraries

If we set aside for a moment the traditional hierarchy between text and image, there was something in the topos we are exploring that encouraged collaboration between its two components. If reading involves an encounter with the author, this encounter will be made more vivid and intense by evoking this author's features and even, almost, his physical presence, and this rite will be accomplished with the aid of a portrait, by means of which words and images may come together and support one another. The link between writers' portraits and "speaking" books was already visible in a passage from Pliny's *Naturalis historia* (XXXV, 9) in which a Hellenistic custom, newly imported to Rome, is described: "We must not pass over a novelty that has also been invented, in that likenesses made, if not of gold or silver, yet at all events of bronze are set up in the libraries in honor of those whose immortal spirits speak to us in the same places, nay more, even imaginary likenesses are modeled and our affection gives birth to countenances that have not been handed down to us, as occurs in the case of Homer."[8] If souls speak through books, the need to envisage the shape of the desired object is also prompted by them, and this encourages the production of imaginary portraits, spurred on by the desire to give Homer recognizable features, to really *see* his face.[9] This desire would, over the course of the centuries, be one of the fundamental drives in the creation of many a false likeness.[10]

The passage from Pliny enjoyed lasting fortune. Worth mentioning at this stage of our investigation is Pomponio Gaurico, a man of letters who lived between Padua and Naples, wrote a commentary on Horace's *Ars poetica*, and in 1504 published in Florence a treatise titled *De sculptura*. Among the arts that a sculptor must know, Gaurico explains, physiognomy occupies an important place, as it illustrates the connection between outer physical traits and inner qualities. It is through this art, he feels, that it will now be possible to rekindle the visibility of the great men of the past, because, by interpreting their works and linking this interpretation to what we know of the authors—the twin facets of their writing and what has been written about them—it will be possible to precisely reconstruct their features: "Sculptors shall hold it [physiognomy] in high esteem, because through it they may represent with great ease that very Homer that we so wish to see, as well as the sage men of ancient Greece, Cleobulus, Periander,

Solon, Thales, Chilo, Pittacus, Bias, and, among ours, the two Catos."[11] Homer is the first to be mentioned; he incarnates most forcefully, as it were, the desire to own a portrait, a material image, of the great men of the past. Written at the beginning of the sixteenth century, this passage presents physiognomy as a kind of shortcut to the attainment of the desire Pliny spoke of, as the best instrument for translating into a *visible* portrait the invisible portrait we glimpse through the text.[12] Because physiognomy was considered capable of evoking this subtextual portrait, it played its part in transforming the act of reading into a dialogue.

In the classical world, the tradition of portraits in libraries probably started in the libraries of Alexandria and Pergamon;[13] Pliny (*Naturalis historia,* XXXV, 10–11) sees in this an example of the passionate love of portraits that existed in antiquity.[14] He follows this assertion by noting that Caius Asinius Pollio, "by founding a library, first made works of genius the property of the public"; he created a public library that even contained a portrait of one of his contemporaries, Varro. In other cases, Pliny notes, the portraits intertwine with the writing: Atticus, for example, the friend to whom Cicero addressed his letters, had gathered into one volume the epigrams celebrating the actions of illustrious personages and had placed them beneath their portraits;[15] Varro accompanied his *elogia* with seven hundred portraits of the men he praised, "not allowing their likenesses to disappear or the lapse of ages to prevail against immortality in men. Herein Varro was the inventor of a benefit that even the gods might envy, since he not only bestowed immortality but dispatched it all over the world, enabling his subjects to be ubiquitous, like the gods."[16] Pliny's words are themselves eloquent praise of how portrait and word can defy death and time, creating a semidivine presence that may rouse the anger of the gods. Suetonius recounts that Tiberius, who was particularly fond of certain Greek poets, had their works and their images placed "in public libraries among the most illustrious ancient authors,"[17] and numerous ancient sources record that libraries often featured paintings, statues, and bronzes of celebrated men, often accompanied by inscriptions, a practice that would also be copied in some Christian libraries.[18]

These ancient models enjoyed a particularly marked revival in the fifteenth century, throughout which the example of Petrarch continued to be significant. His complex relationship with images, and above all with portraits, has been at the center of scholarly interest over the past few decades.[19] One need only think of the fascination exerted over him by the portrait of

Portraits, or The Desire to See the Author

St. Ambrose: in a letter to Francesco Nelli, dated 23 August 1353, Petrarch describes in glowing terms his new Milanese house, its breathtaking view of the snow-capped Alps as summer wanes, and above all the pleasure he experiences in its closeness to the church of St. Ambrose, where he could admire both the tomb and the portrait of the saint: "Often I stop, filled with veneration, to admire his image hanging high up on the wall; this portrait, which is said to be an excellent likeness, seems almost to live and breathe and offers no small recompense for my coming here. It is indeed not easy to find suitable words to describe the gravity of his face, the majesty of his expression, or the tranquility of his look. The voice alone is missing for you to imagine Ambrose himself, alive, standing before you."[20] Petrarch here returns to a topos that is especially dear to him: the portrait appears almost alive, though it lacks a speaking voice.[21] Nevertheless, it is described as "no small reward for having come here," as if to justify his move to Milan, where he had been invited by Archbishop Giovanni Visconti, thereby raising violent criticism dictated by political reasons. Extremely interesting in this context is Bettini's observation that "it was precisely during this Milanese period that Petrarch was reading works by St. Ambrose, in fact peppering the margins of the text with many passionate annotations, such as '*lege cum timore et fletu*' or '*si hoc dicit iste, tu quid?*'"[22] The saint's portrait, so expressive and so closely mirroring his true likeness, must have played a part in the ritual of reading his works, evoking his vivid presence throughout an experience that Petrarch describes as highly emotional.

Another portrait, this time of Petrarch himself, is relevant here. It is both the proof and the result of the extraordinary admiration felt for the poet by a goldsmith from Bergamo called Enrico Capra. Petrarch talks about it at length, noting that Enrico "spent a sizable portion of his patrimony in [Petrarch's] honor, displaying the bust, name and portrait of his new friend in every nook of his house, and imprinting his image even more deeply in his heart."[23] The image placed within the heart occupies the privileged position, but it also works in tandem with the exhibited portrait. The goldsmith, furthermore, became the protagonist of an exemplary tale, as, thanks to his friendship with Petrarch, he abandoned his art to pursue literary studies. These and other passages in the letters testify to the fact that, as Monica Donato has observed, "Petrarch is the first known subject of a widespread practice of individual portraiture, a fact even more noteworthy in that he was a private individual who was painted during his lifetime exclusively because of his fame."[24]

Petrarch's antiquarian passion also led him to turn his attention to ancient coins in order to retrieve a likeness of those great men of history whose actions he had read about. According to the Roman tradition, the image of a hero can inspire both memory and emulation, thus performing an exemplary function. Therefore, Petrarch recounts in a letter of February 1355 to Angelo Tosetti that when he met the Emperor Charles IV in Mantua, he gave him as a gift "some gold and silver coins bearing the portraits of our ancient rulers, . . . coins that I treasured, and among them was the head of Caesar Augustus," adding, "'Here, O Caesar,' I said, 'are the men whom you have succeeded, here are those whom you must try to imitate and admire.'"[25]

Petrarch also labored long and hard on the biographies collected in *De viris illustribus*.[26] On his death, his secretary Lombardo Della Seta, who was extremely close to the poet in the last years of his life, completed the section of *De viris* dedicated to the Roman heroes and continued the *Compendium* of the work begun by Petrarch. A set of complex relationships links the *Compendium* to the figurative cycle of illustrious men that the signore of Padua, Francesco il Vecchio da Carrara, the poet's final patron, commissioned to be painted in the Hall of Giants (Sala dei Giganti) of his residence, the present Palazzo Liviano. Only two portraits of that ancient cycle survive, one of Petrarch in his study (see Chapter 1, Figure 1.1), the other of Lombardo della Seta. What is visible today is the sumptuous sixteenth-century decoration with which the older cycle was overlaid.[27] It was long believed that the illustrious men painted at the end of the fourteenth century were based on Petrarch's text, but a reconsideration of what Lombardo della Seta wrote in 1379 in his "Supplementum" to *De viris,* directly addressing the signore of Padua, suggests a different chronology. The iconographic plan would appear to have been earlier than, or at least contemporaneous with, Petrarch's writing of the *De viris*.[28] "You have selected," Lombardo writes to the lord of Padua,

> the deeds of some famous men, which have been described by the greatest writers, you have made these men not only honorably welcome in your spirit and your soul, . . . you have also offered them a splendid part of your great hall, and as the ancients did you have shown your hospitality by dressing them in gold and purple, with images and inscriptions . . . and, without forgetting yourself and your innate

virtue, you have expressed outwardly, by means of excellent paintings, what your supreme ingenuity had conceived should be placed inside, so that you could always have before your eyes the image of those men whom you had undertaken to love for their great deeds.[29]

Furthermore, Lombardo adds, Francesco had asked Petrarch to recount the deeds of these great men: "so that you could not just see, but listen to these virtuous and delectable things, and mold your soul on higher thoughts."[30] Unfortunately, Lombardo comments, death overtook Petrarch when he was more than halfway through the work.

The ways in which Petrarch's text is linked to the ancient frescoes of the court of Padua, as well as the chronology of this connection, must be rethought. What is of interest here is the relationship that Petrarch's secretary posits between the exemplary images transmitted by the texts, by the ancient biographies, and the images that were visible to the eye, resplendent in their place of honor in the great hall. Petrarch's writing is deployed to reinforce the bond between exteriority and interiority, between sight and hearing: it is his words that effect the transformation of the images into exemplary models, into nourishment for the soul.

Let us examine some further examples of how, during the Quattrocento, the models of antiquity took on new life, also through the portraits that decorated libraries and *studioli*.[31] Lionello d'Este, as Angelo Decembrio tells us in a dialogue set in 1441 and titled *De politia literaria,* believed that having paintings and sculptures that transmitted the memory of gods and heroes was highly desirable, adding that the image of St. Jerome writing in his retreat was particularly common and suited to the context, as it taught one how to seek in the silence of a library the isolation necessary for writing.[32] Classical and Christian traditions were interwoven, making the library the new retreat, the ideal site for study and meditation. In the 1540 edition of *De politia literaria,* the image on the frontispiece celebrated the friendly dialogue-banquet that takes place in the library, at a table (see Figure 3.1). In this encounter, mental rather than mensal, as Marc Fumaroli has observed, "the bread is the book."[33]

In Bracciolini's *buen retiro* at Terranuova, he housed his library and his collection of antiquities and, as we have already seen (Chapter 2, section 5), celebrated the pleasures of engaging in dialogue with the ancients. It was here that he located his dialogue on what constitutes the essence of nobility,

Figure 3.1. Angelo Decembrio, *De Politia literaria* (Augusta: Heinrich Steiner, 1540), frontispiece. *Private collection.*

written in 1439 and 1440 but set a few years earlier, since one of the two speakers, Niccolò Niccoli—the other is Lorenzo de' Medici—had died in 1437. Here the tension between portraits and books brings into play the issue of true nobility, by juxtaposing the nobility of blood, exhibited in the gallery by the portraits of ancestors, with the nobility of the soul, which stems from virtue and wisdom and is nourished by books. Lorenzo points to that classical tradition we have been revisiting, that of portraits placed in libraries and gardens, as being proof that images also can act as signs of memory and spurs to imitation.[34] It is this model that Bracciolini is keen to rekindle, and it becomes clear that what is at stake is also his own social affirmation.

It might also be useful to add to our examples Filarete's statement on this subject in his *Treatise on Architecture*. Written in the 1460s, the text paints a vivid portrait of how Piero de' Medici, when rendered infirm by the gout, sought refuge in the studiolo of his palazzo in Via Larga in Florence: "he takes whatever pleasures he can to give recreation to his mind and refreshment to his nature." He looks at his books: "they seem like nothing but solid pieces of gold." He has texts in Latin, Greek, and Italian, each of which "he has honored . . . , as you have understood, with fine script, miniatures, and ornaments of gold and silk, as a man who recognizes the dignity of their authors and through love of them has wished to honor their works in this manner." Furthermore, "he has effigies and portraits of all the emperors and noble men who ever lived made in gold, silver, bronze, jewels, marble, or other materials. They are marvelous things to see. Their dignity is such that only looking at [them] . . . fills his soul with delight and pleasure at their excellence."[35]

The portraits and the books of the great men share a context where the pleasure experienced is also visual and the repast rich and various; the authors are all present, in the manuscripts that contain their works; the miniatures and the precious materials that embellish the codices are a mark of recognition of the greatness of their authors, of the feelings of love and gratitude that the owner of the studiolo feels for them. Filarete, as Stephen Campbell has rightly argued, endeavored to ease the tension between the ideal of the contemplative reader and the material splendor of his studiolo.[36]

The Vatican Library, founded or, rather, reconstituted by Sixtus IV in 1475, was the first library to be decorated with magnificent frescoes; among these were the portraits of the sages of antiquity and the Church Fathers painted in the lunette by Domenico and Davide Ghirlandaio.[37] Even Erasmus—who, as we shall see, harbored some reservations about portraiture—did not fail to decorate with portraits the library in the ideal house described in one of the *Colloquies, The Godly Feast,* which was written in 1522: "Now let's go into the library," says Eusebius, the host, "which is furnished with choice if not numerous books. . . . This hanging globe puts the whole world before your eyes. Here on the wall every region is painted in a larger space. On the walls you will see pictures of famous teachers. To paint them all would have been an endless task. Christ . . . has the foremost place."[38] The humanist tradition was thus upheld but safely brought back within a Christocentric vision.

The place we shall now enter, which has miraculously survived almost entirely intact, is a space where the tension we have seen between the portrait of the face and the portrait of the soul has been entirely superseded, as if it were forgotten.

3. The Studiolo of Federico da Montefeltro: A Theater of Reading

a. The Studiolo as a Micro-Macrocosm

There is a place where we may still see from close up just how the theater of reading comes alive, how it becomes possible to become immersed, beyond the boundaries of time, in an ideal world, where one may rediscover and rebuild the self: this is the studiolo of Federico da Montefeltro (1422–1482) in Urbino. We shall approach it, as in a game of Chinese boxes, guided by the mnemonic reconstruction of the room in Castiglione's *Cortegiano*:

> Among his other commendable enterprises, Duke Federico built on the rugged site of Urbino a palace which many believe to be the most beautiful in Italy; and he furnished it so well and so appropriately that it seemed more like a city than a mere palace. For he adorned it not only with the usual objects, such as silver vases, wall-hangings of the richest cloth of gold, silk and other similar material, but also with countless antique statues of marble and bronze, with rare pictures, and with every kind of musical instrument; nor would he tolerate anything that was not most rare and outstanding. Then, at great cost, he collected a large number of the finest and rarest books, in Greek, Latin and Hebrew, all of which he adorned with gold and silver, believing that they were the crowning glory of his great palace.[39]

The studiolo is situated within this palace-city, mirroring in its space the interplay of perspectives Castiglione hints at, between microcosm and macrocosm: its intarsios and its paintings referencing the library, the musical instruments, and the military and political career of the duke—the quotation of a part, as it were, evoking the whole. It is a sort of *mise en abyme* of all that makes the palace great, but filtered through the lens of the prince's unique and personal view, making it in many ways an ideal portrait of Federico.[40]

It is well-known that the Duke took a personal interest in the building of the palace and the construction of the studiolo. This is testified by Vespasiano da Bisticci in his biography of Federico, but it is also clearly demonstrated by the letters patent to Luciano Laurana, dated 1468, in which he appoints the architect to direct the building of his palace at Urbino.[41]

Federico greatly esteems, we read in the epistle, those men who are experts in architecture, as its virtue is "founded upon the arts of arithmetic and geometry, which are the foremost of the seven liberal arts because they depend on exact certainty": "Architecture furthermore requires great knowledge and intellect and we appreciate and esteem it most highly. . . . And we have searched everywhere, but principally in Tuscany, . . . having decided to make our city of Urbino a beautiful residence worthy of the rank and fame of our ancestors and our own stature."[42] The letter is an extraordinary document, it has been acutely argued, of a new idea of architecture, linked to the "mathematical humanism" that was a defining feature of the court of Urbino and to the influence of Leon Battista Alberti.[43]

Federico showed a similar personal interest in the studiolo he had built for his palazzo: "He was much interested in painting," wrote Vespasiano da Bisticci, "and because he could not find in Italy painters in oil to suit his taste he sent to Flanders and brought thence a master who did at Urbino many very stately pictures, especially in Federico's study, where he represented philosophers, poets, and doctors of the Church, rendered with wondrous art."[44] The Flemish painter has generally been identified as Justus van Ghent, but other artists seem to have worked at the studiolo, possibly the Spaniard Pedro Berruguete, who is documented as being present in Urbino from 1477; it is to Pedro that the portrait of the Duke is attributed (though some scholars believe it to be a work of Justus of Ghent), in which Federico appears in full armor, fully absorbed in reading a book from his library and accompanied by his son Guidubaldo holding his father's scepter (see Figure 3.2).[45] It is a splendid portrayal of the synthesis between arms and letters, between the active and the contemplative life that the Duke wished to embody. Whether or not this portrait was part of the studiolo has long been a subject of debate. What is certain is that a portrait of the Duke is visible among the intarsios: he is dressed in the toga that was the characteristic dress of the humanist and holds a lance that is pointing to the ground. This is the image of a victorious hero, an emulator of the ancients, and a purveyor of peace, but it is only one of the ways in which Federico's self is represented, diffracted, and celebrated within the space of the studiolo.[46] Before these ways are examined, another famous portrait of Federico should be mentioned: the diptych that he commissioned Piero della Francesca to make of himself and his wife, Battista Sforza (see Figure 3.3).[47] The Duke and Duchess are seen in profile, against the backdrop of a landscape whose distinguishing features are the precision of its

Figure 3.2. Justus van Ghent (or Pedro Berruguete), *Portrait of Federico da Montefeltro with His Son Guidubaldo,* oil on canvas, 1470s, Galleria Nazionale delle Marche, Palazzo Ducale di Urbino. *Ministero Beni a Attività Culturali e del Turismo / Scala, Florence.*

perspective and the extraordinary quality of the light; on the back of the portraits are represented two scenes of triumph: the triumph of Fame in the case of Federico and the triumph of Modesty for Battista, who is depicted in the act of reading a book (see Figure 3.4).

The inscription accompanying the triumph of the Duke celebrates the virtues that make him worthy to hold the scepter on a par with the greatest

Figure 3.3. Piero della Francesca, portrait of Federico da Montefeltro and Battista Sforza, oil on wood, 1465–1472, Galleria degli Uffizi, Florence. *Archivi Alinari, Florence.*

Figure 3.4. Piero della Francesca, triumphal scenes on the back of the portraits of Federico da Montefeltro and Battista Sforza, oil on wood, 1465–1472, Galleria degli Uffizi, Florence. *Archivi Alinari, Florence.*

military leaders; Battista, who indeed possessed a high degree of culture (which is perhaps alluded to in the book she is reading) and had held the reins of state during her husband's frequent absences, is feted for her stoical moderation and praised for the glory reflected on her by the great enterprises of her husband.[48] What was the viewer called on to gather from this dual process of seeing and reading required by the physical closeness of the portrait and the triumph? The function of the double structure is clearly encomiastic: the lord and lady must be "seen" as an incarnation of the twin virtues of Fame and Modesty. The viewer is guided along a pathway that connects the individual subject portrayed to the universal dimension of Virtues. The Duke and Duchess must appear as the historical, exemplary embodiment of a model of perfection. On the outside is an allegorical image, but the individual has not disappeared: the portraits of the signore and his wife are always present, even though they have been scaled down and placed at the center of a representation that pivots on the personifications of virtues. The transition that must be made is therefore from the individual to the universal, from the historical contingencies of the world we inhabit to the eternal world of values: it is a passage that both feeds memory and stimulates imitation—it is, in other words, an excellent introduction to the studiolo.

If, however, we want to gain an idea of Federico's true soul, we should probably follow the advice of Sir Thomas Bodley, founder, in 1598, of the Bodleian at Oxford.[49] The inscription placed above his portrait, as already mentioned in the introduction, reads,

> Thomae Bodlaei quicquid mortale Tabella
> ingentemque animam Bibliotheca refert.
>
> (This image portrays the mortal Thomas Bodley, but the library his vast soul.)

Let us therefore look at Federico's library, which benefited from his great personal care and a significant financial outlay.[50] While the volumes collected before 1464 are fewer than 100, at Federico's death, the library counted around 900 codices, 600 in Latin and Italian, 168 in Greek, 82 in Hebrew, and 2 in Arabic. Viewed in this light, the slightly gauche verses that Giovanni Santi, Raphael's father, dedicated to Federico in his *Cronaca rimata* (1492) offer a fairly faithful portrait of the Duke's interest:

principiò cum nobile intellecto
una Bibliothecha tanta e tale
che ad ogni ingegnio è altissimo dilecto
e in tucte facoltà universale.
Ivi adunò de libri un numer tanto,
che ogni chiar spirto li può spiegar l'ale.
. . . .
Po de diverse lingue anco ivi ho visti
Arabi, Greci et venerandi Hebrei,
libri diversi insiem cum gli altri misti

(He set up there with noble intellect
A library of such a size and nature
That every mind there finds such great delight
And universal knowledge therein dwells,
And there so many books he brought together
That every spirit bright and fair may there
Spread wide his wings and there take flight.
. . . .
And also saw I there so many tongues
Of Arabs, Greeks, and venerable Jews,
Books of so many kinds all brought together.)[51]

At least three hundred manuscripts came from Florence, courtesy of Vespasiano da Bisticci, who spared no praise for the library, the fruit of fourteen years of labor: "He alone had a mind to do what no one had done for a thousand years or more; that is, to create the finest library since ancient times. He spared neither cost nor labour," Vespasiano notes, lauding the extraordinary elegance of the bindings and the beauty of the miniatures: "In this library all the books are superlatively good, and written with the pen, and had there been one printed volume it would have been ashamed in such company."[52] While Vespasiano's words are often taken as a testimony to aristocratic resistance to the age of printing, it has in fact been ascertained that Federico's library also held some incunabula, elegant folio editions that would not have looked out of place sitting next to the precious manuscripts.[53]

The library was in a hall to the left of the entrance to the Palazzo Ducale, in the main courtyard. Throughout the centuries, its holdings have

A MARVELOUS SOLITUDE

Figure 3.5. The wood inlays in the Studiolo di Urbino, Palazzo Ducale, Galleria Nazionale delle Marche, Urbino. *Archivi Alinari, Florence.*

remained almost intact; its books were bought by Pope Alexander VII and are now housed as part of the Vatican Library. Federico's studiolo is a small, irregularly shaped room on the first floor (the *piano nobile*), at the heart of the Duke's apartment; it occupies a space halfway between the public and the private rooms. On the ground floor, exactly below it, we find two small rooms: one is dedicated to God (the Chapel of Forgiveness), the other to the Muses (the Temple of the Muses). The inscription exemplifies the desire to reconcile the classical and the Christian traditions, a project that is also visible in the studiolo.[54] What is particularly intriguing, however, is the relationship between the studiolo and the library, which bears some resemblance to the "city in the shape of a palace" mentioned at the beginning of this section. The small space of the studiolo expands illusionistically into multiple dimensions through the variety and position of the intarsia panels and paintings that cover its walls (see Figures 3.5). On the upper level, a wooden board is inscribed with the date 1476 and with the heraldic symbols of the Duke; on the intermediate level, disposed along two parallel lines, are twenty-eight portraits of illustrious men (see Figure 3.6), originally framed by double-arched windows; the

80

Figure 3.6. The portraits of illustrious men in the Studiolo di Urbino, Palazzo Ducale, Galleria Nazionale delle Marche, Urbino. *Archivi Alinari, Florence.*

wainscoting below is a triumph of intarsio perspectives, masterfully executed by Giuliano da Maiano and his workshop.[55]

In this way, the studiolo reflects and somehow condenses the library: the famous men who are also the authors of the works it preserves. Many of the portraits that we see in the studiolo reappear in the manuscript initials of the codices containing their works (albeit with iconographic variations and in a different technique).[56] The intarsios reproduce the space itself of the library and the objects that inhabit it (a lectern, semiopen bookshelves) as well as the volumes of the Duke's favorite authors (Homer, Virgil, Cicero). Occasionally, however, the intarsios do more than simply evoke absent spaces and objects: they embellish an armchair, a table, the back of a folding bench, or the doors of a wardrobe that actually opens. The intarsios serve to conjure up a loggia overlooking the hilly countryside, but they also decorate a hidden door that opens onto a real loggia.[57] It is only by actually knowing, or by experiencing the secrets of the place, that one can distinguish between reality and representation and find a pathway through the labyrinth of illusions created by perspective.[58]

The studiolo is, after all, illusionistically alive: there is a basket of fruit, a parrot, a squirrel, but above all there is an air of casual disorder, the silent wind flapping the pages of the momentarily discarded books, the benches upturned, the musical instruments left on the ledges—all give the impression that Federico has just left and may at any moment return. This is, ultimately, a space of the mind, a theater where the borders between the external and the internal world, between reality and illusion, are subjected to various questionings so that they may be gradually rebuilt and reimagined. It is, as has already been suggested, the ideal space in which to stage a dialogue with the ancients.

While in many ways the studiolo has remained miraculously untarnished by time, the part on which I wish to focus my attention has greatly suffered its ravages. In 1632, a year after the devolution of the duchy of Urbino to the Holy See, Pope Urban VIII gave his nephew Antonio Barberini the studiolo paintings, which had been detached from the walls and deprived of the accompanying inscriptions. In 1644, they were exhibited at Palazzo Barberini and in 1812 divided into two groups: a set of fourteen that remained in the possession of the Barberini family was sold to the Italian state in 1934 and housed in the National Gallery of Le Marche; the other group passed into the hands of the Colonna Sciarra family and, following their bankruptcy, was bought by Napoleon III in 1861. These latter paintings were exhibited at the Musée Napoléon III and then passed on to the Louvre, where they currently remain.

Before the dismantling of the upper level of the studiolo, Laurentius Schrader, to the eternal gratitude of later scholars, transcribed the inscriptions.[59] In 2015, an exhibition reassembled these scattered limbs, celebrating for the brief space of a few months "the return of the illustrious men to the Court of Urbino."[60]

b. A Gallery of Readers

Let us now enter the studiolo and bring it fully back to life, by putting all the portraits that were present in it back in their rightful place, recalling to

Urbino, as it were, also those that are currently housed in the Louvre and accompanying each with its own inscription. The aim of this reconstruction is to understand how the studiolo worked as a whole; how portraits and inscriptions interacted with Federico; how, in particular, they contributed to the functions that the studiolo was called on to perform, that is, not only self-representation and self-celebration but also reading, meditation, and, perhaps, even writing.

What is immediately striking is the variety of the portraits, of the clothes and the faces depicted but especially of the attitudes and gestures. Such variety and vivacity mark a move away from the traditional portrayal of illustrious men from which they undoubtedly stem.[61] The paintings accentuate the theatrical ideal of a living presence, which is also entrusted to the interplay of perspective: the portraits belonging to the upper level exhibit a more pronounced foreshortening so that different points of view are created: as one moves around the studiolo, there is a constant readjustment of the perspective, of the eye-to-eye contact with the figures watching us from above. Indeed some of the portraits seem at times to invite, at times to command, the tribute of direct eye contact with the viewer: they demand our attention.

The specific layout of the portraits and the overall meaning of the iconographic program have been much discussed. What is certain is that the pagan and the Christian worlds are both represented; the literary taste and the pedagogical ideals of modern humanism cohabit serenely with eulogies for the protagonists of scholastic philosophy; literature and science, law and theology are represented through the likenesses of their most exemplary interpreters. The gallery reconstructs an encyclopedia within the mind, albeit an encyclopedia mediated by the tastes and the personal experience of Federico.

The portraits, as we said, were disposed on two levels: on the upper level, the laymen; on the lower, the men of the church, with the exception of Dante and Petrarch. They were arranged in couples, the figure from antiquity on the left, the modern sage on the right; the painter evidently sought to make them recognizable not just through the inscriptions but through their clothes, their gestures, and their attributes. For example, Gregory the Great, Pius II, and Sixtus IV wear the papal tiara (see Figures 3.7–3.9); St. Ambrose and St. Augustine, the bishop's miter (see Figures 3.10 and 3.11); Bessarion and St. Jerome, the cardinal's hat (see Figures 3.12 and 3.13); Duns Scotus, Thomas Aquinas, and Albertus Magnus, the hat of

Figure 3.7. Justus van Ghent, *Gregory the Great,* tempera on wood, ca. 1460–1475, Palazzo Ducale, Galleria Nazionale delle Marche, Urbino. *De Agostini Picture Library/Scala, Florence.*

doctors of the church (see Figures 3.14–3.16). The clothes worn by the illustrious men are extremely varied and imaginative: generally speaking, as observed by Luciano Cheles, the Greeks wear Oriental garments, which succeeds in bestowing an exotic aura on them, in that they are non-Latins; modern fashions are projected onto antiquity, so that Cicero, for example, wears the modern costume of the doctor of civil law (see Figure 3.17).[62]

Figure 3.8. Justus van Ghent, *Pope Pius II,* tempera on wood, ca. 1460–1475, Palazzo Ducale, Galleria Nazionale delle Marche, Urbino. *De Agostini Picture Library/Scala, Florence.*

There is one element common to all the portraits: all the figures are holding a book; the only exception is Ptolemy, who is holding an astrolabe in his left hand (see Figures 3.18), while another scientific instrument, a pair of compasses, features next to a book in the portrait of Euclid (see Figure 3.19).

It is primarily on the book, therefore, that the construction of knowledge pivots, supplemented, in some cases, as, for example, in mathematics,

Figure 3.9. Justus van Ghent and Pedro Berruguete, *Pope Sixtus IV*, tempera on wood, ca. 1460–1477, Palazzo Ducale, Galleria Nazionale delle Marche, Urbino. *Archivi Alinari, Florence.*

geography, and astronomy, by scientific instruments. Moses is also distinguished by the unique text he is holding, the tables of the law, whose contents he indicates with his left hand, paradoxically pointing out to the viewer the prohibition against graven images (Exodus, XX, 4; see Figure 3.20).[63]

Some of the books in the portraits may be open so as to allow us to view the pages: this is so in the case of Plato, who points to a passage with his

Figure 3.10. Justus van Ghent, *St. Ambrose,* tempera on wood, ca. 1471–1475, Palazzo Ducale, Galleria Nazionale delle Marche, Urbino. *Archivi Alinari, Florence.*

right hand while using his left hand to communicate with us, inviting us to understand and learn (see Figure 3.21); and in the case of Augustine, who holds his book wide open with his left hand and with his right hand invokes God's blessing, accompanying this gesture with his eyes fixed on a distant point; and in the case of the portrait of Albertus Magnus, in which a light wind is rustling the edge of the right-hand page. Here, as with St. Jerome, we see that the open text is the Psalms, and we even glimpse a few

Figure 3.11. Justus van Ghent and Pedro Berruguete, *Augustine*, tempera on wood, ca. 1460–1477, Palazzo Ducale, Galleria Nazionale delle Marche, Urbino. *Archivi Alinari, Florence.*

lines (from Psalms 53 and 117 for Jerome and Psalm 30 for Albertus Magnus)—in the latter case, the portion of Castilian text visible has led some scholars to hypothesize the intervention of a Spanish painter, possibly Berruguete. The portraits thus allow us to penetrate the inner world of the character—something that was usually considered to be the prerogative of the word rather than the image, in the sense that they reveal what is engrossing his mind and occupying his soul.[64] Cicero and Seneca are also holding open books, but the pages are barely visible (see Figure 3.22); So-

Figure 3.12. Justus van Ghent and Pedro Berruguete, *Cardinal Bessarion,* tempera on wood, ca. 1460–1477, Palazzo Ducale, Galleria Nazionale delle Marche, Urbino. *Archivi Alinari, Florence.*

lon's attention is concentrated on a page that he seems about to turn (see Figure 3.23); Bartolo da Sassoferrato is looking forward to one side, and it is difficult to say whether he is about to open or close the pages of his book (see Figure 3.24); St. Ambrose and Pius II hold their books wide open, but we can only see their covers—the former is raising his hand in a gesture of benediction, and the latter is portrayed in profile, as if immersed in his own private dimension.

A MARVELOUS SOLITUDE

Figure 3.13. Justus van Ghent and Pedro Berruguete, *St. Jerome*, tempera on wood, ca. 1460–1477, Palazzo Ducale, Galleria Nazionale delle Marche, Urbino. *Archivi Alinari, Florence.*

In other portraits, the book is closed: Aristotle's left hand is placed firmly on his book (see Figure 3.25); Solomon holds his book up with his right hand, his left hand holding his scepter (see Figure 3.26), in a posture, it has been suggested, that recalls the figures of the Pope and the King from the so-called Mantegna Tarot;[65] Homer's left hand is on his book, his blind eyes hidden by their closed lids (see Figure 3.27); Virgil appears to be almost caressing his book and is perhaps captured as he is

Portraits, or The Desire to See the Author

Figure 3.14. Justus van Ghent, *Duns Scotus,* tempera on wood, ca. 1471–1475, Palazzo Ducale, Galleria Nazionale delle Marche, Urbino. *Archivi Alinari, Florence.*

about to open it (see Figure 3.28); Euclid's compasses are placed on his book; and Vittorino da Feltre points to the book with the index finger of his right hand, a gesture indicating authority (he had been Federico's teacher and was, as we shall see, expressly mentioned by him; see Figure 3.29).[66] Peter Abanus seems to be embracing his book almost lovingly (see Figure 3.30), while Hippocrates and Dante are depicted in the act of teaching the content of their own books, as may be seen by the movement of their right

Figure 3.15. Justus van Ghent and Pedro Berruguete, *Saint Thomas Aquinas,* tempera on wood, ca. 1477, Musée du Louvre, Paris. *RMN-Grand Palais/Scala, Florence.*

hands (see Figures 3.31 and 3.32). In other cases—Boethius (see Figure 3.33), Aquinas, Duns Scotus, Petrarch (see Figure 3.34)—the closed book is accompanied by a gesture of the hand (or hands, which in the first two portraits is particularly lively), indicating that they are engaged in a *disputatio*.[67] Such is the strength of the speakers' memories, it is to be inferred, that the content of the book is firmly imprinted in their minds, from whence they bring forth, one by one, the subjects to be analyzed and discussed.[68]

Figure 3.16. Justus van Ghent and Pedro Berruguete, *Albertus Magnus,* tempera on wood, ca. 1460–1477, Palazzo Ducale, Galleria Nazionale delle Marche, Urbino. *Archivi Alinari, Florence.*

Looking down from the walls of the studiolo, therefore, was a gallery of authors-readers. The book is a constant feature in the portraits, but the minute variations in the way it is represented graphically express different moments in the reading process. The gestures, from the more sedate to the more excited, breathe life into the figures, showing the different ways in which great men of the past and present, from the classical and the Christian worlds, communicate their wisdom to Federico and to those who frequented the studiolo. The gestures of the hands involved in

Figure 3.17. Justus van Ghent, *Cicero*, tempera on wood, ca. 1471–1475, Palazzo Ducale, Galleria Nazionale delle Marche, Urbino. *Archivi Alinari, Florence.*

the *disputatio* are particularly effective in accomplishing this. Vespasiano da Bisticci's biography of Federico repeatedly points out his ability in disputations ("He began to study logic with the keenest understanding, and he argued with the most nimble wit that was ever seen"), as well as his interest in "the modern doctors who proceed through arguments."[69] The gestures in the portraits of the "modern doctors" would perhaps have served to stimulate an ideal, closely argued, *disputatio* between themselves and the Duke.[70]

Portraits, or The Desire to See the Author

Figure 3.18. Justus van Ghent and Pedro Berruguete, *Ptolemy*, tempera on wood, ca. 1477, Musée du Louvre, Paris. *RMN-Grand Palais/Scala, Florence.*

c. Federico; or, The Reader's Gratitude

The dialogue with the wise men in the portraits was not, however, a one-way exchange. This is shown clearly by the inscriptions that originally accompanied the portraits.[71] Here Federico features as the main protagonist of this pictorial enterprise; it was he who desired and commissioned the portraits and oversaw their placement: the inscription "Federicus dicavit" (Federico dedicated) appeared below Plato; "Federicus posuit" (Federico

Figure 3.19. Justus van Ghent, *Euclid*, tempera on wood, ca. 1460–1467, Palazzo Ducale, Galleria Nazionale delle Marche, Urbino. *Archivi Alinari, Florence.*

placed), below Aristotle, Boethius, Cicero, Vittorino da Feltre, Solon, Bartolo da Sassoferrato, St. Jerome, St. Ambrose, Duns Scotus, Pius II, Bessarion, and Albertus Magnus; "Federicus dedit" (Federico gave), under Ptolemy, Virgil, and Euclid; "Federicus erexit" (Federico set up), below Seneca; "Federicus dicat" (Federico dedicates), below St. Thomas Aquinas and Sixtus IV; "Federicus poni curavit" (Federico had it placed), below Peter Abanus and Solomon: everything indicates the personal attention bestowed by

Portraits, or The Desire to See the Author

Figure 3.20. Justus van Ghent, *Moses,* tempera on wood, ca. 1471–1475, Palazzo Ducale, Galleria Nazionale delle Marche, Urbino. *Archivi Alinari, Florence.*

the Duke on the project but also underscores how he delegated its actual realization.

The message is a very specific one: Federico was paying homage to these great men but also thanking them, moved by a strong sense of admiration and gratitude; it is, in other words, an act of justice. Even in the few cases in which Federico's name does not appear, his place is filled by the personification of a virtue, as if to emphasize the same message, to give it universal

Figure 3.21. Justus van Ghent and Pedro Berruguete, *Plato*, tempera on wood, ca. 1460–1477, Musée du Louvre, Paris. *RMN-Grand Palais/Scala, Florence.*

resonance. Thus, in the case of Homer's portrait, the agent is Gratitude herself ("gratitudo posuit"); "gratitudo christiana memor erexit" (Christian Gratitude, in memory, placed) the portrait of Gregory the Great, an inscription that highlighted the central theme of the connection between memory and gratitude (here viewed in a Christian light, given the figure of Gregory). The perspective of posterity is interwoven into the personifications that appear on the labels, as in the case of Hippocrates, the benefits

Figure 3.22. Justus van Ghent and Pedro Berruguete, *Seneca*, tempera on wood, ca. 1460–1477, Musée du Louvre, Paris. *RMN-Grand Palais/Scala, Florence.*

of whose labors endure through time ("bonae posteritatis valetudo dicat": the good health of lucky posterity dedicates), or in the case of Petrarch, where an elegant variation highlights the pleasure and the sense of play communicated by his poetry ("posteritatis laeticia lususque dicavere": the joy and amusement of posterity dedicated). Later generations become the actual agents in the case of St. Augustine ("posteri . . . fieri curaverunt": posterity . . . ensured that it was accomplished) or in the case of Moses,

Figure 3.23. Justus van Ghent and Pedro Berruguete, *Solon*, tempera on wood, ca. 1460–1477, Musée du Louvre, Paris. *RMN-Grand Palais/Scala, Florence.*

where the Christian connotation returns ("posteritas christiana posuit": Christian posterity placed this). Dante is the only case in which a subject is missing: the inscription reads "posita benemerenti" (placed for him who has well deserved); "effigies" (image) is probably to be understood.

Gratitude, however, is not the only sentiment that appears to animate Federico; as the director of this iconographic enterprise, he wished to be indirectly portrayed himself through these inscriptions as a passionate but also as a careful reader, capable of expressing critical and moral opinions.

Portraits, or The Desire to See the Author

Figure 3.24. Justus van Ghent, *Bartolo da Sassoferrato,* tempera on wood, ca. 1471–1475, Palazzo Ducale, Galleria Nazionale delle Marche, Urbino. *Archivi Alinari, Florence.*

The words that accompanied the paintings register the emotions that animated Federico and led him to this undertaking: the Latin phrases ("ex observantia" for Plato and "ex gratitudine" for Aristotle) underscore how the care lavished on their portraits stems from respect and gratitude, is indeed almost their natural consequence, their visible manifestation. The same formula ("ex" + abstract noun) is used to represent the effects produced by the work of those whose portraits are displayed. "Ex persuasione" is used in the case of Cicero, master of the art of persuading, of swaying the souls

Figure 3.25. Justus van Ghent and Pedro Berruguete, *Aristotle*, tempera on wood, ca. 1460–1477, Musée du Louvre, Paris. *RMN-Grand Palais/Scala, Florence.*

and ideas of men, as well as being "father of the motherland."[72] The formula is also used in those cases in which Federico more clearly saw himself as mirrored in the works of the wise men whose portraits he had commissioned and from whom he drew examples and encouragement for his own actions as a ruler. We see this in the case of Solon, the author of the Athenian laws on which the Roman legal system was modeled; "Federicus posuit"—we read—"ex studio bene instituendorum civium" (Federico

Portraits, or The Desire to See the Author

Figure 3.26. Justus van Ghent, *Solomon*, tempera on wood, ca. 1471–1475, Palazzo Ducale, Galleria Nazionale delle Marche, Urbino.
Archivi Alinari, Florence.

placed this on account of his desire to rightly orient the citizens); and in the case of Bartolo da Sassoferrato, an acute and impartial interpreter of the law: "Federicus posuit ex merito et justitia" (Federico placed this to justly recognize his merit).

The ethical thrust of these paintings was accompanied by brief but significant interpretative glosses, a sort of footnotes, we may venture to call them, in a larger book. Plato and Aristotle were placed side by side but are

Figure 3.27. Justus van Ghent, *Homer*, tempera on wood, ca. 1471–1475, Palazzo Ducale, Galleria Nazionale delle Marche, Urbino. *Archivi Alinari, Florence.*

viewed in different lights: Plato is the authority in the field of human and divine philosophy, while Aristotle is praised mainly for his method ("posuit ex gratitudine ob philosophiam rite exacteque traditam": placed out of gratitude for having passed on philosophy in the due and exact manner). Similarly, in the praise for Hippocrates, the *way* in which his medical wisdom was made available to everyone is foregrounded: "brevibus . . . demostratam comprehensibus" (it was expounded through the use of aphorisms).

Portraits, or The Desire to See the Author

Figure 3.28. Justus van Ghent and Pedro Berruguete, *Virgil*, tempera on wood, ca. 1460–1477, Musée du Louvre, Paris. *RMN-Grand Palais/Scala, Florence.*

The celebration of exactitude and precision is also to be found in the inscriptions dedicated to Ptolemy and Euclid, in whose portraits, as previously noted, scientific instruments appear. The inscription for Euclid refers to the compasses, observing that with lines and compasses, he marked out accurately the spaces of the world ("ob comprehensa terrae spacia lineis centroque Federicus dedit, invento exactissimo"), while in the case of Ptolemy, praise for the accuracy of his map of the heavens and the Earth is colored by admiration for the long vigils and the infinite exertions it cost

Figure 3.29. Justus van Ghent and Pedro Berruguete, *Vittorino da Feltre,* tempera on wood, ca. 1460–1477, Musée du Louvre, Paris. *RMN-Grand Palais / Scala, Florence.*

him: "ob certam astrorum dimensionem, inductasque orbi terrarum lineas, vigiliis laborique aeterno Federicus dedit." Ptolemy is not looking at the viewer, because he is entirely engrossed in his astrolabe; he wears a crown, which was his customary attribute until the end of the fifteenth century, when he was no longer confused with King Ptolemy of Egypt. Overall, the portrait is reminiscent of what Boccaccio had depicted in his *Amorosa visione* (IV, 59–63): "modest in his gestures, / sat Ptolemy, who was specu-

Figure 3.30. Justus van Ghent and Pedro Berruguete, *Peter Abanus*, tempera on wood, ca. 1460–1477, Musée du Louvre, Paris. *RMN-Grand Palais/Scala, Florence.*

lating on the heavens / with a most subtle mind, / looking at a sphere that stood / stationary before him."[73]

Medicine is represented by Hippocrates (praised, as we have seen, for his useful and succinct teachings) and by a medieval sage, Peter Abanus, a figure who may have appeared somewhat disturbing in this context.[74] A doctor, astrologer, alchemist, and professor in Padua at the beginning of the fourteenth century, Peter had sojourned in Constantinople to study

Figure 3.31. Justus van Ghent, *Hippocrates*, tempera on wood, ca. 1471–1475, Palazzo Ducale, Galleria Nazionale delle Marche, Urbino. *Archivi Alinari, Florence.*

Greek and familiarize himself with Greek-Byzantine and Arabic traditions; he had introduced the works of Averroes to the West and had been accused of heresy and necromancy. He had, among other things, explained Christ's resurrection as the result of an apparent death. His fame as an expert of the occult had gathered strength during the fifteenth century, contributing to the tradition that his remains had been exhumed and burned. It is therefore significant that Federico should have included him in his anthology of illustrious men. The inscription exalts his medical knowledge without ne-

Figure 3.32. Justus van Ghent and Pedro Berruguete, *Dante*, tempera on wood, ca. 1460–1477, Musée du Louvre, Paris. *RMN-Grand Palais/Scala, Florence.*

glecting to refer to the occult sphere, to the "most recondite" disciplines that had nourished it: "medicorum arbitro, aequissimo ob remotiorum disciplinarum studium insigne" (to the most impartial arbiter of doctors, for his exemplary study of the most recondite fields of knowledge). At the same time, Peter's ability to reconcile divergent ideas is noted. It was following this principle that Plato and Aristotle were placed side by side, and the same principle was applied to the Dominican Thomas Aquinas and the

Figure 3.33. Justus van Ghent, *Boetius,* tempera on wood, ca. 1471–1475, Palazzo Ducale, Galleria Nazionale delle Marche, Urbino. *Archivi Alinari, Florence.*

Franciscan Duns Scotus, "the most acute among doctors." The inscriptions are exactly echoed in Vespasiano da Bisticci's account of Federico, who, he records, enjoyed having Aquinas read out to him, "thus acquiring a strong predilection for St. Thomas's doctrine, which seemed to him very clear and eminently defensible. He rated St. Thomas as clearer than Scotus though less subtle."[75]

The pleasure the Duke took in eloquence was, as we have seen, reflected in the praise bestowed on Cicero, but it also reappears in the inscriptions

Portraits, or The Desire to See the Author

Figure 3.34 Justus van Ghent and Pedro Berruguete, *Francesco Petrarca,* tempera on wood, ca. 1460–1477, Palazzo Ducale, Galleria Nazionale delle Marche, Urbino. *Archivi Alinari, Florence.*

that accompany the doctors of the Church, such as St. Gregory the Great, St. Jerome, and St. Ambrose, who incarnate the union of saintliness, doctrine, and formal elegance.

Classical poetry is represented by Homer, who is lauded for his encyclopedic qualities ("ob divinam disciplinarum varietatem") as well as his unparalleled greatness, which has excited admiration throughout the ages; and by Virgil, who is remembered as the epic singer of the origins of Rome and as an inspired poet, animated by a sublime fervor, in accordance with a recurring paradigm of Florentine Neoplatonism. Dante and Petrarch are the representatives of modern poetry, but while the former is praised for the way in which his poem in the vernacular transmitted a vast amount of knowledge to a wide public ("ob propagatos numeros poëticamque varia doctrina populo perscriptam"), Petrarch is described as the poet whose works communicate sweetness and pleasure.

The contemporary world is represented in the gallery by Sixtus IV, whose philosophical and theological wisdom is celebrated, as well as his recent ascent to the papal throne. Strong political connections justified this: in 1474, Federico had received from the pope the title of Duke and that of Standard Bearer of the Holy Roman Church.

A more personal note is sounded in the praise of Seneca, the teacher of Stoic serenity ("cuius praeceptis animus liberatur perturbationibus excoliturqe tranquillitas": thanks to whose teachings the soul is freed from its troubles and achieves tranquility), and in the words dedicated to Pius II, celebrating his skills in both warfare and eloquence, an interplay of arms and letters in which Federico evidently recognized facets of himself. With Sixtus IV and Pius II, therefore, contemporary characters enter the gallery of portraits of illustrious men—an innovative and highly personal take on tradition.[76]

The theme of personal friendship emerges in the praise of Bessarion, who is remembered primarily for his attempt to reconcile the Eastern and Western churches: "Federico dedicated to his excellent and most wise friend, who brought peace between the Greek and the Latin churches, because of his outstanding seriousness and learning" (Graeci Latinique pacificatori, ob summam gravitatem doctrinaeque excellentiam, Federicus amico sapientissimo optimoque posuit). The two men shared a love of books: Bessarion had entrusted to Federico the precious coffers containing his manuscripts, and Federico, keeping the promise made to his friend, delivered them in 1474 to the secretary of the Signoria of Venice.[77]

Another particularly moving and personal inscription commemorates Vittorino da Feltre, Federico's teacher: "Federico dedicated to his teacher, full of saintliness, Vittorino da Feltre, because of the learning and humanity which he passed on through writing and example" (Victorio Feltrensi, ob humanitatem literis exemploque traditam, Fredericus praeceptori sanctissimo posuit). Vittorino embodied the true spirit of *humanitas,* an interpenetration of life and doctrine: he is the "teacher full of saintliness," who was known as the Christian Socrates. Federico had not forgotten how formative had been those adolescent years that he had spent at Vittorino's school. Between the ages of twelve and fourteen he had studied at the Ca' Gioiosa, where particular care was bestowed on the individual propensities of each pupil, through games, physical exercise, and music, as well as through a syllabus in which mathematics and letters were taught together with drawing and the natural sciences; indeed, just as the fond memory of Vittorino hovered around his portrait, so did the example of his method live on in the very structure of the studiolo.[78]

The portraits of the illustrious men, the inscriptions that accompany them, and their placement along the upper level of the studiolo thus constitute a living, and highly personalized, theater of memory: a memory that selected the treasures held in the library and gave its authors not just a face but a liveliness of expression and gesture that almost invited them to participate in the creative dialogue of reading, writing, and meditation. The *auctoritas* belonging to these cultural giants from both antiquity and modernity, to both the classical and Christian worlds, was certainly the foundation on which this dialogue was built, but it was also a two-way exchange with someone capable of judging and selecting, of viewing those exemplary personages from a very specific angle, a man who could both see himself reflected in them and use them to first build and later reinforce his identity as a scholar and a prince. Federico most certainly agreed with the exalted praise of reading that we find in the famous letter, dated 31 May 1468, that his friend Bessarion had written to the Doge of Venice Cristoforo Moro, in whose hands he left his Venetian library: "There is no object more precious, no treasure more useful and beautiful than a book. Books are full of the voices of the wise; they live, dialogue and converse with us, inform, educate and console us; they show us that things belonging to the remotest past are in fact present—they place them before our very eyes. Without books, we should all be brutes."[79]

4. Erasmus and the Limits of the Portrait

Federico's studiolo makes a powerful case for the ways in which books and portraits can interact in the silent dialogue with viewer and reader. Nevertheless, the traditional mistrust of portraiture had not abated, and it was still regarded as providing a likeness that was inferior to that true inner portrait that can only be provided through words. It was an age-old mistrust fueled by modern arguments, and it triumphed, albeit somewhat paradoxically, in an age that saw the ascendency of portraiture also through the growing popularity of prints and medals.[80]

Viewed in this light, the position of Erasmus in the *Ciceronianus* is particularly intriguing. This dialogue was published in 1528, in the wake of the sack of Rome, an event viewed by some people as the symbolic condemnation of the dominant culture embodied by the papal city, and its primary polemical objective was to combat the fanaticism of the Roman Ciceronians.[81] These admirers of the Roman orator idolized his work, believing that all the terms necessary to talk about the Christian religion could be culled from his texts alone. Driven by nationalistic arrogance, they strove to impose their value criteria onto the whole world, discounting the cultural regeneration that was under way in other European countries. The dialogue also stages a pedagogical itinerary, a therapeutic ritual carried out by Bulephorus (the Advisor) for the benefit of Nosoponus (he who is afflicted by the malady), his young friend who has been ensnared by the Ciceronian cult.

This text is examined in greater detail in Chapter 4, sections 2–3. What is relevant to my argument here is that in the *Ciceronianus*, the theme of the portrait is often associated with canonical examples from antiquity: thus Zeuxis, who in order to paint the portrait of Helen chose his models from among the five most beautiful girls of Croton, is mentioned as proof that in writing, it is preferable to use a variety of models. The most interesting passages are those in which the outcome of the process of imitation is foregrounded: comparison with the portrait is here used to gauge the extent to which the new text is capable of representing the features either of the chosen model or of its writer. The Ciceronian who is obsessively dedicated to imitating his literary idol will therefore risk producing a bad portrait of Cicero, who paradoxically will need to be defended precisely against those whose cult for him has been carried to excess. What is at stake, Bulephorus argues, is in fact Cicero's reputation: "in that I hope to prevent us producing a bad copy of him that will give him a bad name, just as a portrait by an incompetent painter who cannot reproduce the features properly makes the sitter an object of ridicule." Ultimately, however, he continues, it is we ourselves who run the risk of "misplacing our affections and suffering a fate as humiliating and miserable as Ixion's, who . . . embraced an empty cloud-form instead of his desired Juno," or Paris, who fought a long war, "all the time . . . embracing a false image of Helen, because the real Helen had of course been carried off to Egypt by stratagem by the gods."[82] The two mythological comparisons are particularly thought-provoking: both exemplify a form of erotic desire whose satisfaction is, however, deceitful; it is not the body of the beloved that is embraced but an empty simulacrum. Such, for Erasmus, is the desire that drives the Ciceronians, a desire destined to end in frustration, a never-ending quest. A text produced by a Ciceronian can only be an unfaithful portrait of Cicero, unable to capture his true soul; it is destined to failure because, instead of establishing a dialogue, it vainly attempts to copy his external features.

Nosoponus, the fanatical Ciceronian, explains how he thrives on, indeed how he cannot survive without, the constant presence of his beloved author's portrait: "I have a picture of him, nicely painted, not only in my private chapel and in my study, but on all the doors too; and I carry his portrait around with me, carved on gems, so that all the time he's present to my thoughts. I never see anything in my dreams but Cicero."[83] Nosoponus's admiration for Cicero takes on the contours of a cult ("I have reserved for him," he explains, "a place in my calendar among the apostles"), and the physical object that is the portrait of Cicero is invoked, as if it were an icon, to perform the miracle of entirely transferring the qualities of a text read into those of a text written, into the very fibers of the prose, so that Cicero may come back to life and the past may be revived in the present—an endeavor that, for Erasmus, is equivalent to pursuing a ghost or embracing a shadow.

Not only will the text of a Ciceronian be a mediocre and unfaithful likeness of Cicero; it will also be a bad *self*-portrait, like that of someone who wishes to be portrayed as more handsome than they actually are or who chooses to disguise their true self with a mask: "Besides, decent men, even if not particularly blessed with fine features, don't wish to wear a mask in order to make themselves look handsome, and wouldn't even agree to be painted with features other than those nature gave them. It's dishonest to impose on others by disguising oneself, and the idea of a lying mirror or portrait that represents a man not as he is but as he would like to be is quite ludicrous."[84] But, setting aside the quality of the portrait, it is the nature of the genre itself that, Erasmus believes, prevents it from going beyond an external and superficial level: "Let us assume that this person is as adept in recreating Cicero as Zeuxis was in representing the female form. Zeuxis was able to depict his subject's features, complexion, age, even a suggestion of his feelings. . . . Now the man who could offer all this surely realized the full potential of his art? As far as was possible, he transferred the form of the living person to the mute image. Nor can we ask anything more of a painter. . . . But what an enormous amount of the real person is missing from the portrait!"[85]

In this way, the portrait may become a useful term of comparison with the written text, but only in order to observe its differences and weaknesses. The image it transmits is purely exterior, like that created by someone who can only imitate the rhetorical flourishes and the formal elegance of the author on whom they have chosen to model their prose. Erasmus believed the painter could not imitate the essential qualities that defined a person: "Likewise, no mere attempt to reproduce an effect is going to develop the real oratorical virtues. We have to produce them from within ourselves." Erasmus enjoys recounting the ridiculous attempts of a painter who had been engaged to paint their mutual friend Murius but focuses on one detail after another, breathlessly trying to capture the minute changes that time and the passage of the seasons produce in his sitter. This was probably an enactment of what had happened to Erasmus himself during the various sittings for his portrait by Quentin Matsys.[86] He knew from personal experience how impossible it was for a portrait to be situated outside time, observing in a letter to Willibald Pirckeimer, dated 30 July 1526, just how different he was then from the man whom Dürer had portrayed five years previously (see Figure 3.35).[87]

We thus come to a somewhat contradictory but nevertheless intriguing aspect of Erasmus's thoughts on portraiture. Although he frequently highlights the limits of this art, he was very close to painters such as Dürer, Hans Holbein the Younger, and Quentin Matsys, and he commissioned them to paint portraits of himself. In fact, as Lisa Jardine has argued, the diffusion of portraits of Erasmus (whether painted or engraved in the frontispieces of books or on medals) runs parallel to the diffusion of his works throughout Europe and is an important element in the construction of that image of himself and the self-myth to the promotion of which Erasmus devoted so much care, resorting to all the available new *media* of his time.[88]

Figure 3.35. Albrecht Dürer, *Portrait of Erasmus,* engraving, 1526, Gabinetto dei disegni e delle stampe degli Uffizi, Florence. *Antonio Quattrone/Electa/Mondadori Portfolio.*

5. Portraits of Friends

An extraordinary example of how the book and the portrait may not simply collaborate but also interact so as to evoke a whole world of thought and feeling is provided by the twin portraits commissioned by Erasmus and Peter Gilles from the painter Quentin Matsys in 1517 (see Figures 3.36 and 3.37).[89] Their plan, which followed an established tradition for the

Figure 3.36. Quentin Matsys, *Portrait of Erasmus,* oil on canvas, 1517, The Royal Collection, Hampton Court. *Eric Vandeville/akg-images/Mondadori Portfolio.*

portraits of friends, was to make a gift of the portraits to Thomas More, who was in London, while Erasmus and Gilles were in Antwerp. The two portraits, now separated, were originally placed next to each other: Thomas More, in a letter to the painter, speaks of a *tabula duplex.*[90] They are also visually linked by the shelves of a bookcase full of books that appears in both portraits, clearly signaling how books, both those read and those written, create the bond between the two men and their absent interlocutor, the absent friend, whose attention, complicity, and almost physical presence Gilles seems to evoke through his gaze. The books that appear behind Gilles are the Latin classics that Erasmus had edited; he was in that precise period beginning to write his *Paraphrase to Paul's Letter to the Romans.* He there-

Figure 3.37. Quentin Matsys, *Portrait of Peter Gilles*, 1517, oil on canvas, Longford Castle, Salisbury, Wiltshire, England. *Longford Castle.*

fore both reevokes and reembodies St. Jerome. Visible on the shelf behind him is the edition of the New Testament which he began in 1516, while the other volumes testify to his friendship and close collaboration with Thomas More: there is Lucian (whose *Dialogues* More and Erasmus had translated) and his *In Praise of Folly*, which was influenced by Lucian and dedicated to Thomas More.[91] What is conjured up here is therefore a close-knit circle of friends, their intense affective and intellectual complicity; it is a lively dialogue not only with one another but also with the ancient authors they

A MARVELOUS SOLITUDE

Io. Clemens.   Hythlodæus.   Tho. Morus.   Pet. Aegid.

Figure 3.38. Thomas More, Peter Gilles, and Raphael Hythlodaeus in Gilles's garden, in Thomas More, *Utopia* (Leuven: Dirk Martens, 1516). *Ann Ronan/Heritage Images/Scala, Florence.*

admire. Nor should it be forgotten that the double portrait is chronologically located between the two editions of *Utopia* of 1516 and 1518, in which images also play an important role. The 1516 text opens with a woodcut showing Peter Gilles welcoming into his garden both Raphael Hythlodaeus, the traveler who has visited Utopia, and Thomas More (see Figure 3.38); in the 1518 edition, the two friends appear at the borders of the woodcut, with Hythlodaeus pointing to the island that is featured at the center (see Figures 3.39). The 1518 paratext of *Utopia* is further enriched by images and letters from friends; among these, there is a letter written by Erasmus, who has decided to play a part—and a public one at that—in his friends' *serio ludere* on the theme of utopia.[92] It was a game that presupposed, and indeed contributed to creating, this group of cultured and supportive friends, united in dialogue by the books they read and the letters they wrote.

A similar game is played within and around the double portrait. Gilles is holding in his left hand a letter by Thomas More, in which he thanks his friends for their gift.[93] In the letter, More includes two epigrams; in the first, the painting itself speaks ("tabella loquitur"): "I," it says, "testify that Erasmus and Peter Gilles are as fast friends as Castor and Pollux"; More is saddened by the distance that separates him from them but is

Figure 3.39. Raphael Hythlodaeus shows Peter Gilles and Thomas More the island of Utopia, in Thomas More, *Utopia* (Basel: Johann Froben, 1518). *Mary Evans/Scala, Florence.*

joined to them in love, almost as closely as anyone could be to his own self. His friends, themselves saddened that their other friend should miss them, have tried to bring More some comfort: a loving letter conveys their most intimate thoughts, but I, the portrait states, bring him their external appearance, "so that the affectionate letter may conjure the soul, I the body" ("ut horum / reddat amans animum littera, corpus ego").[94]

The second epigram, however, complicates this hierarchy between letter and portrait, by extolling the painter as the new Apelles, capable of giving a new lease of life to dead images ("mire composito potens colore / vitam adfingere mortuis figuris"), even as he breathes this life into such a perishable medium as wood; in the following part of the letter, More expresses his satisfaction at how well his handwriting has been imitated in the letter that Peter Gilles is holding in his hand. It signals clearly, he stresses, how he himself is also present in the painting, next to his friends; in fact, he asks Gilles to return his letter, if he still has it in his possession: he will place it next to the painting, so as to double the miracle it performs ("remitte rogo ad me: duplicabit miraculum apposita cum tabella").

The boundary line between text and portrait is thus drawn once again, but only to be blurred. The images of distant friends continue to speak to their absent friend and re-create his living presence within a network forged through their shared dialogue with classical authors, their epistolary exchange, and that form of writing that can only be the result of an ongoing conversation. Portraiture and letters were originally located within the private sphere, but, as early as 1518, when, thanks to the medium of print, Erasmus's letters were first published, they opened up this dialogue for the common reader, who could now step into that space and re-create it through memory and imagination.

6. Paolo Giovio's Passion for Collecting and Gabriel Naudé's Detachment

As we reach the Cinquecento, the taste for collecting the portraits of famous men reaches its climax, so to say, with the passionate collector's drive of Paolo Giovio (ca. 1483–1552). A doctor, humanist, and historian, Giovio possessed an intimate knowledge of courtly life and was the first theorist of the modern genre of the emblems or "imprese."[95] In the Museum (this is how he refers to the villa he built on Lake Como between 1537 and 1543), atmospheres and themes are combined that hark back to antiquity but also reference modernity: the site (Borgo Vico) and its design recall the villa that Pliny the Elder had built on that very spot; Giovio's collection of the portraits of illustrious men started with those representing men of letters and developed into an encyclopedic project that included literary men both alive and dead, artists, popes, kings, and military commanders but also displayed a strong interest in the Turkish world. The almost four hundred portraits are part of a complex allegorical and commemorative itinerary that transforms the Museum into "a temple consecrated to virtue," a theater of wisdom, closely following Giulio Camillo's project as well as mirroring the inventiveness of Anton Francesco Doni.[96] The paintings were intended to be "verae imagines," faithful depictions of the features of the characters portrayed, and in the case of great men from the past, use was made of ancient coins, recently made available through collections and catalogues. Between word and image, between the portraits, the biographical accounts, and their succinct version in the eulogy, a rich and complex relationship was set up. The text of the *Elogia* would have been placed below the portraits, so as to allow the viewer to recognize the subject but also to direct the *way* in which the painting was viewed, how, in other words, it was to be read, by selecting and recalling aspects of their lives and works: "to each of these images correspond individual sheepskin parchment cartouches, containing the salient points of their lives and works," we read in a letter to Daniele Barbaro dated 5 December 1544.[97]

Giovio very soon started to envisage a double version of his project, something that would develop both in the rooms of his villa and in the pages of a book, but as with all encyclopedic endeavors, its accomplishment was difficult and its outcome predictably poor, one of the reasons being the expense that an illustrated tome forced the printer to incur. Thus, in 1546, Giovio succeeded in publishing with Tramezzino in Venice only the text of the eulogies of the men of letters, with a title hinting at the possibility of viewing the actual portraits in his Museum: *Elogia veris clarorum virorum imaginibus apposita quae in Musaeo Joviano Comi spectantur* (The eulogies of the illustrious men that may be found below their portraits in Como in Giovio's Museum). Alessandro Farnese, to whom the work is dedicated, had actually asked to have the portraits, but as Giovio explained, "It is not possible to paint a suitable likeness on small panels except by much hard and time-consuming labor." Here the topos of the superiority of word over image once again makes its appearance: "it seems much more worthy and important to admire the virtues of these great men as they are described precisely for that purpose within their *elogia,* rather that observe their images, which, however accurately they may be executed, cater only to the enjoyable but sterile pleasure of the eye."[98] We see here Giovio bent on promoting his work (the *Elogia*), without, however, neglecting to exalt the skill and accuracy of the portraits in his Museum.

The decision to publish only the textual part of the *Elogia* was the result of compromise and was, in a sense, a concession. In the previously quoted letter to Daniele Barbaro of 5 December 1544, Giovio had emphasized precisely the vital link between word and image that was the hallmark of his project: the printers, he complained, wanted to publish the eulogies without the portraits, "but such a request is absurd: without the images they would seem dumb and characterless."[99] It was only after Giovio's death that his editorial project was partly accomplished: in Basel, between 1575 and 1578, the Protestant printer Petrus Perna published two of the planned volumes of the *Elogia,* accompanied by portraits engraved by Tobias Stimmer.

It is worth briefly pointing out here that, while the fortune of Giovio's *Elogia* is part of a long tradition of illustrated biographies, the spread of the printed book also fostered the increasingly common practice of accompanying an author's work with his portrait.[100] The portrait of Ariosto offers a particularly fascinating case in point. Apparently engraved by Francesco Marcolini after a drawing attributed to Titian, it was placed at the end of the 1532 edition of the *Furioso,* the last to be overseen with equal measures of lovingness and anxiety by the poet himself.[101] On the right-hand side of the portrait, which is to be found at the end of the book after the octaves, the surviving examples have either the simple motto "Pro bono malum" (which in the first edition accompanied the image of golden honeybees driven away by the fire; see Figure 3.40) or a small, poor-quality, but highly significant woodcut, depicting a ewe suckling the wolf cub that would later devour her (see Figure 3.41).

If, as I have been arguing, the text is the *speculum animi* of its author, the interplay with the reader becomes ever more complex. At the end of the text, we come face-to-face with its author, and this image serves the purpose of reinforcing the dialogue between Ariosto and his reader, who may now compare it to the ideal portrait that the act of reading has painted in their mind. At the same time, what the last pages of the book offer is a *double* portrait of the author: the motto, or its accompanying image of the ewe and the wolf cub, suggests a further dimension and allows us a glimpse into his inner life and/or his, arguably highly pessimistic, vision of the

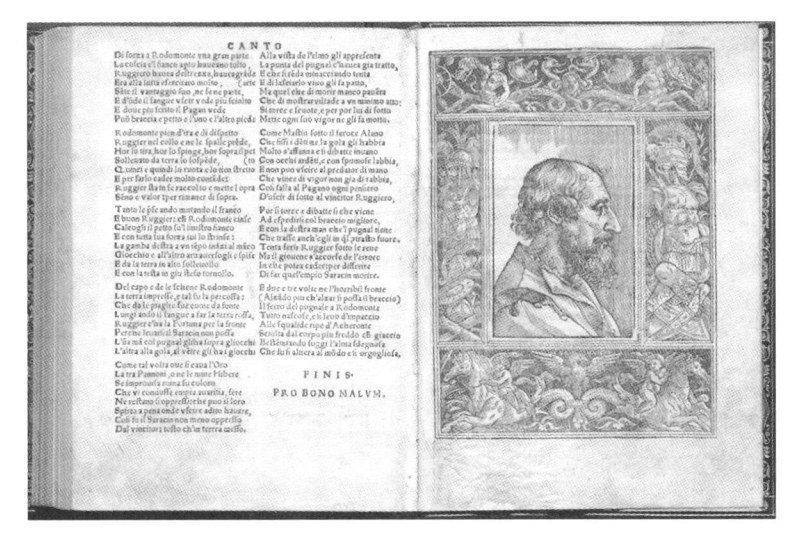

Figure 3.40. Portrait of Ariosto and the motto *pro bono malum* in Ludovico Ariosto, *Orlando Furioso* (Ferrara: Francesco Rossi da Valenza, 1532). *Private collection.*

Figure 3.41. A ewe suckling a wolf cub, in Ludovico Ariosto, *Orlando Furioso* (Ferrara: Francesco Rosso da Valenza, 1532). *Private collection.*

world. The reader's dialogue with the poet thus opens up onto unexpected vistas, the book's visual features transforming it in ever more complex and elusive ways.

The subject of portraits in libraries and the relationship they entertain with books is once again thrown into relief in what is considered to be the first textbook on library practice, *Advis pour dresser une bibliothèque,* written in 1627 by Gabriel Naudé, one of the *libertins érudits,* who dedicated most of his life to libraries, in the service of Cardinals Richelieu and Mazarin and, later, for a brief and disappointing spell, of Queen Christina of Sweden.[102] The long-standing duality of inner and outer portrait—the former a textual constituency, the latter the province of painting and sculpture—is intriguingly re-presented. In chapter 1, Naudé explains "the reasons which are most likely to persuade you that it is to your advantage . . . [to] establish a Library": "it is altogether laudable, generous, and worthy of a courage which defies mortality, to save from oblivion, preserve, and erect again, like another Pompey, all these images, not of the bodies, but of the minds of so many distinguished gentlemen, who have spared neither time nor industry in transmitting to us a lively portrait of what was most noble to themselves."[103] Later, in chapter 9, which is devoted to the decoration suitable for libraries, he reflects on the ancient testimonies describing the precious marbles and the gold and the silver ornaments that embellished the libraries of antiquity, dwelling in particular on the portraits:

> Nor is there any point in seeking out and amassing in a library all the pieces and fragments of old statues,
> Half Curii, Corvinus short a shoulder,
> Galba, too, minus a nose—and his ears,
> since it is enough for us to have good copies carved or cast of those which portray the most famous literary men, so that we may at one and the same time form a judgment of the minds of authors by their books and of their bodily shape and facial expression by means of these pictures and statues, which—joined to the accounts which many have made of their lives—may serve, in my opinion, as a powerful spur to excite a generous and well-born soul to follow in their footsteps and continue steadfastly in the spirit of some noble enterprise resolved upon, and to follow the established path.[104]

Naudé's view is sober. He too believes that the portraits of the great men of the past form part of a virtuous circle of words and images: while the words evoke the spirit of those who wrote them, the portraits together with the biographies shape in the mind an image endowed with exemplary value that encourages imitation.[105] Naudé's perspective is also pragmatic and, in some ways, antiantiquarian.[106] It is sufficient to have some copies of statues and of ancient portraits; there is no need to pile up old junk or amputated body parts. Intriguingly, in order to express his contempt, his annoyance, his impatience even, he quotes, without acknowledgment, the verses of the ancient satirist Juvenal (*Saturae*, VIII, 4–5):

> Et Curios iam dimidios, humerosque minorem
> Corvinum, et Galbum auriculis nasoque carentem

Juvenal juxtaposes the exhibition of the time-worn portraits of the forebears with real nobility, which is achieved through one's own actions and behavior; his verses therefore resonate with Naudé's argument. At the same time, the echoing of those verses points to the fact that his mind-set was very different from that perceivable in the works of Petrarch, Bracciolini, and Bembo, in which strong feelings of pain and desire colored the observation of ruins or the mutilated bodies of statues and manuscripts. The myth of the lacerated body of Hippolytus, pieced back together and brought back to life by Asclepius, has lost its fascination and credibility. The dialogue with past authors continued, and portraits could still have played a role in fostering this dialogue; but it took on new forms. Sainte-Beuve's incisive description of Naudé as "a skeptic moralist hiding behind the mask of an erudite" certainly comes to mind.[107]

Only a few decades later, Naudé's friend Guy Patin, a doctor and man of letters who was professor at the Collège de France, mentioned the portrait of Naudé as being among those of the illustrious men (also present were Erasmus and Rabelais) that decorated his study. It was here, he says, that he celebrated with his colleagues his election as president, with excellent Burgundy and conversation—a conversation that the surrounding portraits contributed to feeding: "Were my guests not, then, in good company? Company that was all the better because, without denigrating the prepared celebration, it provided agreeable subjects of conversation. All were given accolades, and at times we noted the excellent qualities of their works.

Thus the living spoke with the dead and the dead brought pleasure to the living."[108]

The by-now-familiar themes are rehearsed here in an academic and convivial context, and it would certainly be interesting to retrace the history of portraits in libraries—especially portraits of writers—down to the present day. If we ask ourselves what has survived of this desire to "see" the author or how it has evolved, we should probably take a careful look at the media ritual that is the modern literary festival. But it has also survived in such creative forms as Tullio Pericoli's portraits, a long and copious production that may be read as an experiment in how visual shorthand may be applied to the critical essay, in which the physiognomy of the author and the effect of his words intertwine.

> When I find myself . . . looking at a writer's face, I am searching it for his ideas—I must track them down. If I am drawing Montale, I cannot avoid looking for them (and finding them) on his lips or in his eyes, that bare and essential language of his; in the same way I cannot help chasing the geometric lightness of Calvino on the shape of his forehead, or tracing the lines of Beckett's dry prose in the intricate map that is his face. . . . I look for a face that, while similar to the real face, is even more real, because it tells its story.[109]

Pericoli applies his unique approach to a creative dialogue with writers, his work aiming to bring together the two foci—the text as a portrait of the soul, and the portrait as a way to engage with the author—the complex interactions of which we have seen enacted.

4

Reading, Writing, and the Construction of the Self

"The mirror will lie unless it reflects the true-born image of the mind": these words come from the *Ciceronianus,* a work by Erasmus that we have already encountered (Chapter 3, section 4). In this dialogue, published in 1528, Erasmus launches a fierce attack against the Roman Ciceronians, who proclaimed that Cicero was the sole universal model for Latin prose. This was no secondary matter, since Latin was then the common language in the republic of letters, nor was it a question exempt from religious, political, and even personal tensions. Valuable material relevant to the theme under discussion may be garnered from early sixteenth-century texts such as this, which discussed models to be imitated and engaged in lively polemics that carved out the canon, first of Latin and then also of Italian literature. We shall see how the dialogue with authors that reading entails is closely linked to the modes of imitation and therefore of writing, how, through the text, readers sought to see and know the soul of the writer and in that mirror also recognize their own features.

Reading thus becomes an encounter with the other, and this encounter helps to build up the reader's self and give it a voice; if the process is not transparent, the result is negative: as Erasmus writes, "the mirror will lie unless it reflects the true-born image of the mind." To be sure, in Petrarch's work, a strong link may also be found, and indeed is theorized, between ways of reading and ways of writing (one need only think of the image of the bee flying from flower to flower and gathering the substance that honey is made of), but in general, if we compare his thought with that of the humanists, there is an evident transition from the practice of reading in order to live better, obtain a remedy against melancholy, or escape the evils of the present times toward reading as a stepping stone toward writing, as part, in other words, of a professional training.

1. The Debate on Imitation

Between 1512 and 1513, Giovanfrancesco Pico (the nephew of the more famous Pico) and Pietro Bembo (who had been made Secretary of Briefs by Pope Leo X in 1513) exchanged letters on the subject of imitation (*De imitatione*), which partly picked up the debate between Paolo Cortese and Poliziano in the fifteenth century.[1] While Pico defended his decision to follow a variety of models, Bembo argues in favor of following the path laid out by the best, Cicero for prose and Virgil for poetry, as well as Petrarch and Boccaccio for literature in Italian. In Bembo, the distinctive features of the classicist canon are clearly visible; its values are put forward as universal. This canon extolls the idea of unity against the risky degradation of multiplicity, the eternal against the uncertain variety of the present and the past; its underlying assumptions are powerfully pedagogic, its aim being, as we have seen, to link the practice of reading to that of writing. It does so by supplying the framework through which the beauties deposited in an exemplary text may be redeployed in new texts, decanted, as it were; it sets itself up, in other words, as a grid that may be used to exert control over literary memory and its creative powers.[2]

The theme we are exploring, however, seems to have been more popular among those who did not believe in the absoluteness of the model but sought rather the path that led to the recognition of specific individual natures. We see, for example, from Pico's letters to Bembo that he considers the perfection of unity to be incompatible with the world of humanity.[3] In the sublunary world, he observes, the one is expressed through multiplicity; thus the idea (the perfection of the model) may not be embodied, "because it has distributed its splendid resources, not giving it to one alone but to all and each, so that beauty is constituted by the variety of all."[4] This is why, also with regard to imitation, we must follow that "instinct and that propensity of the soul that are proper and innate to us"; "if we break this propensity, or invert it, what we are doing amounts to violating nature itself."[5] Viewed in this light, style becomes the faithful image of individual nature, so that spontaneity in taste and individual preferences signals a correspondence between natures, a similarity between reader and writer. This is what Pico writes.

> Some may perhaps say that we should imitate especially those writers we like most; I have nothing to object: we may like Plato, we may like Cicero, who is a Platonist not just in his ideas but also for his style: let us follow these writers. Although the soul of each one of us has features that are unique to it, just as the features of one's body, so that it is not easy to find two who are entirely alike, nevertheless the difference between our soul and those of other men may be smaller in the case of some, and it is for this reason that it will be easier for us to become similar to these men.[6]

Reading in this way becomes a way to discern, within a plurality of texts, the image of a soul similar to our own. If the text is a mirror of the soul, the reader themselves may look into that same mirror and recognize something familiar; here they may find their true self. Writing, in turn, should resemble the features that readers have glimpsed and recognized, or it will be a distortion of their own nature, a violation of their own identity. The same ideas will be seen in Erasmus.

For Bembo, on the other hand, the search for one's true self, for a form of writing that could manifest one's soul, was just a step in a journey that has started off in the wrong direction but eventually found the right path. In his answer to Pico, he reminds him that he himself had at first tried to express himself originally and then taken as his models middling writers, in the hope that they could be a sort of intermediate step. Only after having experienced the limits and errors of these other choices—he tells us—did he make his final decision: "and having arrived thus far, I am much more willing to rest, because, after having diligently experimented all the other routes, this one has been to me as a safe harbor, following a long and tempestuous peregrination."[7] The idea of reading as a dialogue and a mirroring is replaced here by a pedagogical model: one must find the right teachers and follow their lead.

There is an intriguing recurrence of images inspired by the motif of the journey: for the Ciceronians, there do not exist different routes leading to beauty, only dangerous deviations that cause us to lose our way, that sidetrack us into briers, or trick us into undertaking uncertain routes, beset by dangerous storms, without the safety net of a guide, without a safe harbor in which to drop anchor.[8] The image of the journey, used with reference to either the act of writing or reading, has a long history. In Seneca, for example, the different types of journey that reading involves are classified according to a moral and psychological typology. The opening words of the letter to Lucilius that we find near the beginning of Book I are particularly eloquent on this point:

> From your letter and from what I hear, I am becoming quite hopeful about you: you are not disquieting yourself by running about from place to place. Thrashing around in that way indicates a mind in poor health. In my view, the first sign of a settled mind is that it can stay in one place and spend time with itself. Be careful, though, about your reading in many authors and every type of book. It may be that there is something wayward and unstable in it. You must stay with a limited number of writers and be fed by them if you mean to derive anything that will dwell reliably with you. One who is everywhere is nowhere. Those who travel all the time find they have many places to stay, but no friendships.[9]

The necessary condition for us to become friends with an author and rediscover our own selves is therefore to take time over a text in order to enter into a dialogue with it. The various moments presented by the text become the places where we stop in the course of this journey. In Bembo, as well as in those authors who were inspired by classical literature, as we have seen, the journey may also be deployed to represent different ways of reading and of linking reading to writing. The point of arrival, however, the safe harbor, is not the encounter with the author-friend—and through them, with ourselves—but rather with the masters: there the conversation between friends gives way to the relationship of a student with their teacher.

We can get a better sense of Bembo's position through an author who is in a way more radical, though still essentially very close to him: Giulio Camillo (ca. 1480–1544), known for his famous theater of memory.[10] Erasmus is right, Camillo explains in his *Trattato dell' imitazione*, when he argues that the nature of a writer cannot be imitated; we should therefore seek not to discover our own nature but rather the artistic skill that allows us to capture the idea of beauty that shines through the work of exemplary authors.[11] In this vision, there is no dialogue, no personal relationship; it is

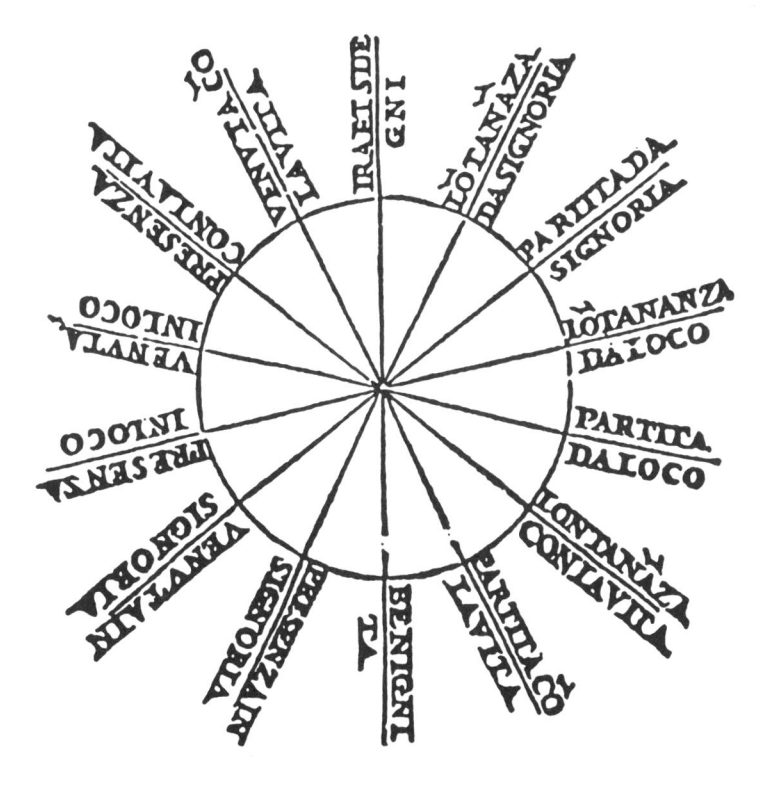

Reading, Writing, and the Construction of the Self

Figure 4.1. *Gorgo dell'artificio,* in Giulio Camillo, *Trattato delle materie,* in *Tutte le opere* (Venezia: Gabriele Giolito, 1552). *Private collection.*

through rhetorical constructions, "whirlpools of artifice," that our aims are achieved (see Figure 4.1).

For Camillo. the object of our quest as readers is not the effigy of a soul in which we may find a reflection of our own selves; our task is to "anatomize" a text and track down its secrets. Here the "anxiety of influence" is neither sublimated nor exorcized—as elsewhere in the tradition we have been reconstructing. It is taken by the horns, subdued almost, with the aid of a truculent imagination inspired by the anatomical experiments that were beginning to be performed and that Camillo claimed he had personally witnessed.[12] As in the topos we have been examining, the text here looks very much like a body; it is not, however, a living body, albeit one conjured up by the imagination; this text is a corpse, to be dissected in an anatomical theater, in the hope that, as if in the hands of an alchemist, it may be brought back to life.

In addition to the anatomical model, we find Camillo deploys a magico-astrological model to describe the process of grasping the secrets of beauty, so that the fruits of reading may be transformed into writing:

> We find in some of the lapidaries that precious stones become such after many years and through the favorable influence of the Sun, which cleanses them of all the ugliness they have imbibed and prepares them so that they may be ready to absorb the power of their star; nor could they before the Sun has rendered them pure receive the virtue that belongs to them, even if they were bound to the celestial body of their star for one hundred thousand years. And indeed their powers are as diverse as their species, because jasper serves to stem blood and lustful concupiscence, topaz is useful in extinguishing heat and drunkenness, ire is tempered with cornelian. To such stones I compare those who have an inclination toward some liberal art and who have not been taught to fully express this predisposition. And, although they may desire to excel in it, nevertheless, until they have been purified by some expert, who, like the Sun, removes any incorrect idea they may thus far have cherished, they will never achieve truth. Many I encounter who, just because they have heard Cicero and Virgil being praised, have abandoned all the others, Apuleius, Quintilian, Pliny, Lucan, and Statius, and spend all day with Cicero and Virgil in their hands. And yet, the virtue of neither of these stars will attach itself to their ill-trained soul, nor will it ever do so, were they to be eternally chained to them, unless they are first purified by some Sun, and those ideas that were imperfectly received by their tainted minds are flushed out. And indeed, while it cannot be denied that the books of Cicero and Virgil could be found and were read in the past centuries, it was not until the present times that their virtues have succeeded in permeating the more purified readers. Similarly, two or four hundred years ago, sculptors and architects had before their eyes the same statues and buildings we see now, and while they always admired and measured them, yet it is only in this age of ours, which we must greatly thank God we were born in, that they have infused their virtues in sculptors and architects.[13]

Camillo likens the beauty to be found in exemplary texts to the magical virtue transmitted by the stars to precious stones: for this power to be activated, the sun must first purify the stone. The action of the sun is likened to that of the interpreter, who knows how to elicit a virtue that would otherwise remain dormant in the most beautiful works of art (books, statues, buildings) that have come down to us from the ancient world. The classicism of his times ("this age of ours, which we must greatly thank God we were born in") is viewed by Camillo as the fruit of a more widespread predisposition to the reception of classical works of art; this translates into what he sees as the greater ability on the part of his contemporaries to revivify the power that is deposited in such works of art and to harvest them, through a process of opportune selection and reading, as sources and models for new works. Clearly Camillo claims for himself a crucial role in such a process: it is his work that helps to bring ancient models back to life; Camillo makes the idea of eloquence once again visible and active. The relationship between reading and writing becomes in Giulio Camillo both artificial and magical; his nets are cast so wide that they take in a whole era.

2. Erasmus and the Pact with the Reader

Erasmus's position on the subject of imitation is at the very antipodes; his dialogue *Ciceronianus* is nevertheless of central importance because of the way it presents the interrelationship between reading and writing.[14] Against the all-encompassing and authoritarian model of Cicero, which seeks to mold the mind of the reader, and thence be transferred onto the written page, Erasmus evokes the ancient tradition of style as *speculum animi*: in this way, reading embraces plurality, possibility, and the relationship with the self. Here we once again come across the by-now-familiar comparison with the portrait. To imitate Cicero alone is an impossible quest: the idea of reproducing in one's writings a faithful portrait is doomed to failure. Moreover, by doing so, the risk is that the self-portrait itself will be distorted and lifeless. Erasmus revisits a theme dear to Poliziano, the search for self, and for identity: "'You do not write like Cicero?' someone says? 'Well? I am not Cicero, it is myself I express, I think.'"[15] In the debate on imitation, the alternative to expressing one's true self is to wear a mask and renounce life: to dress our thought in Ciceronian garb is, as Pico wrote, "as if one dressed in the clothes and adopted the colors of another man; we shall not call these men but rather larvae and ghosts and evanescent shadows, similar to those they wish to represent but lacking all vital strength and soul."[16] A similar attitude is to be found in Erasmus's dialogue: the

Ciceronians, says Bulephorus, are monkeys, mere shadows of Cicero: "Personally I wouldn't want to be called even Apollo's reflection. I would rather be a genuine living Crassus than a reflected Cicero."[17] The shadow motif, the lifeless ghost, appears again and again in the *Ciceronianus:* mention has already been made of the comparison between the Ciceronian and Ixion attempting to clasp a shadow to his bosom, or Paris, embracing the phantom image of Helen (Chapter 3, section 4). Submitting to such a powerful external model carries with it also the idea of *hubris,* enacting a sort of violence against oneself, against one's very nature. "I can wish that we had the ability and natural gifts of Cicero, but I can't give them to us. Every one of us has his own personal inborn characteristics, and these have such force that it is useless for a person fitted by nature for one style of speaking to strive to achieve a different one. As the Greeks say, no one ever succeeded in battling with the Gods."[18]

To fight against one's natural bent is a struggle doomed to defeat; what is possible, however, is the search for one's identity, in which reading does play an important role. "When I was young," writes Erasmus, "I adored all the poets, but as soon as I became better acquainted with Horace, the others by comparison began to stink in my nostrils, though marvelous enough in absolute terms. What do you think was the reason, if not a certain affinity of spirit sensed through the silent letters?"[19] It is therefore possible to find an image of ourselves in those writers with whom we discover a secret affinity, to offer them hospitality as one would with friends, thus reconciling the self with the other.[20] This in its turn guarantees truthful, authentic writing. The writer who was once a reader is thus bound to their own readers by a vital pact. If this pact is broken, reading loses its fascination, and the rite of evocation fails. To imitate another writer, to the point of becoming their slave, Erasmus observes, amounts to renouncing ourselves; it means placing a mask over our face that obliterates our features and makes us unrecognizable by the reader. Nature itself rebels against such folly, that very same nature that intended the text to be the mirror of the soul ("quae voluit orationem esse speculum animi"): "The mirror will lie unless it reflects the true-born image of the mind. The very thing which the reader enjoys is getting to know the writer's feelings, character, disposition, and type of mind from the way he writes, just as he would by living on familiar terms with him for several years. This is why different people display such different attitudes towards the various writers, according to whether the moving spirit appears congenial or antipathetic, attracts or repels, just as a person's physical appearance pleases some and gives offence to others."[21] If a writer therefore wears too heavy a mask, the vital mechanism of reading breaks down; the mirror that allows us to "see" not only the author but also ourselves becomes clouded—the possibility is lost of recognizing something of our own soul through the words and the images of someone else.

Erasmus reproves the Ciceronians for using a mask, which makes their writing opaque; it is a form of deceitfulness that falsifies their interiority: "It is after all a form of imposture not to express yourself but to perform a kind of conjuring trick and to appear as somebody else." Shortly afterward, he adds, "Speech reveals the features of the mind much as the mirror reflects the face, to change the natural image into something different is surely the same as appearing in public wearing a mask."[22] At the very moment the Ciceronian renounces themselves, they are doomed to alienation, and because this practice perverts nature, it amounts to a kind of vampirism: Nosoponus, who embodies in the dialogue the typical Ciceronian, is consumed by his total dedication to the new cult and to the solitary toils it involves. He has lost all pleasure in life, all jolly companionship, and ekes out a larval existence, unrecognizable to his old friends. The enterprise to which he has devoted himself, the folly that grips him—of which he is cured through the help of his friends and by the use of reason—is a distortion of nature: the impossible quest on which he has embarked is to become someone else.

Underlying Erasmus's position is a radical mythologization of transparency: the dialogue-mirroring established through the act of reading is transformed and given new life through writing. The idea of the mask was the focus of a violent attack made in 1535 by Étienne Dolet (1509–1546), the future publisher of *Gargantua*, who was burned as a heretic in 1546. The truth, he says, is that Erasmus is an old man, who is jealous of young people who no longer choose him as their master and prefer Cicero to him; indeed his idea of the Ciceronian as someone who masks their own identity is pure folly: "Who can such an idea come from if not from an ignorant madman? To wish for no one to be different from what they are."[23] The truth is that he, Erasmus, was wearing obscene masks when he imitated Apuleius and Lucian: it is clear that "he himself has for a long time been appearing on stage masked in the most depraved and obscene fashion."[24] Despite the heightened tones of a polemic, Dolet does actually succeed in bringing to the fore the oversimplified mystifications in Erasmus's idea of a transparent style, of the text as the mirror of the writer's soul. It is madness to denounce another man's mask, says Dolet, when we do not see our own. Personal style appears to him in any case to be the outcome of a negotiation with other texts; the physiognomy of writing is unarguably masked.

Like other critics of the *Ciceronianus,* Dolet was right in discerning a strong personal motive underpinning the work: Erasmus wished to reaffirm the value of his own teaching, his own authority, as a judge in the international republic of letters, as clearly emerges from the last part of the dialogue. However, the theme of the mask also had a particularly serious religious dimension. Erasmus believed that the Roman Ciceronians did not merely mask the variety of human nature but did violence to history, concealing behind the features of antiquity the radical novelty of Christianity, at the risk of hiding and even negating it. On both the rhetorical and the religious plane, they contravened the criterion of *decorum,* of *apte dicere:* "Since the entire scene of human activity has been transformed, the only speaker who can respond to it appropriately [*apte dicere*] is one who is very different from Cicero.... Wherever I turn I see everything changed, I stand on a different stage, I see a different theatre, a different world."[25] The Ciceronians throw time out of joint, deluding themselves into thinking that the Rome in which they live is the same as that of the ancient world, but "in short, Rome is not Rome. It has nothing but ruins and rubble, the scars and signs of the disasters that befell long ago."[26] One might almost say—to redeploy the metaphor whose fortune we have already seen—that this Rome was a wounded, scarred body that could not, however, be resurrected. The Ciceronians lived in a world that no longer existed; they re-created artificially a spectacle that could never truly be restaged and wore masks that most definitely belonged to the past. For Erasmus, formalism was a kind of idolatry, a cult that concentrated on words and assigned absolute value to elegance of expression, separating it from the world of things (*res*) and with it, crucially, from the mysteries of faith. The mask of the Ciceronians thus showed its dark side: to speak of the Christian God with pagan words was not just ineffective; it ran the risk of becoming the breeding ground for a masked form of paganism. "It's paganism, believe me, Nosoponus, sheer paganism, that makes our ears and mind accept such an idea. The fact is we're Christians only in name. Our bodies may have been dipped in holy water, but our minds are unbaptized.... We must destroy this paganism, tear it out, expel it from our minds."[27] The *Ciceronianus,* as we mentioned, was published in 1528; the sack of Rome, which had taken place a year earlier, may well have appeared to sanction the merciless accusation of paganism that Erasmus, the great literary man of the north, had hurled against papal Rome.[28]

3. Reading as an Encounter with the Word

The theme of reading, and the close encounter with the other that reading makes possible, is also addressed in an extremely interesting way in some of Erasmus's religious writings.[29] Let us look at some passages from the *Enchiridion militis christiani* (The handbook of the Christian knight), a devotional text from 1503, addressed to a Flemish noblewoman, Anna van Borsselen, Marchioness of Veere, who had offered Erasmus help and protection.

> With great veneration you revere the ashes of Paul, which I do not condemn, if your religion is consistent with your devotion. If you venerate mute and dead ashes and ignore his living image still speaking and breathing, as it were, in his writings, is not your religion utterly absurd? You worship the bones of Paul preserved in a relic casket, but do not worship the mind of Paul hidden away in his writings? You make much of a piece of his body visible through a glass covering, and you do not marvel at the whole mind of Paul shining through his writings? You worship ashes, which are sometimes of some efficacy in removing bodily imperfections; why do you not honor the written word more, by which vices of the soul are healed?
>
> You give homage to an image of Christ's countenance represented in stone or wood or depicted in color. With how much more religious feeling should you render homage to the image of his mind, which has been reproduced in the Gospels through the artistry of the Holy Spirit. No Apelles has ever portrayed with his brush the shape and the features of the body in the way that speech reveals each person's mind and thought. This is especially so with Christ, for as he was the essence of simplicity and truth, there could be no dissimilarity between the archetype of the divine mind and the form of speech that issued from it. Just as nothing is more like the Father than the Son, the Word of the Father emanating from the innermost recesses of his spirit, so nothing is more like Christ than the word of Christ uttered in the innermost sanctuary of his most holy mind.[30]

Exaltation of the reading of the Bible is here intertwined with a polemic against the outward cult of relics. The written word offers a full and faithful insight into the mind of the author: the familiar comparison with Apelles ("No Apelles . . .") is brought in to bolster a traditional theme, which here, however, acquires a specific theological dimension: the New Testament allows us to see the real image of Christ, which is manifested there with absolute clarity, through the workings of the Holy Ghost. The sacred text thus acts as a guarantee of the idea of transparency, of mirroring, which in works written by human beings can be no more than a myth, their success beset by the risks posed by the mask and the artifice. Because of the similarity between the Father and the Son, who is the word of the Father, the form of the discourse faithfully and immediately reflects "the archetype of the divine mind."

Paraclesis, That Is, an Exhortation to the Holy and Health-Giving Study of the Philosophy of Christ, which preceded Erasmus's edition of the New Testament in Greek, was published in Basel by Johann Froben in 1516 and dedicated to Leo X (other editions followed in 1519, 1522, 1527, and 1535). In this preface, Erasmus made an impassioned statement in favor of reading the Scriptures, which should be accessible to all: "I disagree entirely with those who do not want divine literature to be translated into the vernacular tongues and read by ordinary people"; the word of God, which can bring peace, should not be the reserve of a handful of theologians. "Why do we unhesitatingly prefer to learn the wisdom of Christ from the writings of human beings rather than from Christ himself, who in these books especially fulfils what he promised, that he would be with us always, 'even unto the end of the world'; for in them he lives even now, breathes and speaks to us, I might almost say more effectively than when he lived among men. The Jews saw less and heard less than you see and hear in the gospel writings, provided you bring eyes and ears by which he can be seen and heard."[31] The religious nature of the texts lends new depths to the idea of reading as a personal encounter, since the text communicates the living presence of its author. An encounter of this type is not just a possibility made available through style, which reflects the writer's soul; it is rather a certainty guaranteed by God's promise. The presence of Christ in the New Testament is so strong that readers will know him even more intimately than if they had met him in person.

Erasmus next explores in this light an essential component of the theme we are investigating: the idea of friendship and the image of the letter, which makes an absent friend present. Immediately after the previously quoted passage, we find, "What kind of behaviour, I ask you, is this? We preserve the letters written by a dear friend, we admire them greatly, we carry them about, we read then over and over again; yet there are thousands and thousands of Christians who, although learned in other respects, have never even read the Gospels and Epistles in their whole life." We should read the sacred texts, Erasmus continues, allow them to work within us, to transform us:

> Therefore, let us desire these books eagerly; let us embrace them; let us live with them constantly; let us admire them greatly; let us die in them; let us be transformed into them, since "our preoccupations affect our character." Whoever cannot pursue this course—but who cannot if only he so desires?—Let him at least honour those writings as the repository of the divine mind. If someone exhibited a print made by the feet of Christ, how we Christians would prostrate ourselves, how we would adore! Why, then, do we not rather venerate his living and his breathing image, preserved in these books? If someone displayed the tunic of Christ, would not we fly to the ends of the earth to kiss it? But even if you were to produce every possession he owned, there is nothing that would show Christ more clearly and more truly than the written Gospels. Through our love of Christ we enrich a statue of wood and stone with jewels and gold. Why do we not rather adorn these books with gold and jewels and anything more precious, for they recall Christ to us more vividly than any little statue. A statue shows only the appearance of his body—if indeed it shows anything of that—but these books show you the living image of his holy mind and Christ himself, speaking, healing, dying, rising to life again. In short, they restore Christ to us so completely and so vividly that you would see him less clearly should you behold him standing before your very eyes.[32]

Following St. Paul's trope of the inner and the outer man, relics (like portraits) are opposed to the living image of interiority (the texts). It is not the writings of theologians or relics or sacred images but the Gospels that bring the living Christ among us, that allow us to know him as a friend and ensure that his action is felt in our lives. "It is therefore as if Erasmus," as Michel Jeanneret has observed, "transported by the magnetic attraction the biblical text exerts over him, had forgotten the Fall, the progressive distancing from God, and the opacity of signs. Where less confident theologians—and indeed he himself on other occasions—remark on the lack of power of human language, on its insufficiency, here he sees words that are perspicuous and efficacious, capable of expressing fully, and without any loss of meaning, the truth of the divine message."[33]

It is worth noting that although the writings we have mentioned—*Enchiridion* and *Paraclesis*—were written before the *Ciceronianus*, they were reprinted over the years, accompanying Erasmus, we could almost say, into the later decades of his life. While these texts explore the theme of reading as an encounter and a dialogue through a theological lens, they also reveal the intransigence of the polemic against the Ciceronians, allowing us to glimpse how theology could snake its way into modern declensions of the idea of the book as *speculum animi*.

5

Machiavelli's Letter to Vettori

> And if this material amounts to little,
> and seems pretty thin stuff,
> from a man keen to be thought wise and dignified,
> excuse him for this reason: he grapples with these trivial musings,
> to make his miserable life more agreeable,
> because there is nothing else
> he can turn his sights to;
> for he has been prevented
> from showing his skills in other fields,
> and no one rewards him for his labors.

As is well known, Machiavelli offers the most celebrated example of our topos, as well as its most evocative literary consecration. The theme immediately calls to mind the famous passage from the letter to Francesco Vettori of 10 December 1513, which was written from Machiavelli's farm, the Albergaccio, at Sant'Andrea in Percussina. Here the former secretary of the Florentine republic had retired in exile, following the return of the Medici to Florence, when he had been suspected of taking part in a republican plot:[1]

> Venuta la sera, mi ritorno in casa, et entro nel mio scrittoio; et in su l'uscio mi spoglio quella veste cotidiana, piena di fango e di loto, e mi metto panni reali e curiali; e rivestito condecentemente entro nelle antique corti degli antiqui uomini, dove, da loro ricevuto amorevolmente, mi pasco di quel cibo, che solum è mio, e che io nacqui per lui; dove io non mi vergogno parlare con loro, e domandarli della ragione delle loro azioni; e quelli per loro umanità mi rispondono; e non sento

per 4 ore di tempo alcuna noia, sdimentico ogni affanno, non temo la povertà, non mi sbigottisce la morte: tutto mi transferisco in loro. E perché Dante dice che non fa scienza sanza lo ritenere lo avere inteso, io ho notato quello di che per la loro conversazione ho fatto capitale, e composto uno opuscolo *De principatibus*.

(On the coming of evening, I return to my house and enter my study; and at the door I take off the day's clothing, covered with mud and dust, and put on garments regal and courtly; and reclothed appropriately, I enter the ancient courts of ancient men, where, received by them with affection, I feed on that food which only is mine and which I was born for, where I am not ashamed to speak with them and to ask them the reason for their actions; and they in their kindness answer me; and for four hours of time I do not feel boredom, I forget every trouble, I do not dread poverty, I am not frightened by death; entirely I give myself over to them.

And because Dante says it is no true knowledge unless we remember what we have understood, I have noted everything in their conversation which has profited me, and have composed a little work *On Princedoms*.)[2]

The magic ritual of reading, its incantatory force, its pleasures and benefits are here described with extraordinary vividness, through a unique and extraordinarily effective kneading together of formal elegance and syntactic irregularities, the balanced rhythm of the parallelisms and correspondences suddenly veering into unexpected harshness, or surprising us with its intarsio of Italian, Latin, and Latinisms. Thus we see one of the founding myths of classical humanism expressed through a style that does not shy away from expressionistic and irregular effects. In the privacy of his study, Machiavelli performs a rite of evocation: the ancient authors are present and alive; they speak to him and discuss their ideas with him, in a "conversation" that would later flow into *The Prince*. Compared with the other occurrences of the topos that we have looked at, Machiavelli's version is notable for the radical displacement it describes: "entirely I give myself over to them" marks the culmination of a ritual, whose various steps lead the reader into a different world, where he can find his true self and set aside the anguish of everyday life. The process of this transference is rhetorically staged through negation and *climax:* "and for four hours of time I do not feel boredom, I forget every trouble, I do not dread poverty, I am not frightened by death." Palpably, this passage echoes the language and the ritual of the eucharist: Machiavelli changes his clothes; he talks of a "food which only [*solum*] is mine and which I was born for"; it is the word (the written word of books that relives through the dialogue of reading) that brings about salvation.[3] This language, however, and this sacred ritual are reinscribed in an entirely lay and secular context. This is quite different from Erasmus's revisitation of the topos in an evidently religious dimension (Chapter 4, section 3), through the deployment of theological language.

It is possible that the intensity of Machiavelli's account is due to the visual memory of the portraits of the great writers of antiquity, which, as we have seen (Chapter 3), decorated studies and libraries, where they contributed to enhancing the magical rite of evocation that was accomplished through reading. This almost sacral aura of Machiavelli's letter inspired Michele Mari's surreal and amusing desecration: in his parody, after Machiavelli has stepped into "a sumptuous robe of crimson velvet and soft rabbit-skin booties," and after the austere encounter with the ancient authors in his study, he finds himself "in a whirlwind of passion"; he descends into the cellar, where "a naked woman, an infant, a sheep and a capon" are chained to the wall; he tears off his robes, turns into a centaur (the creature who, according to mythology, was entrusted with the upbringing of young princes), and begins to feed on that "food which only is his and which he was born for."[4]

1. An Unequal Exchange

Much has been written on Machiavelli's letter to Vettori, one of the most memorable pages of Italian literature. Here I shall discuss only some of the points made by critics that seem relevant to the underlying theme of this book. First, I believe that a merely formal analysis is misleading. It is of course right that the letter to Vettori, and the passage we are primarily concerned with, should be viewed against the background of the epistolary exchange between the two friends, which shows clearly how the letter itself is part of an ongoing dialogue that forms, as it were, a larger text. As Ferroni has pointed out, the letter's "discursive mode" is part of the characteristic code of correspondence between friends in the Florence of Machiavelli's time, with its humorous tone, its forays into obscenity, and its carnivalesque debasement.[5] However, two factors should not be forgotten: the first is the painful context that determined the exchange in the first place: Machiavelli wrote to Vettori on 13 March 1513 telling him he had just been released from prison. Two days later Vettori replied, "'caro compare' In the last eight months I have experienced the greatest sorrows of my life, including some that you don't know about. But the worst of these came only when I learned that you had been arrested, because I knew right away, that without any error or cause on your part, you would have to undergo torture, as has in fact happened."[6] The epistolary exchange is therefore occasioned by the experience of prison and the still vivid memory of torture ("six hoists of rope on my back") that Machiavelli had endured. Moreover, it should be borne in mind that although this is an exchange between friends, there is a deep imbalance in the relationship of power between them: Machiavelli was condemned to a state of impotence, while Vettori was ambassador to the papal court, where indeed a Medici pope had been elected. From the very start, we see that Machiavelli is counting on his friend in order to work his way back into a political role and that Vettori is trying to pull back, repeatedly pointing out that he is unable to help, that he is placed in a difficult situation, that he is unsure about the best way to proceed, preemptively using his own doubts and anxieties to justify his own impotence.[7] As a result, Machiavelli is placed in the difficult position of actually having to comfort *Vettori* for the failure of his (one feels, half-hearted) attempts and to declare his ascetic (and ultimately impossible) detachment from any desire for political engagement. "I grieve over any notion you have that I am angry," he wrote on 9 April, when Vettori had been unable to obtain what Machiavelli had asked of him, "because I am trained no longer to wish for anything with passion." Then on 16 April, he wrote in a sort of Freudian denial, "I don't write this to you because I want things too much, nor because I want you to undertake for my love any burden or trouble or expense or anxiety."[8]

Machiavelli and Vettori had shared memories, as well as similar codes of language and behavior: their group of Florentine friends had a taste for pranks and cultivated a low, "carnivalesque" style that was resorted to in recounting the erotic adventures they either undertook themselves or witnessed in others. A good example of this is Machiavelli's letter of 16 April 1513, in which he laments, "the company that you know all about seems as though it were lost . . . all its leaders have been boiling": from Marione, who thought he had spent too much on veal and wanted to find somebody who would share the cost, to the recently widowed Girolamo del Guanto, who was dazed "for three or four days," then came back to life and "wanted to get another" wife, to "Count Orlando all torn up again over a fellow from Ragusa and unable to get any kindness from him," to the sodomite Donato del Corno, who "has opened another horn shop where doves are sold, and . . . goes all day from the old one to the new one like a crazed man."[9] It is amid such a colorful account that we come across the aforementioned statement that he no longer wished for anything and has renounced political passion. However, what comes (textually) between the light comedy of the evocation of the "boiling" group of friends and this stoic renunciation should be duly noted: Machiavelli asks Vettori to help him find some political appointment, either in Florence or in Rome, and prefaces his request with a quotation from Petrarch (*Canzoniere,* 102, 13–14), significantly modified by a slip of the memory:

> Però se alcun volta io rido o canto,
> follo perché io non ho se non questa una
> via da sfogare il mio acerbo pianto[10]

> (So then if sometimes I laugh or sing,
> I do so because I have just this one
> way of giving vent to my bitter sorrow.)

Machiavelli substitutes "sfogare" (give vent to) for the "celare" (conceal) of the original. The choice, as Najemy has pointed out, lies between political discourse and silence; Petrarch's "celare" (concealing) has been suppressed, in a move that Giorgio Inglese has linked to the interplay of laughter and tears that is a constant in Machiavelli's writing.[11] The original context of the quotation from Petrarch is, as noted by Federico Baricci, also significant.[12] The octave of Petrarch's sonnet gives two, diametrically opposite, examples: Caesar, who cries when he sees Pompey's severed head "celando l'allegrezza manifesta" (concealing his clear joy), and Hannibal, who laughs when fortune rages against Carthage. The moral, expressed in the sestet, is both universal and personal:

> Et così aven che l'animo ciascuna
> sua passïon sotto 'l contrario manto
> ricopre co la vista or chiara or bruna:

però s'alcuna volta io rido o canto,
facciol, perch'i' non ò se non quest'una
via da celare il mio angoscioso pianto. (*Canzoniere,* 102)

It is clear that Machiavelli identifies with Hannibal, who laughs "per isfogare il suo acerbo despitto" (to give vent to his bitter resentment) against "Fortuna sì molesta." The misquotation is extremely significant, and it must have had a strong impact on Vettori's literary memory, following a recurring pattern that we will be returning to in greater detail later.

It should also be observed that this letter, dated 16 April, is best appreciated if one reads it in relation to the December epistle that is the focus of this section: here too we encounter a double register, one mundane, burlesque, disparagingly (or at least self-disparagingly) comic; the other political, serious, and veering toward the tragic. An unresolved tension between friendship and power is in ferment below the surface of the letter, between an erotic drive and an opposing but equally unstoppable need "to talk about the government" (i.e., politics), between the low, "shared" dimension and a "high" political dimension that is, and looks likely to remain, tragically separate, a dimension from which Machiavelli feels painfully excluded.[13]

2. An Orderly Path, a Polemical Mirroring

The letter of 10 December is, in a sense, the last round of an ongoing game, whose various moves, as we have seen, were already visible in the letter of 16 April. In the letter of 10 December, it is easy to discern, as many critics have pointed out, an oppositional structure that emerges in terms of time, space, and expressive codes. In the account Machiavelli gives of his typical day, we *feel* the outside world, bathed in the light of day, marked by activities and encounters that take place in a sequence of clearly distinguished steps (the grove, the spring, the aviary, the inn): in this world, says Machiavelli, "I sink into vulgarity" (m'ingaglioffo), he immerses himself in the "tastes" and "fantasies" of the lower classes and embraces his primary needs almost as if to challenge fortune. Then comes the intimate and solitary world of the night, when he retires to his study—a world of separation and of dialogue with the dead. These different times and spaces, it has been noted, are associated with different types of reading: outdoors, immersed in nature, Machiavelli reads the love poets that he has brought along with him in his exile: "I have a book, either Dante or Petrarch, or one of the lesser poets such as Tibullus, Ovid and the like. I read about their tender passions and their loves, remember mine, enjoy myself a while in that sort of dreaming."[14] This type of reading involves an emotional mirroring: the love poems prompt memories of his own loves, and this memory, which feeds on comparison, prolongs pleasure.[15]

What Machiavelli reads in the evening behind the closed doors of the study has an entirely different flavor. Here Machiavelli solemnly describes how the great writers of classical antiquity condescend to talk with him, in an atmosphere redolent of sacrality. The two types of reading, Grafton has stressed, are also linked to two different textual formats: the books of love poetry that Machiavelli says he carried around with him must have been small practical octavos, while the great classics with which he dialogued when the evening closed in were probably folios, to be read and questioned in the study.[16]

The oppositional structure (which juxtaposes places, times, and modes of reading) follows an itinerary that culminates in Machiavelli's encounter with the great writers and the writing of *The Prince*. At the same time, the letter suggests a series of correspondences, a mirroring of different moments in time: "Then I move along the road to the inn," Machiavelli says after he has described his reading of love poetry; "entirely I give myself over to them," he states at the culminating moment of his dialogue with the ancients; "I speak with those who pass"—he says, on the road to the inn—"ask news of their villages, learn various things, and note the various tastes and different fancies of men." He asks questions, gathers information, and observes. This choice of verbs, as well as the ternary arrangement, will reappear in the passage on the dialogue with the classics: "where I am not ashamed to speak with them and to ask them the reason for their actions"; "I have written a little book." In describing his partaking of food with his family, he writes, "I eat such food as this poor farm of mine and my tiny property [*paululo patrimonio*] allow"; while in the evening, "I feed on that food that only [*solum*] is mine," where the use of the Latin word *solum* echoes the earlier *paululo,* which masked the Latin word behind what looks like an Italian diminutive.[17] This parallelism suggests the work of a single director moving from low to high, from comic to sublime, from the wayside inn to the intellectual's study.

It is most markedly in the letter addressed to Vettori on 23 November that this direction shows its strength. If we examine the two texts side by side, we observe correspondences that manifest themselves through a systematic recalling and reversing of previous points. If Vettori's letter proceeds from high to low (what he is trying to show in the description of his day is that, although he is an ambassador, he lives a simple life), Machiavelli's letter moves from low to high, from the "ingaglioffamento" of the countryside and the inn to the great ritual reading of the night: although in exile and tormented by adverse fortune, he wishes to show that he is more than ever capable of reasoning about politics and, if given the opportunity, to act as a politician. This is also an implicitly polemical riposte to the comparison with card playing that Vettori had used at the beginning of this letter of 23 November:

> I made no reply to you at the time because I was afraid the same thing might happen to you and me as once happened to me and Panzano when we began to play cards with an old and tired deck even as we sent for a new one. When the errand-boy returned with the new cards, one of us had already lost his money. Similarly, you and I spoke of making peace among the princes of Europe, and they went right on playing: so, I feared that while we were using up our letters getting them to agree, one or another of them would lose his money. After we stopped writing, we saw some [new] things: and although the party isn't over yet, it still seems to have slowed down some; and until it ends I think it best not to talk about it.[18]

The two friends' intense discussions about politics, their attempt to understand and give an account of what was happening in the world around them, is compared to a game with old cards, during which at a certain point new cards are sent for, but by then they have run out of money, which is the essence of the game itself.[19] As events precipitate, the cards become useless, and there is no time to get new ones: politics is here reduced to a game, cards standing in not just for the playing cards but for the papers (*carte*) that are used in writing, to which is entrusted the effort made by reason to make sense of events. The description of Vettori's typical day, which immediately follows, is the result of his acknowledgment of this cognitive impasse and instances his decision to "speak of other things": "and it was because of this letter that I have decided to write to tell you about my life in Rome" (E per questa lettera ho fatto pensiero scrivervi qual sia la vita mia in Roma).[20] It is here that we see the technique of reversal I referred to earlier: Machiavelli declares that he has nothing else to do but describe his daily life to his friend—"and if you judge that you would like to swap with mine, I shall be glad to" (et se voi giudicate che sia a barattarla con la vostra, io sarò contento mutarla).[21]

If Vettori, who lives in the city, describes in detail his solitary abode, the walks he takes by himself in the mornings, Machiavelli, who is confined to his villa, tells him of his thrush snaring, his orders to have a grove cut down for firewood, and the petty arguments and quarrels that ensue. If Vettori sees the pope, the cardinal de' Medici, or some ambassadors and sometimes eats with the cardinal, Machiavelli eats with his family, and his choice is restricted to what is yielded by his poor lands. In the afternoon, Vettori would like to play but can find no suitable companions, whereas Machiavelli spends his time at the inn, happily gaming away and consorting with the vulgar (m'ingaglioffo).

Both men spend the evening reading, but in a very different spirit and with entirely different results: Vettori writes, "At night I return home. I've managed to get a lot of history books, especially those of the Romans, Livy, with the epitome of Lucius Florus, Sallust, Plutarch, Tacitus, Suetonius, Lampridius and Spartianus, and the other three who write of emperors, Erodianus, Ammianus Marcellinus and Procopius. With them I pass the time, and I think about what kind of emperors poor Rome, which used to make the world tremble, has endured, and that it's no wonder that [Rome] has also put up with two popes of the sort that recent ones have been."[22] From the ancient historians, Vettori learns about Rome's infinite capacity of endurance: the miseries of the past are reflected in the present, resulting in a bitter acceptance, a resigned submission to the slings and arrows of adverse fortune.

When the evening comes, Machiavelli retires to his study, dialogues with the ancient writers, and works on *The Prince*. If the political activity Vettori halfheartedly dedicates himself to seems senseless (every four days, he says, he writes a letter to the Council of Ten [the Florentine magistrates] and gives them "some worn-out bits of news of no importance," because he has "nothing else to write"),[23] Machiavelli feels the book he has written may be useful: "And if ever you found any of my fantasies pleasing, this one should not displease you; and by a prince, and especially by a new prince, it ought to be welcomed. Hence I am dedicating it to His Magnificence Giuliano."[24] The colloquial term *ghiribizo* (fantasies) marks a lowering of the language compared to the "sublime" tone of the preceding passage describing his dialogue with the ancient writers: Machiavelli now returns to the informal style of friendly dialogue and to shared memories ("If ever you liked . . ."). Vettori had used a denominal verb from the same term (*ghiribizo*) on 9 April, to mark a particular moment when he found himself rethinking yet again his decision to renounce any reasonable discussion of politics: "although I told you that I no longer want to speculate [*ghiribizzare*], or to discuss matters on the basis of reason [*discorrer con ragione*], nonetheless these latest events have made me change my mind."[25] Machiavelli's oscillation in tone seems aimed at rebuilding the relationship, by calling on his powerful friend to show the same understanding, the same willingness to enter into a conversation on equal terms, that he has experienced with the writers of antiquity.[26]

"Sed fatis trahimur" (But we are dragged along by the Fates), Vettori had stated with one of those Latin quotations that he was so fond of and that he used in order to give himself an air of authority.[27] Machiavelli's letter is a polemical riposte to his friend's suggestion that he should submit to fortune; but his stratagem is not so much to adapt to the various changes brought on by Fortune as to seek a way to escape from them. The famous passage on the dialogue with the ancients becomes, as we have seen, the culmination of a carefully constructed and equally carefully described pathway, which turns on its head Vettori's somewhat blasé description of his meaningless and snobbishly disengaged Roman day.[28] Machiavelli's dialogue with the ancients, which takes place in an elevated and refined atmosphere and which signals his rediscovery and recognition that he is their equal, becomes the emblem of possible redemption and a polemical exemplum for his refractory friend. What Machiavelli is trying to say is that Vettori should follow such an example by truly dialoguing with Machiavelli himself and helping him to find the role that "solum" is his.[29]

3. Two Readers Compared

The code that Machiavelli and Vettori share is also made up of literary memories, of the traces that classical and Italian authors have left and that gradually reemerge, occasionally in a fragmentary or distorted form, in key moments of their intense epistolary exchange. A few examples will be sufficient to show this.

We have already seen the case of the quotation from Petrarch, where "giving vent to" sorrow is substituted for the original "concealing": the quotation itself is placed at a very strategic point in Machiavelli's letter, functioning as a link between the "boilings" of the group of friends, the request for political help, and the show of stoical detachment ("I don't write this to you because I want things too much").[30] A similar function may be observed in a quotation from Dante, which Machiavelli positions like a piece of decorative inlay, colored, however, with both bitterness and the utopian desire to control all desires. Here is the beginning of his letter of 9 April 1513:

Magnificent Mr. Ambassador:
and I, who of his color had become aware, said: "How shall I go if you are fearful, who in my timidity are always my encouragement?" [Et io, che del colore mi fui accorto / dissi: Come verrò se tu paventi, / che suoli al mio dubbiare esser conforto?]

This letter of yours has terrified me more than the rack, and I grieve over any notion you have that I am angry, not on my own account, because I am trained no longer to wish for anything with passion, but on yours. I beg you to imitate the others, who with persistence and craft, rather than with ability and prudence, make themselves places.[31]

The quotation (*Inf.*, IV, 16–18) projects onto Vettori the image of Dante's Virgil, the guide who is supposed to offer comfort to the poet but is overcome by fear. What might also be relevant, as Najemy suggests, is the memory of the place where Dante's verses are set: the Limbo where guiltless souls are condemned to live under the burden of a hopeless desire ("Per tai difetti, e non per altro rio, / semo perduti, e sol di tanto offesi / che sanza speme viviamo in disio"; *Inf.*, IV, 40–42).[32] It may be that Machiavelli felt himself to be in a sort of Limbo and wishes Vettori to grasp this; his aim, if we accept this interpretation, is to prompt his reluctant (and / or powerless) friend to resume once more his role as guide and mentor, even if this involves stooping to emotional blackmail: "this letter of yours has terrified me more than the rack," that is, more that the torture he underwent.

Words can cut more deeply that the instruments of torture: the letter of 10 December is also a passionate reaction to Vettori's "sed fatis trahimur." In this dialogue-duel, Machiavelli sets the central argument of his letter between quotations from two writers in the vulgar tongue that had become classics: toward the end are the proverbial-sounding verses from Dante (*Par.*, V, 41–42), which serve to herald the unveiling of *Il Principe* ("and because

Dante says it does not produce knowledge when we understand but do not remember");[33] at the beginning, there is a line from Petrarch's *Triumphus Eternitatis,* 13: "Tarde non fur mai grazie divine" (Never late were favors divine). The latter quotation becomes doubly ironic on account of its reference to God and because Vettori had in fact not written for a long time, so that his "favors" were indeed "late." The quotation from Petrarch also has a proverbial ring and is well suited to marking the distance between the two correspondents by juxtaposing eternity to time, the "divinity" of the powerful man to the earthly and subordinate position of someone who awaits favors.

At the beginning of Machiavelli's description of his day we find, "I have until now been snaring thrushes with my own hands. I got up before day, prepared birdlime, went out with a bundle of cages on my back, so that I looked like Geta when he was returning from the harbor with Amphytrion's books."[34] The reference here is to a Quattrocento *cantare,* attributed to Domenico da Prato, a novella in octaves titled *Geta e Birria.*[35] The story originally came from Plautus's *Amphitryon,* in which Jove turns himself into Amphitryon so as to enjoy his beautiful wife; around the middle of the twelfth century, Vitalis of Blois had reworked it into an elegiac comedy in which Plautus's servant Sosia becomes the two characters Geta and Birria. Boccaccio had transcribed the text and on a number of occasions taken inspiration from it. The *cantare* is attributed—among others—to Filippo Brunelleschi, which is understandable because the themes of the double, of metamorphosis, and of the loss of identity (at one point, Geta comes face-to-face with his alter ego, the god Archas, who has taken on his form) recall the famous prank played by Brunelleschi and a group of friends on Grasso the cabinet maker: as a revenge for having stood them up, they succeeded in convincing Grasso that he had morphed into someone else. Machiavelli is therefore quoting a text that is clearly connoted as Tuscan and in particular Florentine. But what lies behind the comparison of himself with Geta carrying his master's books?

As Najemy reminds us, Birria sees Geta returning home from the port with his master's books, which he knows he will have to take from him and carry home, so he hides in a cave to avoid the task. Machiavelli's point is that by associating himself with Geta, he is expressing his fear that he will have to return home with his *Prince* in his hands without having been properly heard or helped by his friend.[36] Although Machiavelli is portraying himself through the comic light of burlesque self-debasement, there are intriguing points of contact with the character of Geta. In the fifteenth-century *cantare,* Geta is ugly and deformed, a slave to lust and sexually well endowed.[37] He has followed his master, Amphitryon, who has gone to study philosophy in Athens, and he himself becomes a logician, though this turns out to be of little help to him in the sad events that befall him. Amphitryon's other servant, Birria, is the embodiment of laziness, which he has elevated to a form of philosophy. Machiavelli would like the image of himself returning from his expedition loaded with cages to awaken in Vettori the visual and verbal memory of Geta, the servant whom nobody is willing to help, very poorly aided by his great store of knowledge and tricked by the gods into doubting his own identity and even his own existence. If we give full range to these associations, Machiavelli's self-portrait in the guise of Geta is truly significant.

According to Ezio Raimondi, in one of the final passages of the letter of 10 December, we may also detect an allusion to Lucretius, where Machiavelli expresses his anxiety about how to convey his small book, *The Prince,* to the Medici: "The giving of it is forced on me by the necessity that drives me, because I am using up my money, and I cannot remain as I am a long time without becoming despised through poverty. In addition, there is my wish that our present Medici lords will make use of me, even if they begin by making me roll a stone."[38] To "roll a stone," argues Raimondi, is here a reference to the myth of Sisyphus, by way of Lucretius. In Book III of *De rerum natura,* we learn that the infernal torments described in the myths actually represent the suffering endured by men in real life when they allow themselves to be dominated by passions. For Lucretius, Sisyphus represents the man who is devoured by political ambition, pursuing positions that will only disappoint and frustrate him (*De rerum natura,* III, 995–1002). Machiavelli latches onto Lucretius's political reading of the myth, though without endorsing its moral of stoic renunciation and philosophical detachment. The image of the stone resurfaces in a portion of the text describing deprivation and the vital need to be once more engaged in political action; Lucretius's image is therefore evoked only for its interpretation to be rejected—by distancing himself from it, Machiavelli is in fact giving it a new lease of life. As Raimondi observes, the image "newly sanctions the positivity of the art of statesmanship for someone who cannot live without it and is ready to submit to the most obscure toil in order to re-enter that world and put an end to the suspicion of his having lost or betrayed the very reason of his existence."[39]

A MARVELOUS SOLITUDE

It is difficult to say whether Vettori would have immediately grasped the allusion to Lucretius behind Machiavelli's desire to be employed, if only "to roll a stone"—shared memory, after all, does not always work as it should, and sometimes the underlying quotation fails to unleash the meanings and associations it has been charged with. This is what happened with the fable of the fox and the lion that opens Machiavelli's letter to Vettori of 26 August 1513:

> Mr. Ambassador:
> Your letter of the twentieth, now before me, bewildered me, because its arrangement, the multitude of its reasons, and all its other qualities so entangled me that in the beginning I was lost and confused; and if in the rereading I had not been a little reassured, I would have given you a bad card [would not have replied], and would have answered you about other things. But as I get used to it, the same thing has happened to me as did to the fox when he saw the lion: the first time he was ready to die for fear; the second he stopped behind a bush to look at him; the third he spoke to him; and so having reassured myself by getting used to it, I shall answer you.[40]

This is the very heart of the exchange on the contemporary political situation to which Vettori's letter was devoted and which had "bewildered" Machiavelli. The neat summarization of Aesop's fable perfectly epitomizes the moral commonly associated with it—that things that scare us become less daunting as we become accustomed to them and gain a better understanding of them.[41] The fox and the lion reappear, albeit invested with a different meaning, in the famous chapter 18 of *The Prince*. In this letter, the two animals well represent the power relationship between the two men but also the stubborn determination of Machiavelli, the fox, who gets over his "bewilderment" and begins once more to weave his web, putting forward his own interpretation of the political situation and promoting his competence and usefulness. What takes place between the two friends, however, is also a game, an intellectual challenge: "io davo cartaccia" (I would have given you a bad card), Machiavelli writes, using once again what we have seen to be a recurring metaphor in his epistolary exchange with Vettori. At this stage of the game, however, the bandying of quotations seems to go sour and lose its appeal. "I don't imagine that the Swiss can become new Romans,"

Vettori had pointed out in his ("bewildering") letter of 20 August, adding, "because if you read [Aristotle's] *Politics* carefully and the republics that have existed, you will not find that a republic like the confederated one [of the Swiss] can advance very far."[42] To this accusation of being a careless reader, or indeed a bad interpreter, which was nothing short of an open provocation, Machiavelli answered as follows: "I do not know what Aristotle says about states made up of detached republics, but I do consider what reasonably can be, what is, and what has been; and I remember reading that the Lucumnians held all Italy as far as the Alps."[43] "The quip on Aristotle," observes Giorgio Inglese, "cannot be understood unless one is aware that the *Politics* makes no mention of 'detached' republics."[44] Machiavelli answers Vettori's nonchalant (mis)quotation by appealing to reason and by quoting an example from the ancient world; he will never stop looking to facts for answers or attempting to systematize them in the light of reason.[45]

Aesop's fable of the fox and the lion also falls into the vortex of the crisis between the two friends, the great disavowal of their shared memory. Vettori waits until 23 November to answer, months after Machiavelli's last letter; he therefore feels justified in saying that he does not remember at what point they had left off: "Pray remind me, as I think the last letter I received from you began with the tale of the lion and the fox; I have sifted through my letters a bit, but being unable to find it easily, I thought it best to stop looking."[46] Vettori is unable to remember, he cannot find the tale, he lets things go, and this halfhearted search in the library, this distance between their literary memories, is reflected in the sense of uselessness that extends also to their epistolary exchange: immediately after that comes the comparison we saw earlier with a game played with old cards and no money, while the situation spirals out of control and the real game is played far away, by men who are truly powerful. This is followed by an almost regressive return to the quotidian, as Vettori describes his day. Machiavelli replied to this in the manner we have seen.

4. The Painful Triumph of Eros

The pleasures of eros are often touched on in the correspondence, and the two friends often linger over the comic or burlesque aspects of amorous bondage. The evenings in Vettori's home, for example, are described with brilliant theatrical flair, from Filippo Casavecchia's intimate and indiscreet questioning of a fourteen-year-old boy to Giuliano Brancaccio's languishing for the beautiful Costanza and the host's passionate fondness for courtesans.[47] On 16 January 1515, Vettori writes that he has but little to keep him employed and that to escape melancholy, he concerns himself with loving, or rather, with fucking: "I know nothing that gives more delight to think about and to do than fucking [*fottere*]. Every man may philosophize all he wants, but this is the utter truth, which many people understand this way but few will say."[48] The pleasures of eros, and the account given of these pleasures to the group of friends, are part of a way of life characterized by manifold possibilities and diverse interests, reflecting the multiplicity and variety of nature itself. In this light, the famous passage from Machiavelli's letter of 31 January 1515 may be read as a sort of "instructions to the reader":

> Anybody who saw our letters, honored friend, and saw their diversity, would wonder greatly, because he would suppose now that we were grave men, wholly concerned with important matters, and that into our breasts no thought could fall that did not have in itself honor and greatness. But then, turning the page, he would judge that we, the very same persons, were lightminded, inconstant, lascivious, concerned with empty things. And this way of proceeding, if to some it may appear censurable, to me seems praiseworthy, because we are imitating Nature, who is a variable; and he who imitates her cannot be blamed.[49]

The risk of this scenario, however, is that when variety ceases, eros may become the only pleasure practicable and therefore to a certain extent the only alternative to the possibility of Machiavelli's playing an active political role. An example of this may be seen in a letter Vettori sent to him on 9 April 1513, in which he renewed his invitation to join him in Rome: "We'll see who can hoodwink some folks in such a way that will get us somewhere in all this; and if it doesn't work out, we won't lack the company of a girl I know near my house and the chance to while away some time with her. This seems to me the thing to do, and soon we'll be clearer about all this."[50] If the maneuvers to reinstate Machiavelli in a political role were to fail, there would always be, Vettori suggests, the consolation of love. Although love and sex always remain in the background, they become, when disappointment strikes, all-embracing activities—an alternative way of life pitted against what has become impracticable.[51] It is an alternative forged in blood and tears because it involves renouncing one's destiny. As Machiavelli had written on 9 April, "Yet if I could speak to you, I couldn't keep from filling your head with fantastical constructions [*castellucci*], because Fortune has determined that since I don't know how to talk about the silk business or the wool business, or about profits and losses, I have to talk about the government, and I must either make a vow of silence or discuss that."[52]

Let us now examine the traces of the letter of 10 December 1513 in the epistolary exchange of the following year. Here we see that the lives of the two friends are reflected in their treatment of love. As Machiavelli writes on 3 August 1514, "You, my friend, have with many accounts of your love at Rome kept me all rejoicing, and you have removed from my mind countless worries. . . . And truly Fortune has brought me to a place where I can render you just recompense for it. . . . I ought to tell you, as you did me, the beginnings of this love, with what nets he took me." And a little later we find, "May it be enough for you that, already near fifty years, neither do these suns harm me, nor do rough roads tire me, nor the dark hours of the night frighten me."[53] The three negatives remind us of the famous passage on the dialogue with the ancients: "and for four hours of time I do not feel boredom, I forget every trouble, I do not dread poverty, I am not frightened by death." If this may seem a gratuitous association, what follows actually both justifies and reinforces it: "And though I seem to have entered into great labor, nevertheless I feel in it such sweetness, both through what that face so wonderful and soft brings me, and also through having laid aside the memory of all my troubles, that for anything in the world, being able to free myself, I would not wish it. I have abandoned, then, the thoughts of affairs that are great and serious; I do not anymore take delight in reading ancient things or in discussing modern ones; they are all turned into soft conversations, for which I thank Venus and all Cyprus."[54] Eros has become an all-enveloping force, erasing all other pleasure, even that supreme delight that was found in "reading ancient things" and "discussing modern ones."

When reexamined within the wider context of the Machiavelli-Vettori correspondence, the beautiful passage on the dialogue with the great authors of the past that we have been examining loses none of its strength—rather, it is multiplied as if by diffraction. The memory of this passage, down to its formal structure, reappears in different contexts and becomes part of an oppositional pattern in which the virtual and phantasmal evocation of the ancients is constructed as an alternative to the present—polemically pressing at its borders, demanding to be translated into "reason" and action.

The means through which Machiavelli hoped to cross that border was *The Prince,* which Najemy believes underpins the whole of the correspondence. According to this reading, Vettori had already got wind of the book, even before Machiavelli told him about it, and Vettori's letter of 23 November 1513 should therefore be seen as a sort of preventive action, to forewarn Machiavelli that *The Prince* would be useless, that the men he would like to address it to would not be willing to lend him their ears. That Vettori should have heard something of *The Prince* is only a hypothesis, but the link between this book and the dialogue with the ancients is certainly important. The solemn staging of that encounter, Najemy argues, is a dream that only underscores its painful distance from reality: "the more successfully the letter creates and sustains the illusion of presence, of speech, and of the recovery of the past, the more acutely does it impose the realization of absence and loss"; "the book he writes becomes the fruit of his attempt to capture the dream, or at least, as with any dream, those parts he could remember."[55] At the same time, it might be argued, that dream is shaped by a great tradition. From this tradition, Machiavelli brings the dream forth, molding it though his unmistakable style and turning it into a powerful image as a counterpoise to an opaque present, the sign of a change that is possible.

6

Montaigne's Tower

> Withdrawn to this solitary place,
> With a few but learned books.
> I live conversing with the dead,
> Listening to them with my eyes.
> —Francisco de Quevedo, "Desde la torre"

1. The Library as the Site of Memory and Freedom

In the rolling countryside dotted with hills and vineyards between Bordeaux and Bergerac, there is a tower that survived the fire that claimed the ancient abode of which it originally formed part (see Figure 6.1). Here, on the top floor, Michel de Montaigne (1533–1592) created his refuge, a place designedly removed from the theater of the world and from the masks, subterfuge, and slavery to convention that are its characteristics. In 1570, he resigned from, and sold his position in, the Parlement of Bordeaux, and the following year, he had an inscription placed on the wall of the *cabinet* next to the circular room where his books were kept: "In the year of Christ 1571, at the age of thirty-eight years, on the eve of the calends of March, the anniversary of his birth, Michel de Montaigne, long since disgusted with the slavery of the court of *parlement,* and still feeling fit, came away to repose on the breast of the learned virgins in calm and security; there he will pass the days that he has left to live. Hoping that destiny will allow him to perfect this residence, this sweet paternal retirement, he has consecrated them to his freedom, his tranquility, and his leisure."[1] Montaigne, as Jean Starobinski has written, while continuing to engage in public affairs, created a place that secured for him "the *possibility* of occupying his own private territory, the possibility of withdrawing at any moment into absolute

Figure 6.1. Montaigne's tower, Dordogne, Saint Michel de Montaigne. *J.D. Dallet/AGE Fotostock/Mondadori Portfolio.*

solitude, of quitting the game. . . . Thus a hiatus was opened up between the gaze of the observer and the agitation of mankind": this is the space of a new freedom in which he can recapture "self-presence [*présence à soi*]," which is also a rebirth, clearly signaled by the inscription noting the year and his age.[2]

This "other" space, contiguous with but separate from the world, is the library. In the room adjacent to the *cabinet,* as we have seen, Montaigne placed his own books and those that had been left to him by his beloved friend Étienne de la Boétie, who had died in 1563. In 1570, Montaigne published his friend's works, and in 1571, he dedicated his library to him, as a mark—we read in the Latin inscription that he placed there—of his grateful memory, a *monumentum* to their reciprocal love, a precious ornament.[3] The library was therefore both a physical and a mental space: in it were the books owned by his friend and those written by him, as well as Montaigne's own books. It was a place that somehow succeeded in overcoming death, allowing his absent friend to be present once more and enabling Montaigne to continue a dialogue that had been interrupted by death.

Montaigne's Tower

Figure 6.2. Montaigne's tower, inscriptions on the beams. © *Erich Lessing/K&K Archive/Mondadori Portfolio.*

Montaigne arranged his books to line the walls of the library and also arranged for Latin and Greek inscriptions taken from his favorite readings to be carved on the ceiling beams (see Figure 6.2). Not all of these have survived; in the eighteenth century, visitors could read many more, but those that remain are truly fascinating, their position making them particularly impactful, with quotations from Ecclesiastes—often paraphrased—playing a strong role.[4] The impression one gleans is that they were passages mulled over in memory, wrenched apart, often dramatically reduced to their essentials, displaying, for example, the lightning-like clarity of "God gave to man the desire for knowledge for the sake of tormenting him."[5] The *vanitas* against which Ecclesiastes warns is echoed in the skeptical maxims of Sextus Empiricus; in the passages from Sophocles and Lucretius, Pliny and Menander on the dangerous power of illusions, on how we are nothing but shadows, vain semblances; or in those from Proverbs and St. Paul on the vain presumption of those who think they know.

The inscriptions "encapsulate Montaigne's culture," as Armando Torno has written, "his coordinates, as it were, his reference system simplified to a single line. Or, if one prefers, the optical instruments with which to observe the world and men."[6] Petrarch's *De remediis* comes to mind, with its description of the vials and weapons that may be taken from the library, deposited in the safe chest of memory (and the book), so that we may be ready to face (as well as to write about) the vicissitudes of life (see Chapter 1, section 4). Here, however, all this appears in a form that is more concentrated, more incisive, and reduced to essentials.[7] It is worth remembering what Montaigne wrote of Plutarch: "He merely points out with his finger where we are to go, if we like, and sometimes is content to make only a stab at the heart of a subject. We must snatch these bits out of there and put them on display."[8] This is precisely what the inscriptions do, choosing from the vast thesaurus that is the library those fragments that must be "put on display."

The books on the shelves speak through the sayings that have been taken from them, the fragments of wisdom they have furnished. The different directions of the beams allow different pathways of reading, anticipating and stimulating the visitor who moves about the room, who even physically brings the sayings back to life as they read them, taking in, one step after the other, the teachings Montaigne believed were so vital.[9] Montaigne describes himself, within the refuge of his library, as continually in movement: "My thoughts fall asleep if I make them sit down. My mind will not budge unless my legs move it."[10] It is here that he wrote his *Essays*, where those wise words, epitomized in the inscriptions, take on a life of their own, becoming the seeds of his own writing and at the same time reentering the kaleidoscopic game of interpretations, reversals, and variations.

As suggested by Alain Legros, the tradition that Montaigne redeployed and reworked into the library inscriptions was probably also filtered through the teachings of Erasmus, who believed that important maxims should be inscribed on rings, on cups, above doors, on walls, so that they might always be before the eyes and contribute to swelling the storehouse of knowledge.[11] In the imaginary house and garden where one of Erasmus's *Colloquia, The Godly Feast,* takes place (see Chapter 3, section 2), inscriptions mark out the different spaces, about which Eusebius remarks, "Other men have luxurious homes; I have one where there's plenty of talk, in order that I may never seem lonely."[12]

The tower, its top floor, and the inscription that can be read there lead us into a space we are by now familiar with, and we enter the magic circle of the library, where we may enjoy the silent dialogue with books and the separateness from the world that leads us back to our true selves. Here, reading and writing are closely interconnected; indeed this is what is truly gained by seeking "repose on the breast of the learned virgins," in the arms, that is, of the Muses, who bring both wisdom and memory. The work that sprang from this magic space, the *Essays,* presents features that are both familiar and disquietingly different: we encounter once again the principal elements of the topos we have seen so often reappear, but these very elements now seem separate, deconstructed, their clarity streaked with skepticism and self-criticism: no longer stable, they have become fluid and irreducible to a single perspective. Nowhere is this clearer than in that myth of transparency that has featured so conspicuously in the tradition we have retraced. Starobinski has acutely identified the issue, working in parallel on Montaigne and Rousseau: "The point of these parallel studies," he writes, "lies in the similarity of the actions that serve in each case as a point of departure—the criticism of false appearances and their attendant evils—even though the ultimate outcomes are quite different: unable to attain true being, Montaigne acknowledges the legitimacy of appearance, whereas Rousseau, unreconciled, imagines that hostile clouds are gathering all round, in order to preserve his conviction that within his own heart transparency has found its last refuge."[13] The "legitimacy of appearance" corrodes all fixity, becomes the object of implacable study, of experimentation, of translation into ever-changing images and endless negotiations.

2. The Allure and Risk of Dialogue with the Ancients

The tower and the inscriptions on its ceiling beams may be seen as a sort of paratext to the *Essays.* These receive plentiful nourishment from the library, from the books that may be read there. An amazing variety of anecdotes, aphorisms, and verses are summoned up to help solve, or at least debate, the questions Montaigne puts to himself, so that they may dialogue with his inexhaustible curiosity.[14]

At the same time, this constant dialogue with the ancients, this recurrent reuse of their words, is itself a matter of debate.[15] The chapter on pedantry ("Du pédantisme," I, 25) is typical of Montaigne's way of writing and thinking, which has been described as constantly "en mouvement."[16] "I was often annoyed in my childhood," he muses, "to see a teacher always the butt in Italian comedies; and the title of *magister* used to have scarcely a more honorable significance among us Frenchmen"; and yet, he observes, the disparagement of teachers was already widespread in antiquity. "Since then, as I grew older, I found that they had a very good reason for this. . . . But how it is possible that a soul rich in the knowledge of so many things should not thereby become keener and more alert, and that a crude and commonplace mind can harbor within itself, without being improved, the reasonings and judgments of the greatest minds that the world has produced—that still has me puzzled."[17] The fruit of reading is therefore to offer hospitality to the great men of antiquity (to "harbor them within our minds"). The problem, however, is the quality of the hospitality we offer: "We should have asked who is better learned, not who is more learned. We labor only to fill our memory and leave the understanding and the conscience empty. Just as birds sometimes go in quest of grain, and carry it in their beak without tasting it to give a beakful to their little ones, so our pedants go pillaging knowledge in books and lodge it only on the end of their lips, in order merely to disgorge it and scatter it to the winds."[18] Without quoting him openly, Montaigne is here using his beloved Plutarch, who compared the Sophists, with their overriding interest in exhibiting their knowledge, to the bird that carried a grain in its beak solely to nourish its young, without ever feeding on or even tasting it himself—a staging of the old metaphor of reading as food, the corollary of which is the need to digest, ruminate, and appropriate what one reads.[19] At the same time, Montaigne offers a sort of *mise en abyme* of the *Essays*, as we see in the mocking self-representation that follows and that was added only later, in the marginal notes to the 1588 edition: "Isn't it doing the same thing, what I do in most of my composition? I go about cadging from books here and there the sayings that please me, not to keep them, for I have no storehouses, but to transport them into this one, in which, to tell the truth, they are no more mine than in their original place. We are, I believe, learned only with present knowledge, not with past, any more than with future."[20]

Among the 1588 additions, there may also be found a depiction, through a rhetoric of negation, so to say, of Montaigne's relationship with his favorite authors: "I have not had regular dealings with any solid book, except Plutarch and Seneca, from whom I draw like the Danaïds, incessantly filling up and pouring out. Some of this sticks to this paper; to myself, little or nothing."[21] A little further, however, he remembers the pleasure he experienced in discovering in Plutarch his own ideas on imagination. The use of ancient texts thus also becomes the marker of an affinity, of a deep correspondence that builds up over the centuries, although this correspondence is tinged by the recognition of his own inferiority: "If I happen, as I often do, to come across in the good authors those same subjects I have attempted to treat—as in Plutarch I have just this very moment come across his discourse on the power of imagination—seeing myself so weak and puny, so heavy and so sluggish, in comparison with those men, I hold myself in pity and disdain. Still I am pleased at this, that my opinions have the honor of often coinciding with theirs."[22] Montaigne's main focus in this chapter is the education of the young, which explains why it is addressed to Diane de Foix, who is about to become a mother. Montaigne advocates a didactic method based on the recognition of the pupil's personality, a system of education that teaches freedom of judgment and thought, and relies on experience and curiosity rather than on books.

> He will sound the capacity of each man: a cowherd, a mason, a passerby . . . for everything is useful in a household. . . . He will inquire into the conduct of this prince and that. These are things very pleasant to learn and very useful to know.
>
> In this association with men I mean to include, and foremost, those who live only in the memory of books. He will associate, by means of histories, with those great souls of the best ages. It is a vain study, if you will; but also, if you will, it is a study of inestimable value, and the only study, as Plato tells us, in which the Lacedaemonians had kept a stake for themselves.[23]

Here the components of the by-now-familiar topos are duly listed: the dialogic element and the friendly relationship with the great authors of the past made possible by reading ("He will associate, by means of histories, with those great souls of the best ages"). However, the usefulness is not absolute; it depends, as he later explains, on the quality of reading, on the ability to choose, within the ancient text, what is really important—customs, for example, as opposed to dates: "Let him be taught not so much the histories as how to judge them."[24] This conversation with the ancients is viewed from differing perspectives: it continues to be a tool for building and recognizing the self, but it may also contain an element of risk and become, in a certain sense, despotic. One wonders whether this belittling self-representation may not also be a defensive strategy against the "anxiety of influence," whether it may not hide a wish to negate the authoritative, yet authoritarian, presence of the ancients.[25]

Indeed Montaigne does confess to the need to defend himself against the voices coming from the library:

> When I write, I prefer to do without the company and remembrance of books, for I fear they may interfere with my style. Also because, in truth, the good authors humble me and dishearten me too much. . . . But it is harder for me to do without Plutarch. He is so universal and so full that on all occasions, and however eccentric the subject you have taken up, he makes his way into your work and offers you a liberal hand, inexhaustible in riches and embellishments. It vexes me that I am so greatly exposed to pillage by those who frequent him.[26]

The great authors of the past, he argues, are dangerously generous, and one must learn to do without their company and their memory in order to carry out the task of representing one's true self; this remains, however, an impossible challenge—the more so when, as Montaigne confesses, one has "an aping and imitative nature."[27] It is this fear of losing oneself in the encounter with the other that reveals the dark side of this ongoing conversation that in Montaigne so closely intertwines reading and writing, allowing him, as Fausta Garavini has observed, to "try to experience, through others, all those things that cannot be experienced in our everyday life," to "expand our limited experience of reality in the infinite directions of what is possible."[28]

So next to memory, we find a powerful and instinctive *ars oblivionalis*. Montaigne often speaks of his tendency to forget, which extends to the books he has read: "I leaf through books, I do not study them. What I retain of them is something that I no longer recognize as anyone else's. It is only the material from which my judgment has profited, and the thoughts and ideas with which it has become imbued; the author, the place, the words, and other circumstances, I immediately forget."[29] One thinks of the passage from Petrarch (*Fam.*, XXII, 2) discussed in another part of this book (Chapter 1, section 2), in which the poet attempts to justify his slavish borrowings from Virgil by explaining that he has made the Latin poet's verses so much his own that authorship has become a somewhat blurry matter. In Montaigne, this relationship between reading, forgetting, and writing becomes more disquieting. Intriguingly, to the passage quoted earlier from the edition of 1580, Montaigne added, in 1588, a further comment on the power of forgetting: "And I am so good at forgetting that I forget even my own writings and compositions no less than the rest. People are all the time quoting me to myself without me knowing it."[30] "Indeed," as Pierre Bayard has observed, "at this extreme the distinction between quotation and self-quotation vanishes. Having forgotten what he said about these authors and even that he said anything at all, Montaigne has become other to himself. He is separated from the earlier incarnation of himself by the defects of his memory. . . . For Montaigne, therefore, reading is related not only to defective memory, but also, given the contradictions that arise from it, to the anguish of madness."[31]

3. An Ever-Changing Portrait

Kathy Eden has aptly described the *Essays* as a brilliant new version of the familiar epistle: they therefore take on that dimension of intimacy that is the mark of the dialogue between friends.[32] The dedication "To the Reader" is a nod to this tradition, but in a way that also brazenly distorts it. Montaigne forcefully asserts the wholly private and sincere nature of his book, which is addressed exclusively to those who knew him during his lifetime so that they may once more find him, recognize him, after his death. "I want to be seen here in my simple, natural, ordinary fashion, without straining or artifice; for it is myself that I portray."[33] The text therefore traces a self-portrait, whose limits are due exclusively to the pressures of social convention: "Had I been placed among those nations which are said to live still in the sweet freedom of nature's first laws, I assure you I should very gladly have portrayed myself here entire and wholly naked."[34] The pact of truth therefore ideally extends back beyond the origins of culture itself, to a state of nature that had been recently revealed to the eyes of Europe by the people of the New World.[35] This is followed by the "advertisement" for his book, which, having now been published, is before everyone's eyes; but the reader is both summoned and dismissed in a brilliantly provocative move: "Thus, reader, I am myself the matter of my book; you would be unreasonable to spend your leisure on so frivolous and vain a subject. So farewell. Montaigne, this first of March, fifteen hundred and eighty."[36]

Montaigne deploys the pictorial metaphor to speak of his book on a number of occasions in the *Essays*.[37] As we have seen, this comparison rests on a long-standing tradition that ultimately stems from the topos of the text as *speculum animi*. At the same time, however, in Montaigne, everything is exploded and deconstructed, starting from the self. Having retired from the world, in the closed, protective space of the tower and its books, Montaigne sought to find his true self; what he discovered was a universe that lacked all unity, a crumbling stage, an "I" where dreams and uncontrollable fantasies ceaselessly collide and contend:

> Lately when I retired to my home, determined so far as possible to bother about nothing except spending the little life I have left in rest and seclusion, it seemed to me I could do my mind no greater favor than to let it entertain itself in full idleness and stay and settle in itself, which I hoped it might do more easily now, having become weightier and riper with time. But I find—
> Ever idle hours breed wondering thoughts
> LUCAN,[38]
> —that, on the contrary, like a runaway horse, it gives itself a hundred times more trouble than it took for others, and gives birth to so many chimeras and fantastic monsters, one after another, without order or purpose, that in order to contemplate their ineptitude and strangeness at my pleasure, I have begun to put them in writing, hoping in time to make my mind ashamed of itself.[39]

Here again, the declaration of modesty is ambiguous: the novelty of the *Essays* resides precisely in the recording of that unstable "I," that constantly moving self that Montaigne came face-to-face with in his retreat: a realistic and unembellished portrait, whose perfection, however, was destined to endure. It is senseless—Montaigne argued in the chapter on education quoted earlier—to wish to hide what we have learned from reading and used in our writings:

> However that may be, I mean to say, and whatever these absurdities may be, I have no intention of concealing them, any more than I would a bald and greying portrait of myself, in which the painter had drawn not a perfect face, but mine. For likewise these are my humors and opinions; I offer them as what I believe, not what is to be believed. I aim here only at revealing myself, who will perhaps be different tomorrow, if I learn to do something new which changes me. I have no authority to be believed, nor do I want it, feeling myself too ill-instructed to instruct others.[40]

Aside from the profession of modesty, one feels the echo here of some of the passages from Erasmus that we have previously examined on the connection between portrait and text and on the portrait's inability to keep track of the changes brought about by the passage of time (see Chapter 3, section 4).[41] Indeed, it is precisely this constant study of oneself, the self-portrait reflecting continual change, that Montaigne claims as the defining novelty of his work and the quality that ultimately defines its greatness, in which is reflected the rhythm of the universe itself:

> Others form man; I tell of him, and portray a particular one, very ill-formed. . . . Now the lines of my painting do not go astray, though they change and vary. The world is but a perennial movement. All things in it are in constant motion—the earth, the rocks of the Caucasus, the pyramids of Egypt—both with the common motion and with their own. Stability itself is nothing but a more languid notion. I cannot keep my subject still. It goes along befuddled and staggering, with a natural drunkenness. I take it in this condition, just as it is at the moment. I give my attention to it. I do not portray being: I portray passing . . . from day to day, from minute to minute. My history needs to be adapted to the moment. I may presently change, not only by chance but also by intention. This is a record of various and changeable occurrences, and of irresolute, and when it so befalls, contradictory ideas: whether I am different myself, or whether I take hold of my subjects in different circumstances and aspects.[42]

And again: "No man ever treated a subject he knew and understood better than I do the subject I have undertaken. . . . In this I am the most learned man alive. . . . In this case we go hand in hand and at the same pace, my book and I. In other cases one may commend or blame the work apart from the workman; not so here; he who touches the one, touches the other."[43]

The greatness of the *Essays* consists in the text's full acceptance of what tradition had denounced as a risk, as a limit: the variety, mutability, and constant oscillation of the "I." In this way, the *speculum animi* will be intimately bound to its maker, to his body, to his fantasies, and to his "natural drunkenness." There will therefore be no form of censorship: "Each one of my parts makes me myself just as much as every other one. And no other makes me more properly a man than this one. I owe a complete portrait of myself to the public," he writes with reference to his sexual life.[44] This "complete portrait" is introduced by an ironic comment: "I am annoyed that my essays serve the ladies only as a public article of furniture, an article for the parlor. This chapter will put me in the boudoir."[45] The parts played by chance and fantasy also feature prominently in this portrait: the work and its maker are joined at the hip, as it were, though the work can break free and acquire some degree of autonomy:

> Poetic sallies, which transport their author and ravish him out of himself, why shall we not attribute them to his good luck? He himself confesses that they surpass his ability and strength, and acknowledges that they come from something other than himself and that he does not have them all in his power, any more than orators say they have in theirs those extraordinary impulses and agitations that push them beyond their plan. It is the same with painting: sometimes there escape from the painter's hand touches so surpassing his conception and his knowledge as to arouse his wonder and astonishment. But Fortune shows still more evidently the part she has in all these works by the graces and beauties that are found in them, not only without the workman's intention, but even without his knowledge. An able reader discovers in other men's writings perfections beyond those that the author put in or perceived, and lends them richer meanings and aspects.[46]

In this famous passage, the figure of the "able reader" (*un suffisant lecteur*) is first evoked and then anointed: such a reader collaborates with the author, bringing forth from the text other texts, other possible riches, anticipating, one might say, modern ideas about the role of the reader in the generation of a text, through time. Significantly, the comparison with painting reappears here.[47] Once again the text is seen as a changing image that asks to be observed from different perspectives. "I go out of my way, but rather by license than carelessness," writes Montaigne in the long chapter in Book III, titled "Of Vanity." "My ideas follow one another, but sometimes it is from a distance, and look at each other, but with a sidelong glance."[48]

This chimes in with the passage discussed earlier, in which with ostentatious modesty Montaigne compares his own use of quotations from the ancients with the action of a bird that carries in its beak a grain without eating or digesting it (I, 25), and may also be seen as dialoguing with the following:

> I know well that when I hear someone dwell on the language of these essays, I would rather he said nothing. This is not so much to extol the style as to depreciate the sense; the more galling for being more oblique. Yet I am much mistaken if many other writers offer more to take hold of in their material than I do, and, whether for better or for worse, if any writer has sown his materials more substantially or at least more thickly on his paper. In order to get more in, I pile up only the headings of subjects. Were I to add on their consequences, I would multiply this volume many times over. And how many stories have I spread around which say nothing of themselves, but from which anyone who troubles to pluck them with a little ingenuity will produce numberless essays. Neither these stories nor my quotations serve always simply for example, authority, or ornament. I do not esteem them solely for the use I derive from them. They often bear, outside of my subject, the seeds of a richer and bolder material, and sound obliquely a subtler note, both for myself, who do not wish to express anything more, and for those who get my drift.[49]

Significantly, this passage was among those added by hand to the 1588 edition: it feels like a retrospective look at his work and the philosophy that lay behind it. Here Montaigne casts himself as the "suffisant lecteur" of the *Essays* and offers his instructions for reading. The grain or, rather, the infinite grains that, like the bird, he has carried in his beak and sown in his work have now become the seed from which rich and original matter will grow—a soft sound in the background that, for anyone who knows how to listen, may turn into a song.

4. A Frame of Grotesques, Encircling Emptiness

Montaigne's chapter on friendship contains a famous comparison with painting and with grotesques:

> As I was considering the way a painter I employ went about his work, I had a mind to imitate him. He chooses the best spot, the middle of

each wall, to put a picture labored over with all his skill, and the empty space all round it he fills with grotesques, which are fantastic paintings whose only charm lies in their variety and strangeness. And what are these things of mine, in truth, but grotesques and monstrous bodies, pieced together of diverse members, without definite shape, having no order, sequence or proportion other than accidental?

A lovely woman tapers off into a fish
HORACE.

I do indeed go along with my painter in this second point, but I fall short in the first and better part; for my ability does not go far enough for me to dare to undertake a rich, polished picture, formed according to art. It has occurred to me to borrow from Étienne de La Boétie, which will do honor to the rest of this work.[50]

Montaigne's gaze fixed first on the painting's frame, on the proliferation of grotesques that delimit the space, the fantastical monstrous paintings that are here linked to the famous condemnation of this type of painting in Horace's *Ars Poetica* (l. 4). Montaigne chose the fantastical and disorderly proliferation of the grotesque to describe the dominant characteristic of his own writing. The emptiness at the center remained and might, he thought, only be filled by the work of a friend, whose true portrait it would have been. This is where Montaigne thought he would place the text of Étienne de La Boétie's *La servitude volontaire,* which would thus appear as a jewel "*set in the most beautiful place and the center of the first Book of the Essays*"; ranged around it would have been the "grotesques," that is the pages written by Montaigne.[51] This plan was abandoned because of the difficulties that arose in connection with the Huguenots' unlicensed edition of La Boétie's text; Montaigne therefore presented his readers with an enactment of his decision not to publish *La servitude* as part of the *Essays,* producing a variety of reasons for this decision. According to one tradition of studies, the part played by Montaigne in the writing of La Boétie's text was much more significant than is normally conceded, and he either penned the more specifically political portions himself or revised the text by making additions and corrections.[52] If we were to credit such a hypothesis, at the heart of the book, according to the initial plan, there would have nestled a portrait— which was also a self-portrait—a secret *exemplum,* accessible only to those who held the key, depicting that mirroring of souls that took place between the two friends and that was at the core of the tradition that Montaigne revisited and reworked. Friendship is irreconcilable with tyranny and with that "voluntary servitude" that is its hallmark.

After listing the reasons why La Boétie's work could not be part of the *Essays,* Montaigne states in Book I, chapter 29, that he wishes to replace it with twenty-nine sonnets written by his friend and that he dedicates here to Madame de Gramont, Countess of Guissen. In the 1588 edition, however, Montaigne removed the sonnets and added in a manuscript note, "These verses may be seen elsewhere."[53] A void therefore remains, while the verb chosen by Montaigne in the note, "se voient," seems to allude to the powerful pictorial model that underpinned the chapter on friendship.

It is a void whose presence is paradoxically underscored therefore at the center of Book I; it is no longer possible to paint a "a rich, refined, perfectly executed painting," making present, in the pages of his book, the portrait of a man who has been his alter ego; what is left is a frame without a picture, the grotesques encircling the emptiness.[54]

5. "I Have No More Made My Book than My Book Has Made Me"

A number of chapters from Book II (for example, 6 and 18) focus on answering criticism directed against talking, or specifically writing, about oneself. Montaigne defends the importance of making ourselves the object of our study, of truly knowing ourselves, a fascinating and potentially never-ending task, which also addresses the experience of death, or at least preparation for death. He describes the suspended state, hovering between life and death, that he experienced after falling from his horse and comments, "It is a thorny undertaking, and more so than it seems, to follow a movement so wandering as that of our mind, to penetrate the opaque depths of its innermost folds, to pick out and immobilize the innumerable flutterings that agitate it. And it is a new and extraordinary amusement, which withdraws us from the ordinary occupations of the world, yes, even from those most recommended. It is many years now that I have had only myself as object of my thoughts."[55] To those who criticize him and would prefer him to give evidence of his true self with deeds or facts, rather than merely with words, he answers, "What I chiefly portray is my cogitations, a shapeless subject that does not lend itself to expression in actions. It is all I can do to couch my thoughts in this aery medium of words."[56] Once again we find the language of painting deployed to represent to the reader the fascinating and impossible task Montaigne has set himself: to make visible what is not visible and that indeed may only with great difficulty be entrusted to "this aery medium of words"—the creation of something that exceeds common expectations.[57]

For the great men of the past, as we read in Book II, chapter 18, the distance between words and visibility may disappear. To speak of oneself, as the common opinion goes, is acceptable in the case of these rare and famous men: "In the greatness of their deeds Caesar and Xenophon had something to found and establish their narrative upon, as on a just and solid base. Desirable therefore would be the journals of Alexander the Great, and the commentaries of Augustus, Cato, Silla, Brutus, and others left about their deeds. People love and study the figures of such men, even in bronze and stone."[58] This criticism, Montaigne writes, does not concern him: "I am not building here a statue to erect at the town crossroads, or in a church or a public square.... This is for a nook in a library, and to amuse a neighbour, a relative, a friend, who may take pleasure in associating and conversing with me again in this image."[59] Again we find the dimension of intimacy, a style of writing *familiariter;* at the same time, the written word transmits the image of its author, which here is presented strategically through negation and debasement: "Others have taken courage to speak of themselves because they found the subject worthy and rich; I, on the contrary, because I have found mine so barren and so meager that no suspicion of ostentation can fall upon my plan."[60]

The image created through writing, the fruit of incessant observation and experimentation, is not, however, subject to its author's control: "In modeling this figure upon myself, I have had to fashion and compose myself so often to bring myself out, that the model itself has to some extent grown and taken shape. Painting myself for others, I have painted my inward self with colors clearer than my original ones. I have no more made my book than my book has made me—a book consubstantial with its author, concerned with my own self, an integral part of my life."[61] If one reconsiders the empty space surrounded by grotesques described in the essay on friendship, one may perhaps see how that emptiness has gradually taken on a shape, forming a portrait that has in turn influenced its viewer: the mirror has changed the man who has looked into it.

I observed at the beginning of this chapter on Montaigne how difficult it is to follow the various elements of the topos of reading through the labyrinth of the *Essays:* we pursue an image, but the perspective is continually changing; we try to identify its components, but they look at us "with a sidelong glance." And yet, gradually, familiar themes and tones are detected, such as the extolment of the special friendship afforded by books, their complete availability. "Association" with books, writes Montaigne, is safer and longer lasting than the other two forms of commerce: friendship and love.

> It is at my side throughout my course, and accompanies me everywhere. It consoles me in old age and in solitude. It relieves me of the weight of a tedious idleness, and releases me at any time from disagreeable company. It dulls the pangs of sorrow, unless they are extreme and overpowering. To be diverted from a troublesome idea, I need only have recourse to books: they easily turn my thoughts to themselves and steal away the others. And yet they do not rebel at seeing that I seek them out only for want of those other pleasures, that are more real, lively, and natural; they always receive me with the same expression.[62]

I shall close this chapter with a quotation from the long chapter 9 of Book III, titled "Of Vanity," which appears in the 1588 edition. Montaigne describes—among other things—the situation engendered by the civil war and defends his love of travel; then he writes, "Reader, let this essay of myself run on. And this third extension of the other parts of my painting. I add, but I do not correct. . . . My book is always one. Except that at each new edition, so that the buyer may not come off completely empty-handed, I allow myself to add, since it is only an ill-fitted patchwork, some extra ornaments."[63] In addition to the model of the portrait, we find here the image of the intarsio, or patchwork: the additions, the variations, that are continually added to the text are belittlingly described as "some extra ornaments."

Shortly afterward comes a passage in which the themes of reading, traveling, and friendship are closely interconnected: "I hope for this other advantage, that if my humors happen to please and suit some worthy man before I die, he will try to meet me. I give him a big advantage in ground covered; for all that long acquaintance and familiarity could have gained for him in several years, he can see in three days in this record, and more surely and exactly."[64] Here we encounter once again, though reformulated from a point of view that is entirely personal, an idea that was also in Erasmus (see Chapter 4, section 3): reading a book in which we find ideas that are close to our own allows us to establish with its author a deeper and more significant bond of friendship than that which comes from an actual personal relationship. The *Essays* thus become an offering to unknown and distant friends.

7

Tasso and the Dangers of Reading

1. The Library as a Microcosm

Our scene is Ferrara, an elegant palazzo at the center of the city, in one of its busiest streets. The year is 1585. Our host is Vincenzo Malpiglio, a gentleman from the town of Lucca who is acting as treasurer for the Estense court. He is cultured, a lover of letters and the arts, and a good friend of Torquato Tasso, who is still imprisoned in Sant'Anna (he will be released in 1586). Tasso himself introduces us to Malpiglio's home in one of his dialogues, leading us up to the top floor, where, as in Montaigne's tower, the library is situated.[1] Here Giovanlorenzo, Vincenzo's son, finds refuge from his daily occupations, from the duties that tie him to the court.[2] The wealth of the library testifies to that delicate balance of wealth and virtue, exterior and interior, that is characteristic of Vincenzo Malpiglio; indeed the dialogue opens by praising the coexistence in him of traditionally contrasting elements: "Signor Vincenzo Malpiglio is a gentleman whose wealth is not, as it is for many men, an impediment but rather an ornament to his virtue—which indeed can be said for very few of his equals: thus he ensures that not only is his son's mind adorned but also the room he has chosen for his study. This is located on the topmost floor of his house, which is in the busiest part of town."[3] Let us follow him up the long stairway that leads to this privileged place, together with the Neapolitan stranger, the character who represents Tasso, a "stranger" in Ferrara and possibly in the whole world, modeled on the Athenian guest who stands in for the author in Plato's dialogues.[4] The stranger is the "I" of the dialogue who converses with Giovanlorenzo after sitting down to rest and to contemplate the beauty and novelties of his library. What unfolds before his (and our) eyes is not only a rich and elegant collection of books ("and before my eyes appeared a vast quantity of books written in many different languages on all the different sciences; all were beautifully bound with cuts of silk") but also an encyclopedic collection where beauty meets knowledge and where pictures, globes, and maps sit next to mathematical and astronomical instruments: "multicolored marble spheres, and various crystals to gladden the eye, and musical instruments, as well as others to observe the elevation of the Pole and for the various uses of astrology and geometry; and all these things were so arranged that their order as well as their beauty drew praise."[5] Malpiglio's "study" is the image of orderly encyclopedic knowledge, quite unlike the disorderly and pretentious *Wunderkammer* to which Galileo compared the *Jerusalem Delivered;* it is the elegant and extremely fragile mirror of a unitary vision of the world and of knowledge.[6] It is the perfect frame for the dialogue between Giovanlorenzo and the Neapolitan stranger:

> N.S. You, Sir, have lodged the Muses amid your business.
>
> G.M. This is more of a refuge than a lodging house, for in no other place can they as easily escape the multitudes.
>
> N.S. Indeed, solitude, because you live among orators, historians, poets, and philosophers.
>
> G.M. A noble multitude indeed, and you are one of them as I have here your works together with those of certain others, so I am very often in your company when you least expect it.[7]

At the heart of this exchange lies the function of the library, the fact that reading creates a space of solitude, or at least a place where one may choose one's interlocutors. The Neapolitan stranger verbally fills that space with people, evoking a—somewhat menacing—multitude of orators, historians, poets, and philosophers; Giovanlorenzo answers by underscoring the nobility of this multitude and mentions Tasso's books, which are there, next to their author, in the library.

The books open up the possibility of an encounter, a dialogue, that escapes the control of the author himself: "so I am very often in your company when you least expect it," his host observes, mingling homage to his guest with a defense of the autonomous space that reading affords. The Neapolitan stranger responds by questioning the very possibility of solitude: "you are speaking," he remarks to his host, "like the Roman who was never less alone than when he was alone." In making this remark, he is drawing on a common patrimony of shared memory, and indeed its source—the beginning of Book III of Cicero's *De officiis*—is recognized by his interlocutor, who later in the dialogue assigns his proper name (Scipio) to the person who had earlier been generically referred to only as a "Roman."[8] The idea that books are capable of acting as a barrier against the outside world, of defending us against unwanted thoughts and passions, had already appeared in Alberti's *Teogenio* (see Chapter 2, section 5). It is at this point that the Neapolitan stranger launches his attack: "How is it possible to read Petrarch, whom you often have in your hands, and not imagine him, under a laurel tree on the bank of the Sorgue, penning his beautiful noble thoughts as the waters flow by? And when you read anything by him, you must needs hold him in your thoughts and in your imagination and almost, indeed, feel him, because imagination is an internal sense."[9] This is how the pleasures of reading transform into risks, how the dialogue with an author can become a dangerous invasion of one's interiority: the evocative power of Petrarch's poetry makes such an invasion even more perilous, because the images, the sensations, and the passions communicate themselves to the mind first and then to the imagination, until they become a living, shared experience: it is as if "you feel" what you read, says the Neapolitan stranger, because "imagination is an internal sense."[10] The defense adopted by Giovanlorenzo (this may be so, but they are "extremely pleasant thoughts") immediately reveals its fragility, when the Neapolitan quotes Petrarch's verses on the death of Laura, pointing out that when he is "perusing those verses," he himself becomes "melancholy" (*maninconoso*) and filled with distress. It is through texts, therefore, that passions invade the soul of the reader: "Every time the same thing happens with the other lyric poets, and in the same way you feel the same passions: thus, in addition to a multitude of inner senses and imaginations, you have, or rather we all have, a great number of passions in our soul."[11] The same thing happens with heroic poems and tragedy: tempered by the sweetness of their verses, the passions storm the reader's soul, says the alter ego of Tasso, thinking perhaps of his *Jerusalem Delivered*: "Therefore we have a multitude of affects in our soul, which are nourished most sweetly by the verses of the poets; and if perchance there be any bitterness in this admixture, it only makes the sweetness more enjoyable."[12] Another enemy, however, lurks in the library, insinuating itself within its closed, reserved space; this enemy is the multitude of opinions: "N.S. Therefore in addition to the multitude of inner senses, imaginations, and affects, we have within us a multitude of opinions. . . . However there is no great advantage in escaping the outer multitude if we cannot leave the throng within."[13] At this point, the dialogue embarks on another quest, which will turn out to be equally fruitless: Giovanlorenzo hopes to find in philosophy and in science a refuge, a temple, and an asylum.[14] He thus undertakes a journey through the irreconcilable multitude of the various philosophical theories: the image of navigation (which is both an allegory and a mnemotechnical image) develops into a detailed evocation of ports, inlets, fortifications, winds, ships, and beaches with caves and springs. In the distance, shimmering like an illusion, there appears the Temple of Concord between Aristotelians and Platonists; but it is a steep climb up to the top, and so the project is abandoned.

It is at this point that the Neapolitan stranger suggests trying the path of contemplation, a perspective through which everything may be left behind us and the multitude reassembled into unity, as in a theater seen in a dream or in a vision: "There is nothing worth acquiring more than contemplation, and no price would be too high to see a theater full of faces that seem to touch one another, like the eyes on a peacock's tail, which shines from whichever angle one looks at it."[15] And yet here, too, a strong and insoluble doubt creeps in, expressed by the stranger himself: "if we wish to escape the multitude, it is advisable to leave all human thoughts behind and effect the passing, as it is said, of solitary to solitary: but I, hindered as I am by the world and by myself, do not know if I shall accomplish such a noble escape.[16] Many indeed achieve this escape, and no one believes that they are not fleeing from themselves; but when they have fled all multitudes, since they have not fled all solitudes, will they enjoy happiness?"[17] At the conclusion of the dialogue, it achieves a sort of compromise: "Flee whenever it may be from solitude toward the multitude for the good of your motherland," is the final advice given by the Neapolitan Stranger, "and all your escapes will be honored."[18] There are various forms of honorable escape, including, of course, dedication to the public good, but there is also the vital experience of an encounter with great men that is furnished by literature. Yet all these possibilities seem fatally flawed. Not only does the search for a shared truth that may save us from the stormy swell of multiple doctrines appear illusory, but also the prospect afforded by the contemplation of complete detachment from the multiplicity of human experience induces doubt. Does it truly guarantee happiness? "Are those who practice it really happy?" It is in this context that the topos of reading moves forward in its development but also reveals its risky side, the secret poison it carries within. The risk originates in the very element that guarantees its functioning—imagination, the faculty that, as Machiavelli wrote, permits us to "entirely give [ourselves] over to books," to enter into another world, a virtual existence. Imagination, Tasso argues, is an "internal sense": it is for this reason that the passions conveyed by books can penetrate deep into our inner life.

The first of Tasso's dialogues dedicated to Malpiglio, written a little earlier, between 1584 and 1585, also drew on divergent and irreconcilable tensions. The scene in this case is Venice, and the dialogue between Tasso and Giovanlorenzo (or Lorenzo), a young man in search of his path in life, takes place under the protective wing of the father, who is here also present physically and not merely as the silent supervisor of his son's education and the curator of the setting of the library-museum that we have seen earlier. The central issue is Lorenzo's future, the lure of courtly life, and the utopian desire to reconcile the need to seek the prince's favor with that of escaping the envy of the courtiers. At first Lorenzo places all happiness and hope in sincerity and transparency, but he soon comes to accept the need to feign and hide (*celare*). The "portrait" that Castiglione had painted in the *Cortegiano* ("I am sending you this book as a portrait of the Court of Urbino," he had written in the epistle dedicatory of 1528) here becomes a canvas on which the painter must skillfully manage the shading and be a master of artifice: "Not all [virtues] are equally or always manifest, but as in paintings, shadowing accentuates certain parts of the background, while other parts are highlighted through color; thus it occurs with those virtues that appertain to prudence."[19] The courtier's self-fashioning, the self-portrait he must present to the eyes of the public, must at the same time suggest and hide, balancing show with secrecy. By way of conclusion, the young Lorenzo is urged to study and learn but above all to be careful about the way he presents his knowledge at court and to learn "rather to hide it than to show it."[20]

In the first of the two dialogues dedicated to Malpiglio, we therefore encounter an unresolved tension between the desire for knowledge and the search for a form of social recognition based on transparency and authenticity; in the second dialogue, this tension is recast, against the backdrop of the library, as the risky interplay between the solace and refuge afforded by books, on the one hand, and, on the other, the invasion of our interiority that may be unleashed—between the desire for knowledge and the danger of disintegration and wreckage.

2. "Books I Value Almost as Much as Life"

Reading nevertheless remained for Tasso a vital experience, which had involved him deeply since his earliest youth. At the same time, however, the relationship between writer and publisher was always fraught, a fact clearly demonstrated by the intricate history of the publication of Tasso's own *Jerusalem*. Particularly significant, in this light, is therefore a passage from a letter from Tasso to Angelo Grillo, dated 22 February 1585, on the subject of his poems: "If they were printed in large and beautiful characters, similar to those of messer Vittorio Baldini, they would be exceedingly beautiful and make a great show. Therefore I, who have seen them lacerated and torn into many parts, like the limbs of Hippolytus, would rejoice to see them whole, and, as it were, brought back to life thanks to your work and that of my other friends. But this is perhaps one of those dreams that requires a kind and courteous physician to come true."[21] The myth of Hippolytus's lacerated limbs (see Chapter 2, section 3), which were recomposed and brought back to life, resurfaces here; it had been used by the humanists to celebrate the rediscovery of ancient codices and the philological work that gave them new life. Tasso applies it to his own work, entrusting the resurrection symbolized by the appearance of his verses in print to the beautiful characters he hopes will be used in the book.

His need for books, for the vital experience of reading, became even greater during his confinement in the hospital of Sant'Anna; here they are called on to fill the empty spaces of the cell, to keep at bay, through their conversation with him, the ghosts that torment him. There is a little "thieving" sprite, he wrote to Maurizio Cattaneo on Christmas Day 1585, who "has stolen many scudi from me. . . . He jumbles up my books, opens my chests, steals my keys, and I can do nothing to protect myself from him; I am always unhappy, but most during the night."[22] A few days later, on 30 December, he added,

> Know, therefore, that in addition to the wondrous things perpetrated by this sprite, which might well be enumerated for entertainment on another occasion, there are many night terrors, as when, being awake,

I thought I saw little flames in the air, and sometimes there were sparks in my eyes so that I feared I was losing my sight, and they visibly burst out of my eyes. I have seen moreover shadows of mice in the midst of the sparrowhawk, which could not, according to natural reason, be there; I have heard terrifying noises and have often felt in my ears whistling, tinkling, the ringing of bells, and something like the sound of a clock being wound up, often sounding the hour; and when I was sleeping, it felt as if a horse had been thrown upon me.[23]

The barrier erected by books, the safe space they create against the "magic tricks of the sprite" and the "night terrors" is therefore both essential and fragile.

In a sonnet datable to 1583–1584 ("O testimoni del valore illustre"), Tasso describes himself as talking with his books.[24] They are the custodians of, and witnesses to, the memory and renown of illustrious men—they are the tools through which we gain knowledge of truth. Tasso seeks to learn from them "the sweet style and art" (l. 10) that will make his poem great, so great that it will conquer death and hand on to posterity a portrait of Duke Alfonso that may rival that of the ancient heroes. Again we find reading and writing to be deeply enmeshed: the poem's ability to make Alfonso immortal will reflect the fact that books are capable of overcoming death. Despite the encomiastic language, the author's account of his dialogue with books is anything but tepid:

> O testimoni del valore illustri,
> per cui spiando il vero io vo sovente,
> per cui spira e ragiona e m'è presente
> tal che morì già tanti e tanti lustri.
>
> (Illustrious witnesses of worth,
> Through whom in search of truth I often go,
> Through whom there breathes and talks and now is with me,
> He who died so many years ago.)

The particular intensity of the three verbs, "breathes and talks and now is with me" (*spira e ragiona e m'è presente*) creates an almost physical climax, as if the ancient author had been resurrected. "Books," as Ezio Raimondi has pointed out, "establish what in essence is a community based on intelligence and are the companions of an exchange of opinions from which Tasso derives nourishment."[25]

This visceral need for books did not cease after Tasso was released from Sant'Anna, and one finds a particularly moving expression of this in a letter he sent from Rome to Bergamo in 1588, addressed to Giovan Battista Licino, in which the poet talks about having his belongings sent to him and in particular his books:

> My things, apart from my books, are few and of small importance; nor do I know if they will be sufficient to cover my debts and the expense of their transport, as the servant will want to be paid; but books I value almost as much as life. I have two boxes full of them, and in a third there are but a few that could be made into a bundle that may be included in the foreseen expense; but as I have the greatest need of them, I should like them to be sent before Christmas in whatever way possible.[26]

"Books I value almost as much as life"; I have "the greatest need of them": Tasso's words become clear-cut markers of how passionate he is about these particular possessions.

A few years later, on 4 July 1591, Tasso wrote, this time from Mantua, to Maurizio Cattaneo, a gentleman from Bergamo and secretary to Cardinal Giovanni Girolamo Albani, who had recently died (on 25 April). He told his friend that he felt he had reached an advanced point in life (he was forty-seven) and understood the need to make his peace with the passage of time and with the condition of servitude—or at least of nonfreedom—that had so far characterized his life. He explained that he must henceforth make cautious choices:

> I have too long lived according to the wishes and the pleasure of others and have not yet been able to live for myself. . . . The joyfulness and the pleasure of youth no more befit my age than the yellow and turquoise clothes my mother used to sew for me as a child. But it is now convenient that I should dress a habit suited to my years and not merely the different seasons; and that I should rejoice in those things in which someone in my condition may take comfort. Should I have no other occasion for pleasure, I shall at least tear my pleasures from books, which indeed do not exclude me from rea-

soning, and almost talking, with those who are better and more noble than ourselves.[27]

This privileged conversation with books offers here the last possibility for freedom and pleasure, a pleasure that remains untarnished by the passage of time or any change in social condition; though Tasso has now progressed well beyond the golden hours of his early youth and can no longer wear the colorful clothing his mother made for him, this pleasure has not lost its fascination. Reading, Tasso finally points out, also offers compensation for the limits and difficulties that attend modern times, as through them we may enjoy the conversation "of those who are better and more noble than ourselves."

To books and to the written word Tasso ascribes the power of defeating death; unlike the spoken word, which is both the vehicle and the destroyer of changeable passions, the written word is timeless: "The voice affirms and denies, and is often contrary to itself and moved by fear or love or pity— by all the passions it is moved; but writing, which is usually composed when the mind is calm and free from anything that may perturb it, shows not animosity but truth and is always consistent: what it affirms once it always affirms, and in negating, it has the same consistency; it makes distant people present and the dead almost alive, and this is the greatest of wonders."[28] This passage is part of a long and impassioned defense of writing against the accusations of Plato's *Phaedrus* (275c ff.). It comes from one of Tasso's late dialogues, *Il Cataneo overo de le conclusioni amorose*, which was probably written in the period 1590–1591; what is interesting is that Tasso here seems to forget what he had written in the *Malpiglio Secondo* and disengages writing from the passions, setting it in the realm of truth, or at least of stability. Only when writing is separated from the restless mutability of the spoken word can it achieve the same "maraviglia" as reading—the marvel of making "distant people present and the dead almost alive."

3. "A Fearful and Unpleasant Fit of Melancholy"

A few years earlier, in 1589, Tasso had begun another dialogue, *Costante; or, On Clemency*, with a description of his reader-self informed by a sense of distance and detachment, the activity transporting him to a different place and time. In some ways, this opening reminds us of the *Malpiglio Secondo*, but the roles here are inverted: the visitor this time is the eponymous

Costante, and it is Tasso himself—appearing here under his proper name and no longer under the mask of the Neapolitan Stranger—who is surprised in his study.

> Signor Antonino Costante, a gentleman well versed in letters, came suddenly into the room, and seeing me with a closed book before me, looking not like a man intent on contemplation but almost as one who has fallen into a fearful and unpleasant fit of melancholy,[29] he said to me:
> Perhaps this visit of mine is inopportune and causes some impediment to your studies.
> T.T. This is not study but other thoughts, as you may see from the closed book.
> A.C. You study rather by contemplating than by reading.
> T.T. Indeed I used to contemplate much and read little, my youth being entirely subjected to the laws of love; then in my more mature years, well versed in worries, I read much and contemplated little. Now I desire neither to read nor contemplate, but I preserve the same memory of the things I read and contemplated as an old wall does of the now faded and smoke-stained paintings that used to decorate it.[30]

Tasso's portrait calls to mind the suspended and slightly melancholy expression in Parmigianino's portrait of a young man reading (see Figure 7.1), with the difference that in the painting, the book is open, while here, as Tasso underscores, his book is "firmly closed" (*serrato*), as if to clarify that he has reached the end of a journey. Different relationships with reading mark the three phases of life: in youth, there is more contemplation than reading; in middle age, much reading and little contemplation; and little of either in old age. Both reading and contemplation have left on his mind nothing but faint traces, discolored images, such as those one finds on an old wall, once richly decorated but now bearing only the faded, smoke-stained testimony of those former colors.

The varying relationship between reading and contemplation in the different ages of life that Tasso stages in the dialogue would appear to be linked to the workings of the imagination: in the case of contemplation, it works mostly on the plane of interiority (in youth, all this is connected to the prevailing interest in love), while with reading, imagination is mostly engaged

Figure 7.1. Parmigianino, *Portrait of a Man Reading a Book,* oil on canvas, ca. 1524, York City Art Gallery. *Photo © Fine Art Images/Heritage Images/Mondadori Portfolio.*

in a dialogue with the texts and with the images and the passions they awaken in us. Melancholy runs through some of the texts we have examined as a sort of leitmotiv: Tasso in his study, holding a closed book in his hands, appears to have "entered into a fearful and unpleasant melancholy"; and in the *Malpiglio Secondo,* when Petrarch's verses on the death of Laura are read, it seems impossible not to become "maninconoso con esso lui" (melancholic together with him).

Thus the experience of melancholy that so painfully molded Tasso's life—"the melancholy that torments me is always infinite," as he wrote to Maurizio Cattaneo in 1579—forces its way into the subject of the present study.[31] This experience was handed down to posterity by Montaigne in a famous portrait of the poet (whom he never names directly) after he had visited Tasso in his confinement in the hospital of Sant'Anna:

> Plato says that melancholy minds are the most teachable and excellent: likewise there are none with so much propensity to madness. Countless minds have been ruined by their very power and suppleness. What a leap has just been taken, because of the very restlessness and liveliness of his mind, by one of the most judicious and ingenious of men, a man more closely molded by the pure poetry of antiquity than any other Italian poet has been for a long time! Does he not have reason to be grateful to that murderous vivacity of his mind? To that brilliance that has blinded him? To that exact and intent apprehension of his reason, which has deprived him of reason? To the careful and laborious pursuit of the sciences, which has led him to stupidity? To that rare aptitude for the exercise of the mind, which has left him without exercise and without mind? I felt even more vexation than compassion to see him in Ferrara in so piteous a state, surviving himself, not recognizing himself or his works, which, without his knowledge and yet before his eyes, have been brought out uncorrected and shapeless.[32]

Among those "exercises of the mind" that had both made the poet's greatness and been his downfall are therefore reading and the powerful personal encounter with the other that this experience affords. In the *Malpiglio secondo,* as we have seen, this encounter runs the risk of becoming an invasion; the dialogue it fosters may develop into submission, because the passions that are the object of our reading penetrate into the inner theater, because "imagination is an internal sense."

This idea is picked up again but in more strongly moralistic terms in the 1585 dialogue called *Il Cataneo overo de gli idoli,* a reflection on truth and fiction in poetry and on the dangerous presence of classical mythology, which is closely linked to the composition of *Jerusalem Conquered and a Judgement on His Jerusalem Revised by the Poet Himself.* Tasso here compares love poetry to idolatry: all poets, say the Neapolitan Stranger, call their woman an idol, "and in all of them are described the miracles of love and the wonders of the beloved's beauty. . . . Because verses and rhymes are consecrated to an empty name that the poet makes his idol, they should not be read by the young in particular, who taste and enjoy them as if they were the most refined intellectual food." They should therefore be administered, like the universal remedy of theriac, only by "doctors of the soul, who know how easily the sweet poison of love is drunk; and they should not be read, unless a special permission be granted, by those who are infirm or may easily become so."[33]

It falls to one of the interlocutors, Alessandro Vitelli, to attempt to save Petrarch: "Perhaps you refer to children and young women, who indeed should not be allowed such sweet lessons so early, surely not to those of my age, who all day long visit the playhouse; nor can I see how they may be harmed by Petrarch and similar poets, who are amorous rather than lascivious." The Neapolitan Stranger points out that "this is precisely the time of life when one learns about love: therefore for no one else is reading about it so dangerous," concluding that "lovers and poets who sing of love are idol worshippers and idol builders." Just like the miserly and the ambitious, they fix their thoughts and desires on one particular object, "which impresses itself on the imagination; therefore the amorous soul is, almost, the temple of idolatry: and our imagination is the painting in which idols and adored creatures are portrayed no differently than if they were earthly divinities."[34]

The image cluster of the vital dialogue with books is here tainted by fear and a sense of risk: passions may invade interiority; indeed the words of books can build idols in the imagination of those who are weaker or more sensitive, such as the young or women. Here, as in other passages, there seems to be an echo of the suspicious condemnation of poetry and the profane sciences expressed by the fathers of the Church. One such attack came from St. Jerome: "The food of demons are also the poets' songs, secular knowledge, and the pomp of eloquent words. These types of knowledge allure us like delicacies, but while they capture our ears with their rhythmical, softly modulated verses, they also permeate our souls and fetter our heart."[35] The anxieties voiced by Tasso are recognizably similar to those that would later reappear in the long campaign of mistrust or downright condemnation aimed at policing the reading of romances and novels, especially by women, from Francesca da Rimini right down to Madame Bovary. Nevertheless, in accordance with a pattern that has become familiar, it is precisely fear and censorship that paradoxically reveal the profound power of writing and, by extension, the fascination, and perhaps even the hazards, of reading.

Epilogue

Ruskin, Proust, and the "Miracle of Reading"

On 6 December 1864, John Ruskin gave a lecture at the Rusholme Public Hall, in Manchester. Its title, "Sesame. Of Kings' Treasuries," was designedly ambiguous and aimed at perplexing his audience's expectations. Just as in the *Arabian Nights,* "sesame" is the magic word that opens the door to the treasure of the forty thieves, so for Ruskin it would lead his public into the library, to books, which for people are the real treasure, worthy of kings. To those parents who wrote to him asking what education was most suited for their children to attain a better position in life, he answered that education is a value in itself and that the cornerstone of this education lies in cultivating a deep friendship with books.

We encounter here once again, various centuries later, the topos whose history we have retraced: it reappears in a nineteenth-century England riven by social injustice, through the impassioned moral and reformist voice of John Ruskin, whose aesthetic beliefs and love of Italian art and the Middle Ages—which he shared with the Pre-Raphaelite brotherhood—drove him to despise the horrors and misery of industrial society. For Ruskin, the dialogue with books is both a utopian and a realistic alternative to the difficulties one may meet in life in making the proper choice of friends or in successfully ingratiating oneself with powerful people. Our selection of friends, Ruskin writes, is determined by chance and necessity, but

> there is a society continually open to us, of people who will talk to us as long as we like, whatever our rank or occupation;—talk to us in the best words they can choose, and of the things nearest their hearts.

And this society, because it is so numerous and so gentle, and can be kept waiting round us all day long,—kings and statesmen lingering patiently, not to grant audience, but to gain it!—in those plainly furnished and narrow anterooms, our book-case shelves,—we make no account of that company,—perhaps never listen to a word they say, all day long![1]

The act of reading thus opens up a utopian space of equality, where hierarchies may be inverted and kings and potentates must await the will and leisure of the reader. Once again we find the theme of the library as the space that collects within itself all time and all places; the dialogue with the world of the dead is moreover here predicated on the authenticity of the reader's moral qualities, on the validity of their motives for reading:

[You] flatter yourself that it is with any worthy consciousness of your own claims to respect, that you jostle with the hungry and common crowd for *entrée* here, an audience there, when all the while this eternal court is open to you, with its society, wide as the world, multitudinous as its days, the chosen, and the mighty, of every place and time? Into that you may enter always; in that you may take fellowship and rank according to your wish; from that, once entered into it, you can never be outcast by your own fault; by your aristocracy of companionship there, your own inherent aristocracy will be assuredly tested, and the motives with which you strive to take high place in the society of the living, measured, as to all the truth and sincerity that are in them, by the place you desire to take in this company of the Dead. . . . It [this court] is open to labor and to merit, but to nothing else. No wealth will bribe, no name overawe, no artifice deceive, the guardian of those Elysian gates.[2]

This representation of reading as a paradisiacal place where one may encounter the great writers of the past and fine-tune one's virtues reaches its climax, in the final part of the talk, in Ruskin's ardent denunciation of the evils and the cruelty of contemporary society, the wars and the bloodshed that elicit nothing but indifference, people dying of starvation, children cast into prison for the theft of six walnuts, the religious hypocrisy that leads people to forget the message of revelation that money is the root of all evil. When we read, Ruskin argues, we must not merely understand but feel;

Epilogue

feelings and passions are not negative, but they must be just: "We come then to that great concourse of the Dead, not merely to know from them what is True, but chiefly to feel with them what is just."[3] This is a political clarion call to substitute books for weapons:

> That we should bring up our peasants to a book exercise instead of a bayonet exercise!—
> Organize, drill, maintain with pay, and good generalship, armies of thinkers, instead of armies of stabbers![4]

This bloodless revolution will be achieved through the creation of public libraries in all countries: such is the ultimate goal of Ruskin's talk, which in its final passages, returns to its title in order to reveal its ultimate meaning. Corn laws have been passed, he argues; let us see now if we can pass laws on corn that will give us better bread, "bread made of that old enchanted Arabian grain, the Sesame, which opens doors;—doors, not of robbers" but of "Kings' Treasuries."[5]

The metaphor of treasure was taken up and expanded by Ruskin on 14 December of the same year in the talk he gave in Manchester, called "Lilies. Of Queens' Gardens." At its center are women and the idea that, through reading, they may acquire regal power and preside over what Ruskin calls the "gardens of queens." The two talks were published together in London the following year (June 1865) and enjoyed—"Sesame" more so than "Lilies"—great popularity, being frequently reprinted as late as 1900, the year Ruskin died.

In France, Ruskin had one exceptional admirer and translator, Marcel Proust. On Ruskin's death, Proust wrote two obituaries to commemorate him; he translated, together with his mother, *The Bible of Amiens;* between 1904 and 1906, he translated Ruskin's two talks on the subject of reading, at a difficult juncture in his own life following the death first of his father in 1903 and then of his mother in 1905. Proust's work on *Sesame and Lilies* is much more than a translation, and even the label "critical reading" is not entirely correct.[6] In translating, Proust truly measured himself against the rhythm of Ruskin's prose; we feel him engaging in a sort of challenge, wrestling with the text, which he flanks with notes that at crucial moments become extraordinarily long and furnishes with an introduction, "On Reading." This begins with a reevocation of those childhood days when reading a favorite book was like enjoying a precious treasure snatched from the daily routine of family life, defended against the assault of intruders, hidden in inaccessible recesses, consecrated to solitude. These passages, as Antoine Compagnon has rightly argued, herald *Combray;* they were the first to exactly hit the tone of the novel that was to be, revealing how, at precisely the moment he was clearly distancing himself from Ruskin's ideas on reading, Proust was galvanized by his words, driven, by his love and admiration for the writer he was translating, to delve into his innermost self in order to find his own voice.[7] We are made aware of this implicit distance from the translated text through his decision to open with an account of the pleasures of childhood reading; indeed Proust, as if fearing that his reader might not fully grasp this, decided to signal it more clearly in a note to the introduction: "I have only tried, in this preface, to reflect in my turn on the same subject that Ruskin had dealt with in *Of Kings' Treasuries:* the utility of reading. Thus these few pages, which are hardly about Ruskin, constitute nevertheless a sort of indirect criticism of his doctrine. In exposing my ideas, I find myself involuntarily opposing them in advance to his."[8] Proust rejects Ruskin's utilitarian and pedagogical conception of reading and dedicates a generous portion of his notes and his preface to debunking the idea of reading as a conversation with books perceived as friends. He is struck by Ruskin's rhetorical flair and uses a mixture of admiration and irony to underscore the way in which this theme is introduced. Ruskin says that our choice of friends is both difficult and limited. Indeed, Proust comments in his note, this idea attracts us because of its beauty and utility: the friends we cannot choose are merely tokens of those we *can* choose, that is, books, the main subject of his talk, which, however, do not appear at the very beginning but wait, like a prima donna, before making an entrance.[9] Next Proust goes on to state his critical distance from Ruskin's position: the idea of conversation inherently conflicts with what for him is the essential condition of reading, that is, solitude. The presence of the other creates noise, disturbs concentration; comparing reading to a conversation with a friend projects outward and therefore risks jeopardizing an encounter with the self through the interiorization of the other's voice, which is the prize of reading. Significantly, the theme of the silent voice generated by reading emerges twice in the preface, in the passages describing childhood. As a little boy, when he sought refuge in the kitchen and was interrupted by the cook who offered him a more comfortable reading position, he had to answer, "No, thank you": "you had to stop and bring back from afar your voice which from your lips was repeating noiselessly, hurriedly, all the words your eyes had read, you had to stop it, make it come out."[10] The same painful sense of breaking away was felt in the evening, when the book came to an end: "Then the last page was read and the book was finished. I had to stop the headlong rush of my eyes and of the voice which followed noiselessly, stopping only to regain my breath in a deep sigh."[11]

The crux here is not, as for Ruskin, the acquisition of wisdom through book-friends but the mode itself through which communication takes place in the act of reading: "our mode of communication with people implies a diminution of the active powers of the soul which, on the contrary, are concentrated and excited by this wonderful miracle of reading which is communication in the heart of solitude."[12] One receives the thought of another mind, while all the time engaged in a personal activity; "we are that other person and yet all the time we are developing our own personality with more variety than if we thought alone, we are driven by another on our own ways." In conversation, on the other hand, there is the other's presence, the sound of words; "the spiritual shock is weakened, inspiration, profound thinking, is impossible."[13] For this reason, Proust argues, even if Plato were alive, conversation with him would still be a more superficial exercise than reading, "the value of things heard or read being of less importance than the spiritual state they can create in us and which can be profound only in solitude or in that peopled solitude that reading is."[14]

Proust develops these very themes in the preface, tracing Ruskin's ideas back to a statement by Descartes that, however, he believes Ruskin probably did not know: "the reading of all good books is like a conversation with the most cultivated men of the past centuries who have been their authors." This rather dry thought, he observes, "is in fact the one which is found everywhere in his lecture, only enveloped in an Apollonian gold in which English mists blend, similar to the one whose glory illuminates the landscapes of his favourite painter."[15] Ruskin's love of Turner's paintings is here evoked to describe his style. Whether or not it was through Descartes, Ruskin undoubtedly saw his thoughts on reading as part of the rich ancient tradition we have been studying.

Ruskin, writes Proust, is telling us a beautiful Platonic myth, but, if one looks carefully, the comparison with conversation does not hold. Books, unlike friends, do not interrupt solitude because we receive another thought while still continuing to be on our own, "that is to say, while continuing to enjoy the intellectual power that we have in solitude, which conversation dissipates immediately, in continuing to be able to be inspired, to maintain the full fruitful work of the spirit on itself."[16] He believes, he goes on to say, that reading is something more than Ruskin says it is but that it does not have in our spiritual life the preponderant role he assigns to it.

It is precisely here that one can gauge the distance separating Proust from Ruskin and Ruskin's pedagogical view of reading. For Proust, our own wisdom begins where that of the author ends; a book suggests questions to which it gives no answers, and reading can function only as a form of initiation whereby we can penetrate more deeply within ourselves. The pedagogical vision of reading is in effect its limit, and a dangerous one at that: "As long as reading is for us the initiator whose magic keys open to our innermost selves the doors of rooms that we would not have known how to enter, its role in our life is salutary. Reading however becomes dangerous when instead of waking us to the personal life of the spirit, it tends to substitute itself for it, when truth no longer appears to us as an ideal we can realize only through the intimate progress of our thought and the effort of our heart, but as a material thing, deposited between the leaves of books."[17] Here Proust is thinking about the relationship between reading and writing; his polemical objection is the fetishization of books, whereby a writer extracts from books only an extraneous body, a principle of death rather than life.[18] He reproaches Ruskin for not being aware that the affected search for erudition in the choice of words is the mark of a curious but not a great writer; indeed it is Ruskin himself who "has so effectively and so often shown that the artist, in what he writes or in what he paints, infallibly reveals his weaknesses, his affectations, his faults (and, in effect, is not the work of art through the hidden rhythm of our soul—so much more alive than we perceive it ourselves—similar to those sphysmographic traces in which automatically the pulsations of our blood are registered?)."[19]

What remains, in these pages, in this impassioned self-analysis of the reader-writer, of our age-old topos? Is it only, as Emanuele Trevi has written, "an outmoded humanist metaphor," brushed up by Ruskin with rhetorical verve but irredeemably hackneyed and no longer capable of leading anywhere, so that Proust cannot conceal his disappointment or fail to mark his distance from such a scholastic conception?[20] Certainly, his distance from Ruskin's position is clearly marked and closely linked to his experience as a writer, to the way in which reading can play its part in the search for that hidden rhythm, of which we are unaware. It is nevertheless true that, after criticizing the comparison between a book and a friend, Proust takes the idea up again and develops it after his own fashion:

Epilogue

> Without doubt friendship, friendship which has regard to individuals, is a frivolous thing, and reading is friendship. But at least it is a sincere friendship, and the fact that it addresses itself to one who is dead, who is absent, gives it something disinterested, almost touching. It is moreover a friendship unencumbered with everything that makes for ugliness in other kinds. Since we are all, we the living, only the dead who have not yet assumed our roles, all these compliments, all these greetings in the hall which we call deference, gratitude, devotion, and in which we mingle so many lies, are sterile and tiresome. . . . In reading, friendship is suddenly brought back to its first purity. With books, no amiability. Those friends, if we spend the evening with them, it's truly because we wanted to. In their case at least, we leave often only with regret. . . . All the agitations of friendship expire at the threshold of this pure and calm friendship that is reading. No more deference: we laugh at what Molière says only to the exact degree we find him funny . . . and when we have decidedly had enough of being with him, we put him back in his place as bluntly as if he had neither genius nor fame.[21]

The central idea of silence is put forward again in a version of the relationship with the book-friend that marks its distance from the social rituals of friendship and precisely for this reason guarantees maximum transparency and freedom. The idea that "we the living . . . are only the dead who have not yet assumed our roles" gives a new perspective to the theme of dialogue with the dead—it serves to bring them closer, to create an area of intimacy. Moreover, the old theme of reevocation is again presented in this new context, through which "we can take our leave of Molière when we have decidedly had enough of *being with him*."

In this context, strongly imbued with the theme of friendship, some of the ideas we have previously encountered reemerge:

> The atmosphere of this pure friendship is silence, purer than words. For we speak for others, but we keep silent for ourselves. Also silence does not bear like speech the trace of our defects, of our grimaces. It is pure, it is truly an atmosphere. Silence does not interpose between the author's thought and ours these irreducible elements of our different egoisms that are impervious to thought. The very language of the book is pure (if the book deserves this name), made *transparent*

by the author's thought that has removed everything from it that was not itself, to the point of giving it back its faithful image; each phrase, in essence, resembling every other, for all are spoken with the unique inflection of a personality; hence a sort of continuity that relationships in life and the foreign elements they involve our thinking in exclude, and which very quickly allows us to follow the exact line of the author's thought, the traits of his character reflected in his calm *mirror*.[22]

Here again we encounter the idea of the text's transparency, of its being a *speculum animi*. Proust sees the outcome of both reading and writing as something under constant threat: "If words are chosen not by our own thought according to its essential affinities, but by our desire to depict ourselves, it represents this desire but does not represent us," "so that when a book is not the mirror of a powerful individuality, it is still the mirror of curious defects of the spirit."[23] Nevertheless, it is fascinating to observe how, in this brilliant self-analysis of a reader-author preparing to write *La Recherche,* there resurface themes and metaphors that we have seen to be present in different contexts and in distant centuries. With Proust, the moment has finally come for us to take our leave of them.

Notes

Note on translation: Unless otherwise specified in the notes, translations are by Sylvia Greenup.

Introduction

Epigraph: Al Jâhiz, *Le cadi et la mouche. Anthologie du livre des animaux* (Paris: Sindbad, 1988), 147, quoted in Lucio Coco, *La lettura spirituale. Scrittori cristiani tra Medioevo ed età moderna* (Milano: Edizioni Sylvestre Bonnard, 2005), 66.

1. Francesco Petrarca, "De copia librorum," in *De remediis utriusque fortunae,* I, 43.

2. Jacques Derrida, A. Dufourmantelle, *De l'hospitalité* (Paris: Calmann-Lévy, 1997); A. Montandon, *Elogio dell'ospitalità. Storia di un "rito" da Omero a Kafka* (Roma: Salerno, 2004).

3. I follow the chronology adopted by Robert Darnton, *The Case for Books: Past, Present, and Future* (New York: Public Affairs, 2009), ch. 2, "The Information Landscape," 21–42. The author, a book historian, oversaw in his capacity as chief librarian of the University of Harvard Library the Google Book Search Project with regard to the functions of research libraries. See also Gino Roncaglia, *La quarta rivoluzione. Sei lezioni sul futuro del libro* (Roma-Bari: Laterza, 2010); and "Cultures of Reading," ed. Evelyne Ender, Deidre Shauna Lynch, *PMLA* 133, 5 (October 2018).

4. See Lamberto Maffei, *Elogio della lentezza* (Bologna: Il Mulino, 2014); Maffei, *Elogio della ribellione* (Bologna: Il Mulino, 2016); Maffei, *Elogio della parola* (Bologna: Il Mulino, 2018).

5. For another point of view, see Anthony Grafton, *Bring out Your Dead: The Past as Revelation* (Cambridge, MA: Harvard University Press, 2004); Jürgen Pieters, *Speaking with the Dead: Explorations in Literature and History* (Edinburgh: Edinburgh

University Press, 2005); Thomas M. Greene, *The Light in Troy: Imitation and Discovery in Renaissance Poetry* (New Haven, CT: Yale University Press, 1982), 32.

6. Mike Licht, *Portrait of Laura Battiferri with Her iPad, after Agnolo Bronzino*, Flickr, accessed 11 February 2021, https://www.flickr.com/photos/notionscapital/5268001834.

7. See Victoria Kirkham, "Dante's Phantom, Petrarch's Specter: Bronzino's Portrait of the Poet Laura Battiferri," in *"Visibile parlare." Dante and the Art of the Italian Renaissance,* ed. Deborah Parker (Charlottesville: University of Virginia, 1998), 63–139; Deborah Parker, *Bronzino: Renaissance Painter as Poet* (Cambridge: Cambridge University Press, 2000); Lina Bolzoni, *Poesia e ritratto nel Rinascimento,* texts with commentary by Federica Pich (Bari: Laterza, 2008), 55–57, 211–217; *Bronzino pittore e poeta alla corte dei Medici,* ed. A. Natali, C. Falciani (Firenze: Mandragora, 2010).

8. See Stephen Greenblatt, *Renaissance Self-Fashioning: From More to Shakespeare* (Chicago: University of Chicago Press, 2005).

9. Alberto Manguel, *A History of Reading* (New York, Penguin, [1996] 2014). One case mentioned is that of the workers in a Cuban cigar factory, each of whom in 1886 made a contribution in order to pay for a reader during their working hours.

10. Louis Bollioud-Mermet, *Sulla bibliomania,* ed. Pino di Branco (Milano: La vita felice, 2013). The author (1709–1794), who was permanent secretary of the Académie of Lyon and expert in music, had the work published anonymously in the Hague in 1761; it was titled *De la bibliomanie* and was reprinted in 1765 under the title *Essai sur la lecture.* In the final pages, we read, "It is precisely because I love and esteem books that I do not want it to be insinuated that there is the least sign of a fanatic passion in my esteem of them. I have myself been obliged to recognize and experience this danger" (127).

11. Walter Benjamin, "Unpacking My Library: A Talk about Book Collecting," in *Illuminations* (Boston: Mariner Books, 2019), 3, 10. See the comment by Homi Bhabha, "Unpacking My Library Again," *Identities* 28, 1 (Spring 1995): 5–18.

12. Tullia d'Aragona writes a passionate exaltation of the pleasures afforded by reading in the letter to readers with which she presents her rewriting in octaves of a Spanish translation of *Guerrin Meschino*. Reading guarantees pleasures and liberties that those other "honest and agreeable pastimes" do not allow: "In reading we can by ourselves govern ourselves exactly as we wish, alone, in company, as much or as little as we desire, without expense, without damage, without travail, but to our own complete satisfaction and content." It is a pleasure, d'Aragona argues, suitable for both men and women but to women in particular, as we are reminded by Boccaccio, who, however, is guilty of "horrendous lewdness." Tullia d'Aragona, *Il Meschino altramente detto Il Guerrino fatto in ottava rima dalla signora Tullia d'Aragona* (Venezia: Gio. Battista e Melchior Setta, 1560), "Ai lettori," unnumbered pages. This eulogy of reading is extremely interesting, even if its purpose is to exalt the beauty and the usefulness of the work Tullia is presenting to her readers as well as to distance herself from her life as a cour-

tesan, from the days of her youth when she learned through experience just how harmful the reading of lewd books can be. I wish to thank Virginia Cox for bringing this text to my attention. See also Tiziana Plebani, *Il "genere" dei libri. Storie e rappresentazioni della lettura al femminile e al maschile tra Medioevo e età moderna* (Milano: Franco Angeli, 2001).

13. Sylvain Maréchal, *Progetto di legge per vietare alle donne di imparare a leggere*, ed. Enrico Badellino (Milano: Archinto, 2008), 67, 78, 86, 68.

14. Virginia Woolf, *The Essays of Virginia Woolf*, vol. 5, ed. Stuart N. Clarke (London: Hogarth Press, 2009), 582. On women reading, see also Nadia Fusini's *Hannah e le altre* (Torino: Einaudi, 2013).

15. See Mary Carruthers, *The Craft of Thought: Meditation, Rhetoric and the Making of Images 400–1200* (Cambridge: Cambridge University Press, 1998), in particular chs. 2 and 3.

16. George Steiner, *Les Logocrates* (Paris: Éditions de L'Herne, 2003). By the same author, see *No Passion Spent: Essays 1978–1996* (London: Faber and Faber, 1996). The catalogue of the exhibition *Le lecteur à l'oeuvre*, ed. M. Jeanneret, N. Ducimetière, V. Hayart, R. Suciu (Gollion: Infolio, 2013), provides a useful overview and a good bibliography of the various ways in which a reader can be involved. Valuable ideas and bibliographical indications are to be found in Luca Ferrieri, *Fra l'ultimo libro letto e il primo nuovo da aprire. Letture e passioni che abitiamo* (Firenze: Olschki, 2013).

17. See Ezio Raimondi, *Un'etica del lettore* (Bologna: Il Mulino, 2007).

18. Michel De Certeau, "La lecture absolue," in *Problèmes actuels de la lecture*, ed. L. Dahlenbach, J. Ricardou (Paris: Clanciers-Guénaud, 1982), 65–80; and Certeau, "Lire. Un braconage," in *L'invention du quotidien 1. Arts de faire* (Paris: Union Général d'Édition, 1980). See the comment by Christian Jacob, "L'art de lire," in *Des Alexandries II. Les métamorphoses du lecteur*, ed. C. Jacob (Paris: Bibliothèque Nationale de France, 2003), 15–33.

19. Sir Thomas Bodley, *The Autobiography of Sir Thomas Bodley*, introduction and notes by William Clennell (Oxford, UK: Bodleian Library, 2006). The portrait is described in *Catalogue of the Portraits Exhibited in the Reading Room and Gallery of the Bodleian Library* (Oxford: Oxford University Press, 2004), 29n71.

20. Alberto Manguel, *Fabulous Monsters: Dracula, Alice, Superman, and Other Literary Friends* (New Haven, CT: Yale University Press, 2019), 149. Manguel also points out that Verne's publisher, Hetzel, recognized in Nemo a self-portrait of the author and convinced the illustrator, Édouard Riou, to use Verne for his portrait of Nemo.

21. The novel, published in 1935, gained popularity in the 1960s and 1970s. See Lina Bolzoni, "Il gioco degli occhi. L'arte della memoria fra antiche esperienze e moderne suggestioni," in *Memoria e memorie. Convegno internazionale di studi, Roma, 18–19 maggio 1995, Accademia Nazionale dei Lincei*, ed. L. Bolzoni, V. Erlindo, M. Morelli (Firenze: Olschki, 1998), 1–28 (11–14).

22. See Pliny the Elder, *Naturalis historia,* VII, 24; Seneca the Elder, *Controversiae,* I, 18; Francesco Petrarca, *Rerum memorandarum libri,* II, 13; Filippo Gesualdo, "Della libreria della memoria," in *Plutosofia* (Padova: Paolo Megietti, 1592), cc. 55v–56.

23. Bernard Berenson, "On the Future of I Tatti" (Vallombrosa, 18 August 1956), 3.

1. Petrarch and the Magical Space of the Library

1. See Emilio Pasquini, "Due concordanze petrarchesche," *Il Cannocchiale* 3–4 (1965): 59–73; August Buck, *Die Rezeption der Antike in den romanischen Literaturen der Renaissance* (Berlin: E. Schmidt, 1976); Christian Bec, "Dal Petrarca al Machiavelli. Il dialogo tra lettore e autore," in *Cultura e società a Firenze nell'età della Rinascenza* (Roma: Salerno, 1981), 228–244; Michele Feo, "'Sì che pare a' lor vivagni.' Il dialogo col libro da Dante a Montaigne," in *Agnolo Poliziano poeta scrittore filologo,* ed. V. Fera, M. Martelli (Firenze: Le Lettere, 1998), 245–294, which also mentions an important book in which the European idea of conversing with the great writers of the past is carefully reconstructed: Karl Otto Brogsitter, *Das hohe Geistergespräch. Studien zur Geschichte der humanistischen Vorstellungen von einer zeitlosen Gemeinschaft der grossen Geister* (Bonn: H. Bouvier, 1958); Paola Vecchi Galli, "'Leggere,' 'scrivere' nelle 'Familiari,'" in *Motivi e forme delle 'Familiari' di Francesco Petrarca,* ed. Claudia Berra (Milano: Cisalpino, 2003), 323–366; Loredana Chines, "Loqui cum libris," in *Motivi e forme delle 'Familiari,'* 367–384; Giulio Ferroni, "Come essere giudicati dagli antichi," in *Arma virumque . . . Studi di poesia e storiografia in onore di Luca Canali,* ed. E. Lelli (Pisa-Roma: Istituti Editoriali e Poligrafici Internazionale, 2002), 321–329; Kathy Eden, "A Rhetoric and Hermeneutics of Intimacy in Petrarch's 'Familiares,'" in *The Renaissance Rediscovery of Intimacy* (Chicago: University of Chicago Press, 2012), 49–72; *Petrarca lettore. Pratiche e rappresentazioni della lettura nelle opere dell'umanista,* ed. L. Marcozzi (Firenze: Cesati, 2016).

2. See also the bibliography appended to the essays in *Petrarca lettore. Pratiche e rappresentazioni della lettura nelle opere dell'umanista,* ed. L. Marcozzi (Firenze: Cesati, 2016).

3. Francis Petrarch (*Seniles,* I, 5, 63), *Letters of Old Age: Rerum Senilium Libri I–XVIII* (henceforth *Sen.*), vol. 1, Books I–IX, trans. Aldo S. Bernardo, Saul Levin, Reta Bernardo (Baltimore: Johns Hopkins University Press, 1992), 25. See, further, the recent French edition of Pétrarque, *Lettres de la veillesse,* ed. E. Nota, trans. F. Castelli, F. Fabre, A. de Rosny, notes by U. Dotti (Paris: Les Belles Lettres, 2002). On the correspondence between Petrarch and Boccaccio, see Gabriella Albanese, "La corrispondenza fra Petrarca e Boccaccio," in *Motivi e forme delle 'Familiari,'* 39–98 (and 44n7).

4. Francis Petrarch (*Familiares,* III, 18, 2–3), *Letters on Familiar Matters (Rerum Familiarum Libri)* (henceforth *Fam.*), vol. 1, trans. Aldo S. Bernardo (New York: Italica, [1975] 2005), 157.

5. On the redeployment of this topos in Boccaccio, see Christian Bec, "Dal Petrarca al Machiavelli," 234–236.

6. (XXI, 15, 27) *Fam.,* vol. 3 ([1985] 2005), 206.

7. Ernst Robert Curtius, *European Literature and the Latin Middle Ages,* afterword by Peter Godman, trans. Willard R. Trask (Princeton, NJ: Princeton University Press, 1973), 336; this is one of the examples of "the book as symbol" (ibid., 303–337), on which see Hans Blumenberg, *Die Lesbarkeit der Welt* (Frankfurt: Suhrkamp, 1981).

8. (I, 1, 37) *Fam.,* vol. 1, 3, 9. Francisco Rico has suggested that the unfinished work might have been *Africa:* "'Animi effigies.' L'Africa' nel prologo delle 'Familiari,'" in *Verso il Centenario petrarchesco. Prospettive critiche sul Petrarca,* ed. L. Chines, P. Vecchi Galli, *Quaderni petrarcheschi* 11 (2001): 215–228. On Petrarch's vision of his work as self-portrait and on his relationship with classical and contemporary art, see Maria Monica Donato, "'Veteres' e 'novi,' 'externi' e 'nostri.' Gli artisti di Petrarca. Per una rilettura," in *Medioevo. Immagine e racconto, Atti del Convegno internazionale di studi Parma, 27–30 Settembre 2000,* ed. A. Quintavalle (Milano: Electa, 2003), 433–455.

9. Il tomo del Ramusio / dall'alto dello scaffale / occhieggia da molti giorni / russa di notte come un maiale / quando si sveglia vuole / balzarmi sulla schiena / precipitarmi addosso / fracassarmi anche un osso. / Il tomo mi vuole male / digrigna i denti sospira / impreca e si lamenta / perché non l'ho venduto in Giappone / o alla biblioteca di Argenta. R. Roversi, *Libri e contro il tarlo inimico* (Bologna: Pandragon, 2012), 96–97. The reference is to G. B. Ramusio, *Navigationi et Viaggi,* 3 folio vols. (1550–1559).

10. Andrea Torre, *Petrarcheschi segni di memoria. Spie, postille, metafore* (Pisa: Edizioni della Normale, 2007).

11. (XXII, 2, 12–13) *Fam.,* vol. 3, 212–213, with minor changes.

12. (XXII, 2,11) ibid., 212.

13. (XXII, 2,13) ibid., 213.

14. *Against a Physician,* in Franceso Petrarca, *Invectives,* ed. and trans. David Marsh, The I Tatti Renaissance Library (Cambridge, MA: Harvard University Press, 2003), 121.

15. Francesco Petrarca, *My Secret Book* (II, 16, 10), ed. and trans. Nicholas Mann, The I Tatti Renaissance Library (Cambridge, MA: Harvard University Press, 2016), 139–141.

16. Cicero, *De oratore* (III, xxxiv, 138), *De Oratore in Two Volumes,* trans. H. Racham (Cambridge, MA: Harvard University Press, 1952), 109.

17. See Ronald L. Martinez, "Petrarch's Lame Leg and the Corpus of Cicero: An Early Crisis of Humanism?," in *The Body in Early Modern Italy,* ed. J. L. Hairston, W. Stephens (Baltimore: Johns Hopkins University Press, 2010), 42–60.

18. (XXI, 10, 17) *Fam.,* vol. 3, 187.

19. (XXI, 10, 26) ibid., 188.

20. Rinaldi offers a different interpretation: Rinaldo Rinaldi, "'Sed calamo superstite.' La scrittura interna delle Familiari," in *Motivi e forme delle 'Familiari,'* 419–456.

21. Francesco Petrarca, "Lettere varie," in *Lettere disperse,* ed. A. Pancheri (Parma: Ugo Guanda,1994), 46 (Var. 25), 348–349.

22. See Bortolo Martinelli, "Il Petrarca e San Paolo," *Studi petrarcheschi* 9 (1990): 86, which evokes Galatians, VI, 17: "ego enim stigmata Domini Iesu in corpore meo porto"; Andrea Torre, *Petrarcheschi segni,* 299: "*intus et extra . . .* doubles Petrarch's mental memorization of Cicero's work by physically noting on his body its inescapable presence"; *stigma* calls into play St. Francis's religious experience, i.e., the physical experience of a complete immedesimation in Christ (Francis had so deeply meditated on Christ's crucifixion that it seemed to him as though he himself had been crucified, "so that in the end his pious belief transferred the true image of the thing from his soul to his body"; *Sen.,* vol. 1, 282). "The stigmata of Francis started when he embraced Christ's death in such a continuous and powerful meditation that he had mentally transferred it over a long period of time and felt as though he himself were crucified with his lord, eventually his pious belief transferred a true likeness of the thing from his mind into his body—'tandem ab animo in corpus veram rei effigiem pia transferret opinio.'"

23. See Francisco Rico, *Vida u obra de Petrarca. I. Lectura del "Secretum"* (Padova: Antenore, 1974), Victoria Kahn, "The Figure of the Reader in Petrarch's *Secretum*," *PMLA,* 100, 2 (1985): 154–166. On the connections with Augustine's *Confessions* and the differences with the reading practices depicted in the *Secretum,* see Brian Stock, *After Augustine: The Meditative Reader and the Text* (Philadelphia: University of Pennsylvania Press, 2001), 71–85. On the relationships between modes of reading and mnemonic techniques, see Mary Carruthers's two book-length studies, *The Book of Memory: A Study of Memory in Medieval Culture* (Cambridge: Cambridge University Press, 1990) and *The Craft of Thought: Meditation, Rhetoric, and the Making of Images, 400–1200* (Cambridge: Cambridge University Press, 1998).

24. *Prohemium,* 3, 5; Francesco Petrarca, *My Secret Book,* 9.

25. Paola Vecchi Galli, "'Leggere,' 'scrivere' nelle 'Familiari,'" 355.

26. (XII, 8, 1–8) *Fam.,* vol. 2, 153–154.

27. (VI, 2, 7) *Sen.,* vol. 1, 192.

28. Loredana Chines, "Loqui cum libris," 367–384 (374).

29. (XII, 8, 10) *Fam.,* vol. 2, 154.

30. (XII, 8, 11) ibid.

31. Thomas Greene places necromantic metaphors at the heart of the Renaissance and highlights the search for continuity with a very distant past: "That is why even the act of memory always involves an implicit necromantic metaphor: a resuscitation." Thomas M. Greene, *The Light in Troy: Imitation and Discovery in Renaissance Poetry* (New Haven, CT: Yale University Press, 1982), 32.

32. See l. 44; the letter is among those that were traditionally called *Epystole metrice* and that Feo suggests calling *Epystole:* see Michele Feo, "Epystole," in *Codici latini*

del Petrarca nelle biblioteche fiorentine, Firenze, Biblioteca Medicea Laurenziana, 19 May–30 June 1991, catalogue ed. M. Feo (Firenze: Le Lettere, 1991), 421–423 (421). The text of the letter is in Francesco Petrarca, *Rime. Trionfi e poesie latine,* ed. F. Neri., G. Martellotti, E. Bianchi, N. Sapegno (Milano-Napoli: Ricciardi Ricciardi, 1951), 727–741.

33. See Francisco Rico, *I venerdì del Petrarca* (Milano: Adelphi, 2016).

34. *Epystola,* 1.6.110–115.

35. This thesis is put forward by Alessandra Macinante in her doctoral thesis on Petrarch's *Epystole,* which she discussed at the Scuola Normale Superiore of Pisa.

36. *Epystola,* 1.6.129–152; see *Petrarch at Vaucluse: Letters in Verse and Prose Translated by Ernest Hatch Wilkins* (Chicago: University of Chicago Press, 1958), 8.

37. *Epystola,* 1.6.178–200 (*Petrarch at Vaucluse,* 9–10).

38. Loredana Chines, "Loqui cum libris," 378.

39. (XV, 3, 14–15) *Fam.,* vol. 2, 256–257.

40. (II, XIV) translation SG. See also Francesco Petrarca, *La vie solitaire 1346–1366,* preface by N. Mann; ed., introduction, and notes by C. Carraud (Grénoble: J. Millon, 1999).

41. Stephen Campbell, in *The Cabinet of Eros: Renaissance Mythological Painting and the Studiolo of Isabella d'Este* (New Haven, CT: Yale University Press, 2004), 36, points out that the inscription that exalts Federico's library above all other riches ("Bibliotheca parata est, iussa loqui facunda nimis, vel iussa tacere") paraphrases "libros . . . paratosque semper vel tacere vel loqui."

42. The passage is pointed out by Monica Berté, "'Lector, intende, letaberis.' La prassi della lettura in Petrarca," in *Petrarca lettore,* 15–39 (28).

43. "And will you therefore always be alone?" "On the contrary, I will have company." "And who will your companions be?" "They are dead." "Ha! Ha! Ha! Ha!" "Why do you laugh?" "Because you leave the city to be with dead people." "I leave infinite evils, indeed, to be more specific, I leave a never-ending array of troubles and vexations: leaving the city is like escaping a storm at sea!" The original is in *Lettere a Petrarca,* ed. U. Dotti (Torino: Aragno 2012), 504–517 (508–509).

44. (XV, 3, 32), *Sen.,* vol. 2, 567–689.

45. Already for some years, accusations (perhaps better defined as rumors) of practicing magic had been leveled against Petrarch; these were invariably connected to his love of solitude and to his intimate knowledge of Virgil, who was in turn considered to be a magician. See the 1350 letter addressed to the Bishop of Parma, Ugolino Rossi: "Perhaps, I say, by this time I appear to many as a necromancer and a magician. I no doubt appear so because I am frequently alone and because, as all those experts say and I do not deny, I read the works of Virgil, an opinion which elicits bile mixed with laughter. I have indeed read them." (IX, 5, 15) *Fam.,* vol. 2, 16. See Bruno Lavillatte, "Pétrarque et la magie: Une histoire familière," in *Francesco Petrarca. L'opera*

latina. Tradizione e fortuna, ed. Luisa Secchi Tarugi (Firenze: Franco Cesati, 2006), 669–686; and the classic study by Domenico Comparetti, *Virgilio nel medioevo,* published in 1872.

46. Theodore Cachey links Petrarch's exile, his stateless condition, to his constant traveling and his choice of writing itself as a place, as it were, to inhabit. Theodore Cachey, "Poetry in Motion," in *The Cambridge Companion in Petrarch* (Cambridge: Cambridge University Press, 2015), 13–25.

47. (XVIII, 1) *Sen.,* vol. 2, 673–674. See Francisco Rico, "Il nucleo della 'Posteritati' (e le autobiografie di Petrarca)," in *Motivi e forme delle 'Familiari,'* 1–19.

48. Francesco Petrarca, *Rerum memorandarum libri,* ed. M. Petoletti (Firenze: Le lettere, 2014), vol. 1, 19, vol. 4, 54–55 (translation SG). The complaint ("querela") refers to the lack of interest among his contemporaries for the great works of antiquity.

49. (XXIV, 5, 2) *Fam.,* vol. 3, 322.

50. Petrarch's assiduous reading of Cicero created a strong familiarity, intimacy even, with the classical author: "you would have liked the *Aeniad* more than the *Iliad*," he wrote to Cicero, "if I have come to know your mind through your works, which I do seem to know as though I had lived with you." (XXIV, 4, 9) *Fam.,* vol. 3, 320.

51. (XVII, 3) *Sen.,* vol. 2, 671.

52. *De vita solitaria,* I, VI, 6; translation SG.

53. Ibid., I, VI, 12; translation SG.

54. (VI, 4, 4) *Fam.,* vol. 1, 314.

55. (XIII, 5, 23) *Fam.,* vol. 2, 191.

56. Ibid.

57. See Lina Bolzoni, "Memoria e oblio nel *De remediis* di Petrarca e una immagine di Sebastian Brant," in *Il lettore creativo. Percorsi cinquecenteschi fra memoria, gioco, scrittura* (Napoli: Guida, 2012), 85–107.

58. (*De remediis,* I, Prefatio, 4, 11) *Petrarch's Remedies for Fortunes Fair and Foul: A Modern English Translation of* De Remediis Utriusque Fortune, *with a Commentary,* trans. Conrad Rawski (Bloomington: Indiana University Press, 1991), vol. 1, 3–4.

59. (Ibid., Prefatio, 6, 12) *Petrarch's Remedies,* vol. 1, 4.

60. (Ibid., Prefatio, 8, 16) *Petrarch's Remedies,* vol. 1, 6–7. On the relationships between rhetoric and medicine, see *Rhetoric and Medicine in Early Modern Europe,* ed. S. Pender, N. S. Struever (Farnham, UK: Ashgate, 2012).

61. (*De remediis,* I, 43) *Petrarch's Remedies,* vol. 1, 138. The reference to Seneca is to the *Epistulae morales ad Lucilium* 2, 2–4, and to *De tranquillitate animi* IX, 5.

62. (*De remediis,* I, 43, 6) *Petrarch's Remedies,* vol. 1, 216.

63. (XVI, 1, 3) *Fam.,* vol. 2, 291.

64. (XXII, 2, 13) *Fam.,* vol. 3, 213.

65. (I, 8, 20) *Fam.,* vol. 1, 45.

66. (I, 9, 11–12); translation SG.

2. The Text as a Body and the Resurrection of the Ancients

1. Giovanni Boccaccio, *The Elegy of Lady Fiammetta,* ed. and trans. Mariangela Causa-Steindler, Thomas Mauch (Chicago: University of Chicago Press, 1990), 156. The text was written before 1345.

2. Ibid. See Antonio Enzo Quaglio, "Picciolo libretto," *Lingua nostra* 20 (1959): 35–36.

3. Ovid, *Tristia ex Ponto* (I, 1–16), trans. A. L. Wheeler, Loeb Classical Library (Cambridge, MA: Heinmann, 1988), 3.

4. Giovanni Boccaccio, *Consolatoria a Pino de' Rossi,* ed. Giuseppe Chiecchi, in *Tutte le opere* (Milano: Mondadori, 1994), vol. 5, 613–651.

5. Ibid., 650; translation SG.

6. Nicola Gardini, "Osiris and the End of the Renaissance," in *Renaissance Now: The Value of the Renaissance Past in the Culture of Today,* ed. Brendan Dooley (Frankfurt am Main: Peter Lang, 2014), 39–57.

7. A. Bartlett Giamatti, "Hippolytus among the Exiles: The Romance of Early Humanism," in *Exile and Change in Renaissance Literature* (New Haven, CT: Yale University Press, 1984), 12–32; this section is greatly indebted to his work.

8. See also, for a bibliography on earlier material, Leonard Barkan, *Unearthing the Past: Archaeology and Aesthetics in the Making of Renaissance Culture* (New Haven, CT: Yale University Press, 1982), 57–61; Vincenzo Farinella, *Archeologia e pittura a Roma tra Quattrocento e Cinquecento. Il caso di Jacopo Ripanda* (Torino: Einaudi, 1992), 3–19.

9. Giovanni Boccaccio, *Genealogy of the Pagan Gods,* ed. and trans. Jon Solomon, The I Tatti Renaissance Library (Cambridge, MA: Harvard University Press, 2011), I, 40:19.

10. Ibid., I, 50:23.

11. Ibid., I, 41:19.

12. "At the beginning of each of these books I thought it best to append a tree: the father is located at the roots; in the branches in the descending order I have spread out all the progeny so you can see from whom they are born and in what order you will find them later in the work; you will also find these books divided into appropriate chapter headings that will be more memorable because you will already have read that single name on the leaves of a tree." (ibid., I, 47:21–22). On Boccaccio's trees, see also Albertina Catherine de La Mare, Catherine Reynolds, "Arbores genealogicae from '*Genealogia deorum*' (Merton College, ms. 299, cc. 281v–289r)," *Studi sul Boccaccio* (1991–1992): 70–72. On the mnemonic function of trees, see Lina Bolzoni, *La rete delle immagini. Predicazione in volgare dalle origini a Bernardino da Siena* (Torino: Einaudi, 2002), ch. 3, "Alberi e altri schemi. Alcuni esempi d'uso," 103–144.

13. See Alexandre Dumas, *The Count of Monte Cristo,* ch. 14.

14. This is the cod. Lat.7720 in the Bibliothèque Nationale di Parigi. On Petrarch's dense glossing of the manuscript pages that deal with the subject of memory, see Andrea Torre, *Petrarcheschi segni di memoria. Spie, postille, metafore* (Pisa: Edizioni della Normale, 2007), 112–128.

15. Francis Petrarch (*Familiares,* XXIV, 7, 1–2), *Letters on Familiar Matters (Rerum Familiarum Libri)* (henceforth *Fam.*), vol. 3, trans. Aldo S. Bernardo (New York: Italica, [1985] 2005), 392.

16. "I hope to see you in your entirety, and if you are anywhere in such condition, I beg you not to hide from me any longer." (XXIV, 7, 10) *Fam.,* vol. 3, 331.

17. A. Bartlett Giamatti, "Hippolytus among the Exiles," 18.

18. "Poggius to Guarinus Veronensis," in *Two Renaissance Book Hunters: The Letters of Poggius Bracciolini to Nicolaus de Niccolis,* trans. from the Latin and annotated by Phyllis Walter Goodhart Gordan (New York: Columbia University Press, 1974), 193. The verses quoted are from *Aeneid* VI, 496–498. See also Poggio Bracciolini, *Lettere,* 3 vols., ed. H. Harth (Firenze: Olschki, 1984–1987).

19. *Two Renaissance Book Hunters,* 194–195.

20. *Petrarch's Remedies for Fortunes Fair and Foul: A Modern English Translation of De Remediis Utriusque Fortune, with a Commentary,* trans. Conrad Rawski (Bloomington: Indiana University Press, 1991), vol. 1, 142. See Michele Feo, "'Sì che pare a' lor vivagni.' Il dialogo col libro da Dante e Montaigne," in *Agnolo Poliziano poeta scrittore filologo,* ed. V. Fera, M. Martelli (Firenze: Le Lettere, 1998), 245–294 (255–256).

21. Stephen Greenblatt, *The Swerve: How the World Became Modern* (New York: Norton, 2012), 177–179.

22. The full text of the letter in English may be found in *The Life of Poggio Bracciolini,* by William Shepherd (London: Longman, 1837), 69–79; see also the edition and commentary in *Umanisti italiani. Pensiero e destino,* ed. Raphael Ebgi, with an essay by Massimo Cacciari (Torino: Einaudi, 2016), 9–12, 19–26.

23. "He advanced nothing unbecoming a good man; and if his real sentiments agreed with his professions, he was so far from deserving to die, that his principles did not even give just ground for the slightest offence" (W. Shepherd, *Life of Poggio Bracciolini,* 72). This seems, to the letter's addressee, to lack caution, and Bruni advises Poggio that more circumspection is required. Leonardo Bruni, *Epistolarum libri VIII,* recensente Laurentio Mehus (1741), ed. J. Hankins (Roma: Edizioni di storia e letteratura, 2007), vol. 1, 120.

24. W. Shepherd, *Life of Poggio Bracciolini,* 70.

25. Ibid., 71.

26. Ibid., 72.

27. For this, and the preceding quotation, in which Poggio observes that the manuscript is not in a library but "in a foul and gloomy dungeon," see *Two Renaissance Book Hunters,* 194–195.

28. Ibid., 192.

29. Ibid., 191.

30. A. Bartlett Giamatti, "Hippolytus among the Exiles," 25–26.

31. *Two Renaissance Book Hunters,* 199.

32. Ibid., 72–73.

33. See Angelo Poliziano, *Due poemetti latini. Elegia a Bartolomeo Fonzio. Epicedio di Albiera degli Albizi,* ed. F. Bausi (Roma: Salerno, 2003).

34. See Giuseppe Cagni, *Vespasiano da Bisticci e il suo epistolario* (Roma: Edizioni di Storia e Letteratura, 1969), 32.

35. Ibid., 36–39, ll. 210–222. The translation is in Angelo Poliziano, *Greek and Latin Poetry,* trans. and ed. Peter E. Knox, I Tatti (Cambridge, MA: Harvard University Press, 2019), 252.

36. Giuseppe Cagni, *Vespasiano da Bisticci,* 38, note for ll. 215–218.

37. Angelo Poliziano, "Latini dettati a Piero de' Medici," in *Prose volgari inedite e poesie latine greche edite e inedite,* ed. I. Del Lungo (Firenze: Barbera, 1867), 32–34; translation SG.

38. Angelo Poliziano, *Greek and Latin Poetry,* 255.

39. Giuseppe Cagni, *Vespasiano da Bisticci,* 32, note to ll. 183–184.

40. See Antonia Tissoni Benvenuti, *L'Orfeo del Poliziano* (Padova: Antenore, 1986), 138. On the connection that is thus forged between the myths of Orpheus and Aesculapius, see ibid., 86–87.

41. Angelo Poliziano, *Miscellaneorum Centuria secunda,* ed. V. Branca, M. Pastore Stocchi (Firenze: Alinari, 1972), vol. 4, 3; translation SG. See now Angelo Poliziano, *Miscellanies,* ed. and trans. Andrew R. Dyck, Alan Cottrell, 2 vols. (Cambridge, MA: Harvard University Press, 2020).

42. Poggio Bracciolini to Pier Candido Decembrio, 17 September 1438, in *Lettere,* vol. 2, 326–327; translation SG.

43. Poggio Bracciolini to Gerardo Landriani, 20 September 1438, ibid., vol. 3, 325.

44. Cicero, *Epist. ad fam.,* IX, 1, 2, quoted in K. Eden, *The Renaissance Rediscovery of Intimacy* (Chicago: University of Chicago Press, 2012), 65n32.

45. Poggio Bracciolini to Francesco de Lignamine, 26 October 1438, in *Lettere,* vol. 4, 329.

46. See the entry on "Dal Legname Francesco" by Alfred A. Strnad in *Dizionario Biografico degli italiani,* vol. 32 (Roma: Istituto della Enciclopedia italiana, 1986), 92–96.

47. Poggio Bracciolini, *De vera nobilitate,* ed. D. Canfora (Roma: Edizioni di Storia e Letteratura, 2002).

48. Translated from Giovanni di Pagolo Morelli, *Ricordi,* ed. V. Branca (Firenze: Le Monnier, 1956). See also Christian Bec, *Les marchands écrivains. Affaires et humanisme à Florence 1375–1434* (Paris: De Gruyter Mouton, 1967), 53–75ff., where it is also suggested that Giovanni Dominici played an important role in the transmission of the theme we are here discussing; Angelo Cicchetti, Raul Mordenti, "La scrittura dei libri

di famiglia," in *Letteratura italiana Einaudi,* tome III, vol. 2 (Torino: Einaudi, 1984), 1117–1159; Leonida Pandimiglio, *Famiglia e memoria a Firenze, I (secoli XIII–XVI)* (Roma: Edizioni di Storia e Letteratura, 2010), 75–252.

49. Morelli, *Ricordi,* 220, 205, 206.

50. Portions of Morelli's *Ricordi* are in *Merchant Writers of the Italian Renaissance,* ed. Vittore Branca, trans. from the Italian by Murtha Baba (New York: Marsilio, 1999); this passage, which has been integrated, is translated at p. 87.

51. Ibid., 70–71 (with integrations).

52. Ibid., 71 (with integrations and minor changes).

53. Although it focuses principally on a later period, see Gigliola Fragnito, *La Bibbia al rogo. La censura ecclesiastica e i volgarizzamenti della Scrittura (1471–1605)* (Bologna: Il Mulino, 1997).

54. *Cento meditazioni sulla vita di Gesù Cristo,* in San Bonaventura, *Opere ascetiche volgarizzate nel Trecento,* ed. B. Sorio (Verona: Ramanzini, 1851), 91–92; translation SG. For further bibliography, see Bolzoni, *La rete delle immagini,* 190–198.

55. Eugenio Garin, *Educazione umanistica in Italia* (Bari: Laterza, 1966), 48.

56. S. Bernardino da Siena, *Le prediche volgari. Quaresimale del 1425,* ed. C. Cannarozzi (Firenze: Libreria Editrice Fiorentina, 1940), vol. 1, 305.

57. Ibid., 306.

58. S. Bernardino da Siena, *Le prediche volgari,* ed. C. Cannarozzi (Pistoia: Alberto Pacinotti, 1924) vol. 2, 464; S. Bernardino da Siena, *Le prediche volgari. La predicazione del 1425 in Siena,* ed. C. Cannarozzi (Firenze: Rinaldi, 1958), vol. 1, 291. See also Bolzoni, *La rete delle immagini,* 206–217.

59. Leon Battista Alberti, *Theogenius,* in *Opere volgari,* vol. 2, *Rime e trattati morali,* ed. C. Grayson (Bari: Laterza, 1966), 55–104 (74); translation SG.

60. Ibid., 58.

61. Ibid., 74.

62. For this interpretation, see Francesco Furlan, *Studia albertiana. Lectures et lecteurs de L. B. Alberti* (Paris-Torino: J. Vrin, Nino Aragno, 2003), 95–101.

63. Martin McLaughlin, "Pessimismo stoico e cultura classica nel 'Theogenius' dell'Alberti," in *Leon Battista Alberti. La vita, l'umanesimo, le opere letterarie* (Firenze: Olschki, 2016), 125–144, which contains further useful bibliography.

64. *De officiis,* III, 1. "Cato, who was of about the same years, Marcus, my son, as that Publius Scipio who first bore the surname of Africanus, has given us the statement that Scipio used to say that he was never less idle than when he had nothing to do and never less lonely than when he was alone. An admirable sentiment, in truth, and becoming to a great and wise man. It shows that even in his leisure hours his thoughts were occupied with public business and that he used to commune with himself when alone; and so not only was he never unoccupied, but he sometimes had no need for company. The two conditions, then, that prompt others to idleness—leisure and solitude—only spurred him on. I wish I could say the same of myself and say it

truly. But if by imitation I cannot attain to such excellence of character, in aspiration, at all events, I approach it as nearly as I can; for as I am kept by force of armed treason away from practical politics and from my practice at the bar; I am now leading a life of leisure. For that reason I have left the city and, wandering in the country from place to place, I am often alone." *Cicero, in Twenty-Eight Volumes,* vol. 21, *De Officiis,* with an English trans. by Walter Miller (London: Heinmann; Cambridge, MA, Harvard University Press, 1968), 271.

65. On Alberti's relationship with books and on the importance of Petrarch, see Roberto Cardini, "Alberti e i libri," in *Leon Battista Alberti. La biblioteca di un umanista,* ed. R. Cardini, L. Bertolini, M. Regoliosi (Firenze: Mandragora, 2005), 21–35, where the final passage of the Latin dedication of the *Intercenale Uxoria* is also quoted. According to Furlan, the passage quoted from *Theogenius* indicates the order that should be followed in reading, an order of importance that begins with useful knowledge and finally reaches philosophical matters: Furlan, *Studia albertiana,* 35.

66. Leon Battista Alberti, *Theogenius,* 66–67; translation SG.

67. See Pietro Bembo, *Ad Herculem Strotium de Vergilii Culice et Terentii fabulis liber,* ed. Giovan Antonio Nicolini da Sabbio (Venezia, 1530). I have examined the exemplar in the University Library of Pisa, Misc. 467.4. See Maurizio Campanelli, "Pietro Bembo, Roma e la filologia del tardo Quattrocento," *Rinascimento,* 2nd ser., 37 (1997): 283–319.

68. Pietro Bembo, *De Vergilii culice,* c.a IVr.

69. Campanelli, in "Pietro Bembo, Roma e la filologia del tardo Quattrocento" (293n19), quotes Leon Battista Alberti, *De re aedificatoria* (7, 16), ed. G. Orlandi, introduction and notes by P. Portoghesi (Milano: Il Polifilo, 1966), vol. 2, 655: "Tradition relates that there were so many statues in Rome that a second population was said to exist—one of marble"; Pomponio Gaurico, *De sculptura,* ed. A. Chastel, R. Klein (Genève: Droz, 1969), 53. See also, for the occurrence of this image in the *Tebaldeo,* Lina Bolzoni, *Poesia e ritratto nel Rinascimento* (Bari: Laterza, 2008), 52. Also see Alexander de Alexandro, *Genialium dierum libri sex,* IV, 12.

70. "Tot sepulchrorum, tot theatrorum cadavera prostrata et diruta ante oculos iacent" (Bembo, *De Vergilii culice,* c.a IVr).

71. Ibid., c.a Vr.

72. Ibid., c.a IVv.

73. Francesco Paolo Di Teodoro, *Raffaello, Baldassar Castiglione e la Lettera a Leone X* (Bologna: Nuova Alpha, 1994).

74. Translation in *The Neo-Latin Epigram: A Learned and Witty Genre,* ed. Susanna De Beer, Karl A. E. Enenkel, David Ruser (Leuven: Leuven University Press, 2009), 119. See John Shearman, *Raphael in Early Modern Sources (1483–1602)* (New Haven, CT: Yale University Press, 2003), vol. 1, 650–651.

75. Pietro Bembo, *Prose della volgar lingua,* ed. C. Dionisotti (Milano: TEA, 2001), 183; translation SG. See Lina Bolzoni, "Il fascino delle rovine e il fantasma di

Beatrice," in *La parola e l'immagine. Studi in onore di Gianni Venturi,* ed. M. Ariani, A. Bruni, A. Dolfi, A. Gareffi (Firenze: Olschki, 2011), 253–260.

76. Dante Alighieri, *Vita nova,* ed. G. Gorni (Torino: Einaudi, 1964), 159.

77. See ibid., Gorni's observation, "The repeated paronomasia with *miracolo* is by no means casual."

3. Portraits, or The Desire to See the Author

1. See Maurizio Bettini, *Il ritratto dell'amante* (Torino: Einaudi, 1992), 49; Victor I. Stoichita, *A Short History of the Shadow* (London: Reaktion Books, 1997), 11–20. On Pliny the Elder's position on the question of the origin of the portrait, see Georges Didi-Huberman, *Devant le temps. Histoire de l'art et anachronisme des images* (Paris: Les Éditions de Minuit, 2000), ch. 1, 59–83.

2. See Édouard Pommier, *Théorie du portrait. De la Renaissance aux Lumières* (Paris: Gallimard, 1998); Federica Pich, *I poeti davanti al ritratto. Da Petrarca a Marino* (Lucca: Pacini Fazzi, 2010).

3. Book I, xx, *The Letters of Marcus Tullius Cicero: To His Familiars and Friends,* trans. William Melmoth (London: W. Green, 1817), vol. 1, 46–47.

4. Seneca, *Letters on Ethics to Lucilius* (VII, 64, 5), trans. and with an introduction and commentary by Margaret Graver and A. A. Long (Chicago: University of Chicago Press, 2015), 185. On the Romans' relationship with the images of their ancestors, see Yan Thomas, "À Rome, pères citoyens et cité des pères (II siècle avant J.C.–II siècle après)," in *Histoire de la famille,* ed. A. Bourguière, C. Klapisch-Zuber, M. Segalen, F. Zonabend (Paris: Armand Colin, 1986), vol. 1, 195–229.

5. Seneca, *Letters on Ethics to Lucilius,* IV, 40, 120.

6. Camillo Baldi, *Come da una lettera missiva si conoscano la natura e qualità dello scrittore,* foreword by A. Petrucci (Pordenone: Studio Tesi, 1992).

7. See David Ganz, "Mind in Character: Ancient and Medieval Ideas about the Status of the Autograph as an Expression of Personality," in *Of the Making of Books: Medieval Manuscripts, Their Scribes and Readers; Essays Presented to M. B. Parkes,* ed. P. Robinson, R. Zim (Aldershot, UK: Scholar Press, 1997), 280–299 (299). The letter to Jacobi is dated 27 April 1806. I should like to thank Stefano Zamboni, who pointed out this passage to me.

8. Pliny, *The Natural History,* trans. H. Rackham, Loeb (Cambridge, MA: Harvard University Press, 1961–1968), vol. 9, 267. See R. Neudecker, *Die Skulpturenausstattung römischer Villen in Italien* (Mainz: von Zabern, 1988), 70; Sorcha Carey, "Imaging Memory," in *Pliny's Catalogue of Culture: Art and Empire in the Natural History* (Oxford: Oxford University Press, 2003), 138–178; David Petrain, "Visual Supplementation and Metonymy," in *Ancient Libraries,* ed. J. König, K. Oikonomopoulou, G. Woolf (Cambridge: Cambridge University Press, 2013), 332–346 (339–341); I must thank Paul Nelles for pointing out this study as well as for other valuable

suggestions. See also Giandomenico Spinola, "I ritratti dei poeti, filosofi, letterati e uomini illustri nelle biblioteche romane," in *La biblioteca infinita. I luoghi del sapere nel mondo antico,* ed. R. Meneghini, R. Rea (Milano: Electa, 2014), 155–175.

9. On portraits in the Greek and Roman world, see Paul Zanker, *The Mask of Socrates: The Image of the Intellectual in Antiquity,* trans. Alan Shapiro (Berkeley: University of California Press, 1995); in particular, "Wisdom and Nobility: An Early Portrait of Homer," 14–21; "The Divine Homer," 166–170.

10. See, for example, *Fakes, Lies and Forgeries: Rare Books and Manuscripts from the Arthur and Janet Freeman Bibliotheca Fictiva Collection,* ed. Earle Havens (Baltimore: Johns Hopkins Sheridan Libraries, 2014), in which, among other things, is mentioned (24) the discovery of Homer's tomb by a Dutch traveler, Pasch van Krienen, which supposedly took place on one of the Cycladic islands (*Breve descrizione dell'arcipelago . . . e specialmente del sepolcro di Omero* [Livorno: Tommaso Masi, 1773]).

11. Pomponio Gaurico, *De sculptura* (1504), ed. A. Chastel, R. Klein (Droz: Genève, 1969), 131; translation SG.

12. See Lina Bolzoni, *La stanza della memoria. Modelli letterari e iconografici nell'età della stampa* (Torino: Einaudi, 1995), "Il teatro delle passioni fra memoria, retorica, fisiognomica" (164–174) and "La biografia e il ritratto" (227–230).

13. Justus Lipsius paid special attention to portraits in libraries in his extremely influential *De bibliothecis, syntagma* (1602); see ch. 10, "Imagines in Bibliothecis," in Thomas Hendrickson, *Ancient Libraries and Renaissance Humanism: The* De bibliothecis *of Justus Lipsius* (Leiden: Brill, 2017), 160–161. For a history of the buildings that became libraries, see James W. P. Campbell, Will Pryce, *The Library: A World History* (Chicago: University of Chicago Press, 2013).

14. L. Canfora notes that Pollio "merely realized Caesar's project; indeed possibly taking into account that very project." The establishment of great public libraries, on the model of Alexandria, was part of Caesar's decision to "appropriate Hellenistic models of monarchy." "In the great capitals of the Hellenistic world (Pella, Antioch, Pergamon, Alexandria, Carthage) libraries were an aspect or regality." L. Canfora, *Per una storia delle biblioteche* (Bologna: Il Mulino, 2017), 47–48.

15. This is also in Cornelius Nepos (*Atticus*, 18).

16. Pliny (*Naturalis historia*, XXXV, 11), *The Natural History,* vol. 9, 269.

17. Alberti approvingly quotes this passage (*Tiberius,* 70, 2) in *De re aedificatoria,* VIII, ix: "One point not to be overlooked is this: the principal ornaments to any library will be a huge collection of books, drawn, preferably, from the learning of the ancients." He also thought mathematical and astronomical instruments constituted suitable ornaments and added that "Tiberius quite rightly recommended that a library should contain statues of the ancient poets." Leon Battista Alberti, *On the Art of Building in Ten Books,* trans. Joseph Rykwert, Neil Leach, Robert Tavernor (Cambridge, MA: MIT Press, 1988), 287.

18. See Christiane L. Joost-Gaugier, "The Early Beginning of the Notion of 'uomini famosi' and De viris illustribus in Greco-Roman Literary Tradition," *Artibus et historiae* 6 (1982): 95–115. Wolfgang Liebenwein, in *Studiolo. Storia e tipologia di uno spazio culturale*, ed. C. Cieri Via (Roma: Bulzoni, 2005), 17 (trans. from the German, *Studiolo. Die Enstehung eines Raumtyps und seine Entwicklung bis um 1600* [Berlin, 1977]) points out the case of the fifth-century Bishop of Lyon, Rusticus, who had mosaic or wax portraits of rhetoricians and poets, illustrated by epigrams; he also discusses the epigrams in the library of Isidore of Seville, which were placed as inscriptions below the portraits of writers.

19. See Gianfranco Contini, "Petrarca e le arti liberali," in *Francesco Petrarca Citizen of the World*, ed. A. Bernardo (Padova: Albany, 1980), 115–131; Marcello Ciccuto, *Figure di Petrarca. Giotto, Simone Martini, Franco Bolognese* (Napoli: Federico & Ardia, 1991); Ciccuto, "Petrarca tra le arti. Testi e immagini," in *Petrarch and the Textual Origins of Interpretation*, ed. T. Barolini, H. Wayne Storey (Leiden: Brill, 2007); Maria Monica Donato, "'Veteres' e 'novi,' 'externi' e 'nostri.' Gli artisti di Petrarca. Per una rilettura," in *Il Medioevo. Immagini e racconto. Atti del Convegno Internazionale di Studi, Parma, 27–30, settembre 2000* (Milano: Electa, 2003), 432–433; Maurizio Bettini, *Francesco Petrarca sulle arti figurative, Tra Plinio e sant'Agostino* (Livorno: Sillabe, 2002).

20. *Fam.*, XVI, 11, 12–13; translation SG.

21. We need only remember here sonnet 78 of the *Canzoniere*, on Laura's portrait by Simone Martini. See Lina Bolzoni, *Poesia e ritratto nel Rinascimento*, ed. Federica Pich (Bari: Laterza, 2008), 10–14, 75–81.

22. Maurizio Bettini, in *Francesco Petrarca sulle arti figurative*, 10, refers the reader to P. de Nolhac, *Pétrarque et l'humanisme* (Paris: Honoré Champion, 1907), vol. 2, 203 and 206.

23. Francis Petrarch (*Familiares*, XXI, 11, 5) *Letters on Familiar Matters (Rerum Familiarum Libri)* (henceforth *Fam.*), vol. 1, trans. Aldo S. Bernardo (New York: Italica, [1975] 2005), 189.

24. Maria Monica Donato, "'Veteres' e 'novi,' 'externi' e 'nostri,'" 438.

25. (XIX, 3, 14–15) *Fam.*, vol. 3, 79. Quoted in Maria Monica Donato, "Gli eroi romani tra storia ed exemplum. I primi cicli umanistici di Uomini famosi," in *Memoria dell'antico nell'arte italiana*, vol. 2, *I generi e i temi ritrovati*, ed. S. Settis (Torino: Einaudi, 1985), 97–152 (117).

26. On its complex textual history, see the introduction to Francesco Petrarca, *De viris illustribus. Adam-Hercules*, ed. C. Malta (Messina: Centro Interdipartimentale di Studi Umanistici, 2008), ix–ccxxix. See also Francesco Petrarca, *De gestis Cesaris*, ed. G. Crevatin (Pisa: Scuola Normale Superiore, 2003).

27. See Mirella Ferrari, "Tra libri, testi e documenti. Luogo e strumenti di scrittura personale," in *I luoghi dello scrivere da Francesco Petrarca agli albori dell'età moderna*, ed. C. Tristano, M. Calleri, L. Magionami (Spoleto: Fondazione Centro italiano di studi sull'alto Medioevo, 2006), 431–466; and, in particular on the sixteenth-century

decoration, Giulio Bodon, *Heroum imagines. La Sala dei Giganti a Padova. Un monumento della tradizione classica e della cultura antiquaria* (Venezia: Istituto Veneto di scienze, 2009).

28. For the earlier critical tradition, see Theodor E. Mommsen, "Petrarch and the Decoration of Sala Virorum illustrium in Padua," *The Art Bulletin* 34 (1952): 95–116; Maria Monica Donato, "Gli eroi romani." A different chronology is suggested by Vincenzo Fera, "I 'fragmenta de viris illustribus' di Francesco Petrarca," in *Caro Vitto: Essays in Memory of Vittore Branca,* ed. Jill Kraye, Laura Lepschy, *The Italianist* 27, 2 (2007): 101–132.

29. Vincenzo Fera, "I 'fragmenta de viris illustribus' di Francesco Petrarca," 115, quoting from the manuscript in Paris, Bibliothèque Nationale de France, lat. 6069 F, c144r. An old edition of the text, taken from cod. vat. Lat.4523, is in Domenico Rossetti, *Petrarca, Giulio Celso e Boccaccio* (Trieste: G. Marenigh, 1828), 226–232; the translation here is by SG.

30. Vincenzo Fera, "I 'fragmenta de viris illustribus' di Francesco Petrarca," 115; translation SG.

31. See Wolfgang Liebenwein, *Studiolo;* for a general overview, see A. Masson, *Le décor des Bibliothèques* (Genève: Droz, 1972).

32. Angelo Decembrio, *De politia literaria,* ed. N. Witten (München-Leipzig: Saur 2002), lib. I, ch. 3, 5, 150. On this text, see also Michael Baxandall, "A Dialogue on Art from the Court of Lionello d'Este. Angelo Decembrio's *De Politia litteraria,* pars LXVIII," *Journal of the Warburg and Courtauld Institutes* 26 (1963): 304–326.

33. Marc Fumaroli, *The Republic of Letters,* trans. from the French by Laura Vergonaud (New Haven, CT: Yale University Press, 2018), 89. The German edition was published in Augsburg by Heinrich Steiner.

34. Poggio Bracciolini, *De vera nobilitate,* ed. D. Canfora (Roma: Edizioni di Storia e Letteratura, 2002), 7; translation SG.

35. Book XXV, fol. 186v, 187r, *Filarete's Treatise on Architecture,* trans., introduction, and notes by John R. Spencer, vol. 1 (New Haven, CT: Yale University Press, 1965), 319–320; here the account is given as coming from Nicodemo Tranchedini, the ambassador at the court of Milan and Florence.

36. Stephen Campbell, "The Study, the Collection, and the Renaissance Self," in *The Cabinet of Eros: Renaissance Mythological Painting and the Studiolo of Isabella d'Este* (New Haven, CT: Yale University Press, 2004), 29–57 (29–31).

37. See Anthony Grafton, "The Vatican Library," in *Rome Reborn: The Vatican Library and Renaissance Culture,* ed. A. Grafton (Washington, DC: Library of Congress; Biblioteca Apostolica Vaticana, 1993), xi–xv; Antonio Manfredi, "La nascita della Vaticana in età umanistica da Niccolò V a Sisto IV," in *Storia della biblioteca Apostolica Vaticana,* vol. 1, *Le origini della Bibblioteca Vaticana tra Umanesimo e Rinascimento (1447–1534),* ed. A. Manfredi (Città del Vaticano: Biblioteca Apostolica Vaticana, 2010), 147–236; Joseph Connors, Angela Dressen, "Biblioteche. L'architettura e l'ordinamento

del sapere," in *Il Rinascimento italiano e l'Europa*, vol. 6, *Luoghi, spazi, architetture*, ed. D. Calabi, E. Svalduz (Treviso-Costabissara: Angelo Colla, 2010), 199–228 (206). The collection of portraits in the Vatican Library grew and became more specialized over the centuries: see Jorge Card. Mejìa, Christine Grafinger, Barbara Jatta, *I cardinali bibliotecari di Santa Romana Chiesa. La quadreria nella Biblioteca Apostolica Vaticana* (Città del Vaticano: Biblioteca Apostolica Vaticana, 2006).

38. Erasmus, *The Colloquies of Erasmus*, trans. Craig R. Thompson (Chicago: University of Chicago Press, 1965), 77; Desiderio Erasmo da Rotterdam, *I colloqui*, ed. L. D'Ascia (Torino: Loescher, 2017), vol. 1, 436–437. On *The Godly Feast*, see L. D'Ascia, "Introduzione," in *I colloqui*, 20–22.

39. Baldassare Castiglione, *The Book of the Courtier* (bk. 1, ch. 2), trans. and with an introduction by George Bull (Harmondsworth, UK: Penguin, 2004), 70.

40. See also, for further bibliography, Pasquale Rotondi, *Il palazzo ducale di Urbino* (Urbino: Istituto statale d'arte per il libro, 1950); Wolfgang Liebenwein, *Studiolo* (on the studiolo of Urbino, see 122–138); Virginia Grace Tenzer, *The Iconography of the "Studiolo" of Federico da Montefeltro in Urbino* (PhD diss., Brown University, 1985), University Microfilms International, Ann Arbor, Michigan,1985; Luciano Cheles, *Lo studiolo di Urbino. Iconografia di un microcosmo principesco* (Modena: Panini, 1991); Pier Luigi Bagatin, *Le tarsie dello Studiolo d'Urbino* (Trieste: Lint, 1993); Stephen Campbell, *The Cabinet of Eros*, 27–58; Robert Kirkbride, *Architecture and Memory: The Renaissance Studioli of Federico da Montefeltro* (New York: Columbia University Press, 2008).

41. Vespasiano da Bisticci, *The Vespasiano Memoirs, Lives of Illustrious Men of the XVth Century*, trans. William George, Emily Waters, introduction by Myron P. Gilmore (Toronto: Toronto University Press, 1997), 83–113; Vespasiano da Bisticci, "Comentario de la vita del signor Federico, duca d'Urbino," in *Le vite*, ed. A. Greco (Firenze: Istituto Nazionale di Studi sul Rinascimento, 1970), vol. 1 , 355–416 (382–383).

42. Quoted in Margaret L. King, *The Renaissance in Europe* (London: Laurence King, 2003), 118. See also "Patente a Luciano Laurana," ed. D. De Robertis, in *Scritti rinascimentali di architettura*, ed. A. Bruschi, C. Maltese, M. Tafuri, R. Bonelli (Milano: Il Polifilo, 1978), 19–22 (19–21); introductory note by A. Bruschi, 3–17.

43. See André Chastel, *Arte e umanesimo a Firenze al tempo di Lorenzo il Magnifico. Studi sul Rinascimento e sull'Umanesimo platonico* (Torino: Einaudi, 1964), 369ff.

44. Vespasiano da Bisticci, *The Vespasiano Memoirs*, 101.

45. The book has been identified as Gregory the Great's *Morals on the Book of Job*. Marcello Simonetta, "Federico da Montefeltro: The Self-Portrait of a Renaissance Man," in *Federico da Montefeltro and His Library*, ed. M. Simonetta, preface by J. J. G. Alexander (Milano: Y. Press, 2007), 18–27 (18); see *Double Portrait of Federico da Montefeltro and His Son Guidobaldo*, ibid., 102–109.

46. See Luciano Cheles, "'Topoi' e 'serio ludere' nello studiolo di Urbino," in *Federico di Montefeltro. Lo stato. Le arti. La cultura*, ed. G. Cerboni Baiardi, G. Chittolini, P. Floriani (Roma: Bulzoni, 1986), vol. 2, 269–286 (277–279).

47. See also, for further bibliography, Lina Bolzoni, *Il cuore di cristallo. Ragionamenti d'amore, poesia e ritratto nel Rinascimento* (Torino: Einaudi, 2010), 236–241. A recent study, which focuses on a dialogue in which Battista plays an important part, is Virginia Cox, "Cicero at Court. Martino Filetico's 'Iocundissimae disputationes,'" in *The Afterlife of Cicero,* ed. G. Manuwald (London: Institute of Classical Studies, School of Advanced Study, University of London, 2016), 67–81.

48. "Gloriously is he carried in noble triumph he whom the eternal fame of virtue celebrates as equal to the great leaders, fully worthy of holding the sceptre" is the inscription accompanying the triumph of Federico, while the inscription relating to the triumph of Battista reads, "She who was able to preserve measure in good fortune, decorated by the praise generated by the deeds of her great husband, is now praised by all men."

49. Sir Thomas Bodley, *The Autobiography of Sir Thomas Bodley,* introduction and notes by William Clennell (Oxford, UK: Bodleian Library, 2006).

50. Marcella Peruzzi, *Cultura potere immagine. La biblioteca di Federico da Montefeltro* (Urbino: Accademia Raffaello, 2004).

51. Giovanni Santi, *Federico di Montefeltro Duca di Urbino-Cronaca* (lib. XII, ch. LIX, 51–52, 56), ed. H. Holtzinger (Stuttgard: W. Kohlhammer, 1893), 120; translation SG.

52. Vespasiano da Bisticci, *The Vespasiano Memoirs,* 202, 104.

53. See Luigi Michelini Tocci, "La formazione della biblioteca di Federico da Montefeltro. Codici contemporanei e libri a stampa," in *Federico da Montefeltro. Lo stato. Le arti. La cultura,* vol. 3, 9–18; Martin Davies, "'Non ve n'è ignuno a stampa.' The Printed Books of Federico da Montefeltro," in *Federico da Montefeltro and His Library,* 63–80; Marcella Peruzzi, "La biblioteca di Federico da Montefeltro," in *Principi e signori. Le biblioteche nella seconda metà del Quattrocento,* ed. G. Arbizzoni, C. Bianca, M. Peruzzi (Urbino: Accademia Raffaello, 2010), 265–304.

54. "You see two sacred rooms linked by a small space; one part is dedicated to the Muses, the other to God." Lorenzo Cheles, *Lo Studiolo di Urbino,* 12.

55. See André Chastel, "Les marqueteries en trompe-l'oeil des 'studioli' d'Urbin et de Gubbio," *Art et décoration* 16 (1950): 13–17; Massimo Ferretti, "I maestri di prospettiva," in *Storia dell'arte italiana,* ed. F. Zeri (Torino: Einaudi, 1982), 488, 516–524, 577–585.

56. See the examples given by Fabrizio Fenucci and Marcello Simonetta, "The Studiolo in the 'Cube.' A Visual Guide," in *Federico da Montefeltro and His Library,* 88–99.

57. See Pier Luigi Bagatin, *Le tarsie dello Studiolo d'Urbino* (Trieste: LINT, 1993), 13; and Lorenzo Cheles, *Lo Studiolo di Urbino,* 69–70, fig. 69.

58. One intarsio door did in fact represent a labyrinth.

59. Laurentius Schrader, *Monumentorum Italiae quae hoc nostro saeculo et a christianis posita sunt libri quatuor* (Helmstadt: Iacobi Lucij Transyluani,1592), 283–284.

60. *Lo Studiolo del Duca. Il ritorno degli Uomini Illustri alla Corte di Urbino*, ed. A. Marchi (Milano: Skira, 2015).

61. See Virginia Grace Tenzer, *The Iconography of the "Studiolo" of Federico da Montefeltro in Urbino:* the figures portrayed "exhibit a broad spectrum in their attire, ages, postures, gestures, facial types, and even their size" (95), while the famous men and women who feature in Andrea del Castagno's fresco in Villa Carducci di Legnaia, carried out 1448 and 1451 for the Gonfaloniere di Giustizia Filippo Carducci, are all the same height and display little variety in their poses. See Maria Monica Donato, "Gli eroi romani tra storia ed *exemplum*. I primi cicli umanistici di Uomini famosi," in *Memoria dell'antico nell'arte italiana*, vol. 2, *I generi e i temi ritrovati*, ed. S. Settis (Torino: Einaudi, 1985), 97–152.

62. Lorenzo Cheles, *Lo Studiolo di Urbino*, 39.

63. Stephen Campbell, *The Cabinet of Eros*, 45: "The very existence of the image of Moses calls into question the text he displays. . . . The implication is that the image has a place in the enterprise of reading, that images too can be read, and can even subsume and displace the function of the word."

64. See Novella Macola, *Sguardi e scritture. Figure con libro nella ritrattistica italiana della prima metà del Cinquecento* (Venezia: Istituto Veneto di Scienze Lettere ed Arti, 2007).

65. Lamberto Donati, "Le fonti iconografiche di alcuni manoscritti urbinati della Biblioteca Vaticana," *La Bibliofilia* 60–61 (1958–1959): 49.

66. See Lorenzo Cheles, *Lo Studiolo di Urbino*, 40, quoting André Chastel, "Sémantique de l'index," *Storia dell'arte* 38–40 (1980): 415–418.

67. On the iconography of gestures, see Jean-Claude Schmitt, *Il gesto nel Medioevo* (Bari: Laterza, 1999); C. Frugoni, *La voce delle immagini. Pillole iconografiche dal Medioevo* (Torino: Einaudi, 2010). Lorenzo Cheles reads the gestures of the illustrious men in the Studiolo in the light of Quintilian (*Lo Studiolo di Urbino*, 40–41) and points out, with reference to Boethius, that his gesture was one commonly associated with the personification of mathematics (51n50).

68. See Mary Carruthers, *The Book of Memory: A Study of Memory in Medieval Culture* (Cambridge: Cambridge University Press, 1990); Carruthers, "In memoriae suae bibliotheca. Lecteurs et art de la mémoire dans l'Occident medieval," in *Des Alexandries II. Les métamorphoses du lecteur*, ed. I. C. Jacob (Paris: Bibliothèque Nationale de France, 2003), 221–232. Memory is also one of the virtues that Vespasiano da Bisticci praises in Federico, and mnemonic exercises formed part of the didactic method adopted by Vittorino da Feltre.

69. Vespasiano da Bisticci, *The Vespasiano Memoirs*, 99.

70. There are interesting similarities, I feel, to be found in an entirely different context: the great fresco dedicated to the triumph of Catholic doctrine according to the interpretation of St. Thomas Aquinas, which was painted by Andrea di Bonaiuto, probably in 1366, in the Chapter House of the Convent of Santa Maria Novella in Florence (which later became the "Cappellone degli Spagnoli"). It features a complex system of encyclopedic correspondences; in the lower band are a gallery of illustrious personages, representing the sacred and profane sciences: Cicero, Aristotle, Ptolemy, and Euclid for the profane sciences, among the arts of the Trivium and the Quadrivium, Boethius and Augustine among the exponents of the sacred sciences, are all figures we also find in the studiolo. Almost all of them hold a book, either open or closed, and are characterized by a particular gesture, although this is less expressive than in their Urbino counterparts. See Serena Romano, "Due affreschi del Cappellone degli Spagnoli. Problemi iconologici," *Storia dell'arte* 28 (1976): 181–213; I. P. Grossi, "'Arti' e 'Scienze' nel 'Trionfo di S. Tommaso' di Andrea di Bonaiuto. Ipotesi di interpretazione," *Memorie domenicane* 8–9 (1977–1978): 341–353; Paul F. Watson, "The Spanish Chapel: Portraits of Poets or a Portrait of Christian Order?," *Memorie domenicane* 11 (1980): 471–487; *Santa Maria Novella. La basilica, il convento, i chiostri monumentali,* ed. U. Baldini (Firenze: Nardini, 1981).

71. The text of the inscriptions is in A. Bernardini, "Regesto. Le iscrizioni elogiative degli Uomini illustri," in *Lo Studiolo del Duca,* 147–150.

72. On Cicero's place in the studiolo and on the relationship between philosophy and power, see Virginia Cox, "Cicero at Court," 60–65.

73. See Virginia Grace Tenzer, *The Iconography of the "Studiolo" of Federico da Montefeltro in Urbino,* 249, 321n140; "in atto umile / si sedea Tolomeo, e speculava / i ciel con intelletto assai sottile, / riguardando una spera che li stava ferma davanti," in Giovanni Boccaccio, *Amorosa Visione,* trans. Robert Hollander, Timothy Hampton, Margherita Frankel, with an introduction by Vittore Branca (Hanover, NH: University Press of New England, 1986), 21.

74. See Iolanda Ventura, entry on Pietro d'Abano, in *Dizionario biografico degli italiani* (Roma: Istituto della Enciclopedia italiana, 2015), 437–441.

75. Vespasiano da Bisticci, *The Vespasiano Memoirs,* 100 (slightly adapted).

76. See Wolfgang Liebenwein, *Studiolo,* 132.

77. On the relationship between Federico and Bessarion, see Concetta Bianca, "L'accademia del Bessarione tra Roma e Urbino," in *Federico di Montefeltro. Lo stato. Le arti. La cultura,* vol. 3, 61–79. Bessarion's appearance and significance in Piero della Francesca's *Flagellation* have been much discussed. See Carlo Ginzburg, *Indagini su Piero. Il Battesimo, il ciclo di Arezzo, la Flagellazione di Urbino* (Torino: Einaudi, 1982); Silvia Ronchey, *L'enigma di Piero. L'ultimo bizantino e la crociata fantasma nella rivelazione di un grande quadro* (Milano: Rizzoli, 2006).

78. See Eugenio Garin, *L'educazione in Europa 1400–1600. Problemi e programmi* (Roma-Bari: Laterza, 1976), 136–141; *Vittorino da Feltre e la sua scuola. Umanesimo, pedagogia, arti,* ed. Nella Giannetto (Firenze: Olschki, 1986).

79. See Lotte Labowsky, *Bessarion's Library and the Biblioteca Marciana: Six Early Inventories* (Roma: Edizioni di Storia e Letteratura, 1979), 147–149.

80. See Lina Bolzoni, *Poesia e ritratto nel Rinascimento.*

81. See also, for further bibliography, the introductions and the commentary on the text in Angiolo Gambaro, preface to Erasmus, *Il Ciceroniano o dello stile migliore* (Brescia: La Scuola, 1965), ix–cxii; Betty I. Knott, introduction to Erasmus, *Ciceronianus,* in *Literary and Educational Writings,* ed. C. R. Thompson, vol. 6 in *Collected Works* (Toronto: Toronto University Press, 1986), 324–336; Francesco Bausi, "Introduzione. Le astuzie del batavo," in Desiderio Erasmo da Rotterdam, *Il Ciceroniano,* ed. F. Bausi, D. Canfora, in collaboration with E. Tinelli (Torino: Loescher, 2016), 7–59. See, further, Hugh Macrae Richmond, "Personal Identity and Literary Personae: A Study in Historical Psychology," *PMLA* 90 (1975): 9–22; George W. Pigman, "Imitation and the Renaissance Sense of the Past: The Reception of Erasmus' *Ciceronianus,*" *Journal of Medieval and Renaissance Studies* 9 (1979): 155–177; Pigman, "Versions of Imitation in the Renaissance," *Renaissance Quarterly* 32 (1980): 1–32; John F. D'Amico, *Renaissance Humanism in Papal Rome* (Baltimore: Johns Hopkins University Press, 1983); Marc Fumaroli, *L'âge de l'éloquence. Rhétorique et "res literaria" de la Renaissance au seuil de l'époque classique* (Genève: Droz, 1980), 37–46, 77–115; Jacques Chomarat, *Grammaire et rhétorique chez Erasme* (Paris: Les Belles Lettres, 1981); Luca D'Ascia, *Erasmo e l'Umanesimo romano* (Firenze: Olschki, 1991). For a more general view of Erasmus's role in European culture, see Carlo Ossola, *Erasmo nel notturno d'Europa* (Milano: Vita e pensiero, 2015).

82. Erasmus, *Ciceronianus,* 360. See also Desiderio Erasmo da Rotterdam, *Il Ciceroniano o dello stile migliore* (ed. A. Gambaro), 61–63; and Erasmo da Rotterdam, *Il Ciceroniano* (ed. F. Bausi, D. Canfora). The version of the myth of Helen used by Erasmus goes back to the *Palinody* of Stesichorus.

83. Erasmus, *Ciceronianus,* 346.

84. Ibid., 441.

85. Ibid., 375.

86. Ibid. See also the note on p. 323 of the edition by Bausi and Canfora.

87. "Si minus respondet effigies, mirum non est. Non enim sum is qui fui ante annos quinque," in Erasmus, *Opus epistolarum,* ed. P. S. Allen (Oxford, UK: Clarendon Press, 1906–1958), vol. 6, no. 1729, 371, quoted in Erwin Panofsky, "Erasmus and the Visual Arts," *Journal of the Warburg and Courtauld Institutes* 32 (1969): 200–227 (204).

88. Lisa Jardine, *Erasmus, Man of Letters: The Construction of Charisma in Print* (Princeton, NJ: Princeton University Press, 1993). Another extremely interesting ex-

ample is a medal cast in 1519 by Matsys, displaying the following motto in Greek: "my writings show the best likeness" (Panofsky, "Erasmus and the Visual Arts," 214–217).

89. See Lorne Campbell, Margaret Mann Phillips, Hubertus Schulte Herbrüggen, J. B. Trapp, "Quinten Metsys, Desiderius Erasmus, Peter Gillis and Thomas More," *Burlington Magazine* 120 (1978): 716–725 and 221 (1979): 434–437; Linda Klinger Aleci, "Images of Identity: Italian Portrait Collection of the Fifteenth and Sixteenth Centuries," in *The Images of the Individual: Portraits in the Renaissance,* ed. N. Mann and L. Syson (London: British Museum Press, 1998), 67–79 (70); Peter van der Coelen, *Images of Erasmus* (Rotterdam: Museum Boijmans Van Beuningen, 2008), 50–51; *Renaissance Faces: Van Eyck to Titian,* ed. L. Campbell, M. Falomir, J. Fletcher, L. Syson (London: National Gallery, 2008), 168.

90. Erasmus, *Opus epistolarum,* ed. P. S. Allen (Oxford, UK: Clarendon Press, 1906–1958), vol. 3, no. 684, letter from Thomas More to Peter Gilles, 105. See Lorne Campbell, Margaret Mann Phillips, Hubertus Schulte Herbrüggen, J. B. Trapp, "Quinten Metsys," 717: the epigrams were published in 1518 (Basel: Froben, August 1518) in a collection of letters by Erasmus, *Auctarium selectarum epistolarum,* preceded by a rubric, probably compiled by Beatus Rhenanus, the editor of the collection, who clarifies More's words: in the two portraits, Erasmus is about to write his *Paraphrase to St. Paul's Letter to the Romans,* and Gilles is holding a letter from More. Therefore the earliest copy of the portrait is that in the queen's collection, in Hampton Court, and the earliest portrait of Gilles is that belonging to Lord Radnor, in Longford Castle.

91. See Simon Goldhill, "Learning Greek Is Heresy! Resisting Erasmus," in *Who Needs Greek? Contests in the Cultural History of Hellenism* (Cambridge: Cambridge University Press, 2002), 14–59.

92. See Lina Bolzoni, "Il gioco paradossale dell'utopia fra antico e moderno, fra parole e immagini," in *Dall'antico al moderno. Immagini del classico nelle letterature europee,* ed. P. Boitani, E. Di Rocco (Roma: Edizioni di Storia e letteratura, 2015), 121–134.

93. Erasmus, *Opus epistolarum,* vol. 3, no. 683, 103, letter to Erasmus; no. 684, 105–107, letter to Peter Gilles.

94. Ibid.; translation SG.

95. See also, for further bibliography, Paolo Giovio, *Scritti d'arte. Lessico ed ecfrasi,* ed. S. Maffei (Pisa: Scuola Normale Superiore, 1999), 111–170; and Franco Minonzio, "'Elogi degli uomini illustri.' Il 'Museo di carta' di Paolo Giovio," in Paolo Giovio, *Elogi degli uomini illustri,* ed. F. Minonzio (Torino: Einaudi, 2006), xix–lxxxvii.

96. Camillo is discussed further in chapter 4. See Lina Bolzoni, *La stanza della memoria,* 203–209; Lina Bolzoni, introduction to Giulio Camillo, *L'Idea del theatro con L'idea dell'eloquenza, il De transmutatione e altri testi inediti,* ed. L. Bolzoni (Milano: Adelphi, 2015), 9–127.

97. Paolo Giovio, *Epistularum pars altera,* ed. G. G. Ferrero (Roma: Società Storica Comense e Istituto Poligrafico dello Stato, 1958), vol. 2, 4; translation SG.

98. Paolo Giovio, *Elogi degli uomini illustri,* 5–6. For the Latin text, see Paolo Giovio, *Elogia virorum illustrium,* ed. R. Meregazzi (Roma: Istituto Poligrafico dello Stato, 1972), 33.

99. Paolo Giovio, *Epistularum pars altera,* 4.

100. See Patricia Eichel-Lojkine, *Le siècle des grands hommes. Les recueils de Vies d'hommes illsutres avec portraits du XVI^{éme} siècle* (Louvain-Paris: Editions Peeters, 2001); Tommaso Casini, *Ritratti parlanti, collezionismo e biografie illustrate nei secoli XVI e XVII* (Firenze: Edifir, 2004). "Print publication undoubtedly enhances the general recognition of the identity of the author as the creator and owner of the text. This recognition is reflected in the practice (which has been dated from 1479) of including, on the title page or elsewhere, portraits of the author which became increasingly true to life"; Brian Richardson, *Printing, Writers and Readers in Renaissance Italy* (Cambridge: Cambridge University Press, 1999), 101. See Francesco Barberi, *Il frontespizio nel libro italiano del Quattrocento e del Cinquecento* (Milano: il Polifilo, 1969); Giuseppina Zappella, *Il ritratto nel libro italiano del Cinquecento* (Milano: Editrice Bibliografica, 1988).

101. See Lina Bolzoni, "Sulle soglie del testo. Un autoritratto per immagini nelle prime edizioni del Furioso," in *Galassia Ariosto. Il modello editoriale dell'Orlando Furioso dal libro illustrato al web,* ed. L. Bolzoni (Roma: Donzelli, 2017), 3–34.

102. See also, for further bibliographical indications, the essays on Naudé in *Littératures classiques* 66, 2 (2008): Armand Colin, "L'idée des bibliothèques à l'âge classique"; Bernard Teyssandier, "L'ethos érudit dans l' *Avis pour dresser une bibliothèque* de Gabriel Naudé," 115–131; Lorenzo Bianchi, "L' *Avis pour dresser une bibliothèque* de Gabriel Naudé. Prolégomènes pour une bibliothèque libertine?," 133–142. See also Estelle Boeuf, *La Bibliothèque parisienne de Gabriel Naudé en 1630. Les lectures d'un libertin érudit* (Genève: Librairie Droz, 2007); Anna Lisa Schino, *Battaglie libertine. La vita e le opere di G. Naudé* (Firenze: Le lettere, 2014).

103. Gabriel Naudé, *Advice on Establishing a Library,* introduction by Archer Taylor (Westport, CT: Greenwood Press, 1976), 5.

104. Ibid., ch. 9, 72.

105. Thirteen years later, in 1640, Naudé wrote some epigrams to accompany the portraits in the library of Cassiano Dal Pozzo, his Roman patron (*Epigrammata in virorum literatorum imagines, quas illustrissimus eques Cassianus a Puteo sua in biblioteca dedicavit*): see Gabriel Naudé, *Epigrammi per i ritratti della biblioteca di Cassiano del Pozzo,* ed. G. Ernst (Pisa: F. Serra, 2009).

106. See also the passage in which Naudé explains that one should "consider that libraries are neither built nor esteemed but for the service and benefit which one may receive from them, and therefore one should disregard such books and manuscripts as are valuable only for their antiquity, pictures, illuminations, bindings and other minor considerations" (*Advice on Establishing a Library,* ch. 5, 55).

107. Charles-Augustin Sainte-Beuve, *Portraits littéraires* (Paris: Garnier, 1862), vol. 2, 469, quoted in Vittoria Lacchini, introduction to Naudé, *Avvertenze per la costituzione di una biblioteca,* ed. Vittoria Lacchini (Bologna: Clueb, 1994), ix–xlii (xi), who also points out that Sainte-Beuve himself was conservator at the Biliothèque Mazarine.

108. Guy Patin, *L'esprit de Guy Patin, tiré de ses conversations, de son cabinet, de ses lettres et de ses autres ouvrages, avec son portrait historique* (Amsterdam: Schelten, 1709), 70, quoted in Marc Fumaroli, *The Republic of Letters,* trans. from the French by Laura Vergonaud (New Haven, CT: Yale University Press, 2018), 89.

109. Tullio Pericoli, *L'anima del volto* (Milano: Bompiani, 2005), 34–35.

4. Reading, Writing, and the Construction of the Self

1. See Martin McLaughlin, *Literary Imitation in the Italian Renaissance: The Theory and Practice of Literary Imitation in Italy from Dante to Bembo* (Oxford, UK: Clarendon Press, 1995); Amedeo Quondam, *Rinascimento e classicismo. Materiali per l'analisi del sistema culturale di Antico regime* (Roma: Bulzoni, 1999) and *Rinascimento e classicismi. Forme e metamorfosi della modernità* (Bolona: Il Mulino, 2013); Lina Bolzoni, "La formazione del canone nel Cinquecento. Criteri di valore e stile personale," in *Il lettore creativo. Percorsi cinquecenteschi fra memoria, gioco, scrittura* (Napoli: Guida, 2012), 269–290. The texts may be found in *Le epistole "De imitatione" di Giovanfrancesco Pico Della Mirandola e di Pietro Bembo,* ed. G. Santangelo (Firenze: Olschki, 1954).

2. See Lina Bolzoni, "Imitazione dell'antico e creazione del nuovo. Il ruolo della memoria nel dibattito fra Quattro e Cinquecento," in *Classicismo e sperimentalismo nella letteratura italiana tra Quattro e Cinquecento,* ed. R. Pestarino, A. Menozzi, E. Niccolai (Pavia: Pavia University Press, 2016), 1–18.

3. On Pico, see Charles B. Schmitt, *Gianfrancesco Pico della Mirandola (1469–1533) and His Critique of Aristotle* (The Hague: Martinus Nijhoff, 1967); Lucia Pappalardo, *Gianfrancesco Pico della Mirandola. Fede, immaginazione, scetticismo* (Turnhout: Brepols, 2014).

4. *Le epistole "De imitatione,"* 28; translation SG.

5. Ibid., 27.

6. Ibid., 29.

7. Ibid., 53.

8. Without a sure guide, argued Cortese, one stumbles around aimlessly, among the briers ("devius inter spinas volutatur"), while he who places his trust in Cicero "without difficulty and unerringly reaches his chosen destination, following the path he had determined upon." Pietro Bembo, *Epistola de imitation,* in *Prosatori latini del Quattrocento,* ed. E. Garin (Milano-Napoli: Ricciardi, 1952), 910–911; translation SG.

9. Seneca, *Letters on Ethics to Lucilius,* trans. A.A. Long and Margaret Graver (Chicago: University of Chicago Press, 2017), 26.

10. See Giulio Camillo, *L'idea del theatro con L'idea dell'eloquenza, il De transmutatione e altri testi inediti*, ed. L. Bolzoni (Milano: Adelphi, 2015).

11. Giulio Camillo, *Trattato dell'imitazione*, in *Trattati di poetica e retorica del Cinquecento*, ed. B. Weinberg, vol. 1 (Bari: Laterza, 1970), 161–185 (178–179).

12. I am naturally referring to Harold Bloom's *The Anxiety of Influence: A Theory of Poetry* (Oxford: Oxford University Press, 1973).

13. Giulio Camillo, *L'idea dell'eloquenza*, in *L'idea del theatro*, 243–280 (253); translation SG.

14. Terence Cave underscores how Erasmus envisages a role for the reader and assigns them a space beyond the confines of the text, while others, such as Dolet or Scaliger, seek the "perfect or near-perfect; the reader should, as it were, disappear or be effaced in favour of the paradigm text." Terence Cave, "Representations of Reading in the Renaissance: Readers in the Text-Reading and Imitation; Montaigne and Reading," in *Retrospectives: Essays in Literature, Poetics and Cultural History* (London: Legenda, 2009), 10–47 (13).

15. *Lettera di Angelo Poliziano*, in *Prosatori latini*, 902–903; translation SG. See Jean Lecointe, *L'idéal et la différence. La perception de la personnalité littéraire à la Reniassance* (Genève: Droz, 1993), 325–326, 409, 450; Kathy Eden, "'Familiaritas' in Erasmian Rhetoric and Hermeneutics," in *The Renaissance Rediscovery of Intimacy* (Chicago: University of Chicago Press, 2012), 73–95.

16. *Le epistole "De imitatione,"* 70; translation SG.

17. Erasmus, *Ciceronianus*, in *Literary and Educational Writings*, ed. C. R. Thompson, vol. 6 in *Collected Works* (Toronto: Toronto University Press, 1986), 374.

18. Ibid., 396–97.

19. Ibid., 440.

20. See Terence Cave, "Imitation," in *The Cornucopian Text: Problems of Writing in the French Renaissance* (Oxford, UK: Clarendon Press, 1979), 35–77; Eden, "'Familiaritas' in Erasmian Rhetoric and Hermeneutics," 84–85. On hospitality and its complex nature, see Jacques Derrida, Anne Dufourmantelle, *Of Hospitality*, trans. Rachel Bowlby (Stanford, CA: Stanford University Press, 2000).

21. Erasmus, *Ciceronianus*, 440.

22. Ibid., 441.

23. Étienne Dolet, *Dialogus de imitatione ciceroniana adversus Desiderium Erasmum Roterodamum, pro Christophoro Longolio*, ed. E. V. Telle (Genève: Droz, 1974), 89; translation SG.

24. Ibid., 90.

25. Erasmus, *Ciceronianus*, 383.

26. Ibid., 430.

27. Ibid., 394.

28. For a reconsideration of Erasmus's accusations against the Ciceronians, see John Monfasani, "Renaissance Ciceronianism and Christianity," in *Humanisme et église*

en Italie et en France méridionale (XVe siècle–milieu du XVIe siècle), ed. P. Gilli (Roma: École Française de Rome, 2004), 362–379.

29. See Kathy Eden, "'Familiaritas' in Erasmian Rhetoric and Hermeneutics," 89–95.

30. Erasmus, *Enchiridion*, in *Spiritualia*, ed. J. W. O'Malley, vol. 66 in *Collected Works* (Toronto: Toronto University Press, 1988), 72.

31. Erasmus, *The Paraclesis*, in *The New Testament Scholarship of Erasmus*, ed. Robert D. Sider, vol. 41 in *Collected Works* (Toronto: Toronto University Press, 2019), 410, 417.

32. Ibid., 417–418, 422.

33. Michel Jeanneret, "Je lis, donc je suis. Herméneutique et conscience de soi à la Renaissance," in *Émergence du sujet. De l'"Amant vert" au "Misanthrope,"* ed. Olivier Pot (Genève: Droz, 2005), 151–169 (163); translation SG.

5. Machiavelli's Letter to Vettori

Epigraph: Niccolò Machiavelli, *The Mandrake*, Prologue, ll. 46–56, in *Ariosto's* The Supposes, *Machiavelli's* The Mandrake, *Intronati's* The Deceived: *Three Italian Renaissance Comedies*, ed. Christopher Cairns, trans. Jennifer Lorch, Kenneth and Laura Richards, Nerida Newbigin (Lewiston, NY: Edwin Mellen Press, 1996), 182.

1. The traditional image of Machiavelli's "exile" is significantly revised by William J. Connell's "La lettera di Machiavelli a Vettori del 10 dicembre 1513," *Archivio storico italiano* 171 (2013): 665–723; republished in *Machiavelli nel Rinascimento italiano* (Milano: Franco Angeli, 2015), 51–93.

2. Slightly adapted from Niccolò Machiavelli, *The Letters of Machiavelli*, ed. and trans. Allan Gilbert (New York: Capricorn Books, 1961), 142. Niccolò Machiavelli, *Lettere*, ed. F. Gaeta, in *Opere*, vol. 3 (Torino: UTET, 1984), 426. See also Niccolò Machiavelli, *Lettere a Francesco Vettori e a Francesco Guicciardini (1513–1527)*, ed. G. Inglese (Milano: Rizzoli, 1989); Niccolò Machiavelli, *Dieci lettere private*, ed. G. Bardazzi (Roma: Salerno, 1992).

3. Giorgio Barberi Squarotti, "Narrazione e sublimazione. Le lettere di Machiavelli," in *Machiavelli o la scelta della letteratura* (Roma: Bulzoni, 1987), 63–95; Werner Gundersheimer, "San Casciano, 1513: A Machiavellian Moment Reconsidered," *Journal of Medieval and Renaissance Studies* 17 (1987): 41–58.

4. Michele Mari, "Il centauro," in *Fantasmagonia* (Torino: Einaudi, 2012), 89–90.

5. Giulio Ferroni, "Le 'cose vane' nelle Lettere di Machiavelli," *Rassegna della letteratura italiana* 76 (1972): 215–264; on the tradition of letters between friends, see John M. Najemy, *Between Friends: Discourses of Power and Desire in the Machiavelli-Vettori Letters of 1513–1515* (Princeton, NJ: Princeton University Press, 1993), which calls attention to the fact that Machiavelli and Vettori's epistolary constitutes "a collaborative text" (10).

6. John M. Najemy, *Between Friends* (henceforth *BF*), 96.

7. Letter from Vettori to Machiavelli dated 15 March 1513: "It grieves me that I was unable to help you as your faith in me deserved, and I was very upset when your brother Totto sent me the news and I could do nothing to help. I did so when the new pope was created, and I asked for no other favour than your liberation, which I dearly wished had happened sooner" (*BF*, 96, with integrations).

8. Machiavelli, *The Letters of Machiavelli*, 104, 107.

9. Ibid., 105–107. See also *BF*, 111n23: the doves (colombe), "which can mean either lovers or sweet innocents, or, as in this case, perhaps both, are obviously the boys to whom Donato was so devoted, and the opening of another shop (bottega) . . . must refer to the recent expansion of Donato's erotic activities that Machiavelli reports."

10. Machiavelli, *The Letters of Machiavelli*, 371.

11. *BF*, 109ff.; Inglese, in a note to his edition of Machiavelli's letters, *Lettere a Francesco Vettori*, points out an echo from Strambotto: "io spero, e lo sperar cresce 'l tormento;/ io piango, e il pianger ciba il lasso core. . . . così sperando, piango, rido e ardo/ e paura ho di ciò che io odo e guardo."

12. This is a point made in Federico Baricci's paper "'Però se alcuna volta io rido o canto': Le citazioni letterarie nel carteggio Machiavelli-Vettori," given at my course at the Scuola Normale in 2013.

13. Machiavelli, *The Letters of Machiavelli*,104.

14. Ibid., 141.

15. Given the context, Martelli believes that Machiavelli is thinking of the Dante of the *Rime* and/or the *Vita nuova*. Mario Martelli, "Machiavelli politico amante poeta," *Interpres* 2, 17 (1998): 211–256; John M. Najemy suggests that the idea of exile may also play a part in his choice of love poets (*BF*, 232–234).

16. Anthony Grafton, "L'umanista come lettore," in *Storia della lettura nel mondo occidentale*, ed. G. Cavallo, R. Chartier (Bari: Laterza, 1998), 199–242 (in particular 199–201). On the significance of the different format of books, see Armando Petrucci, "Alle orgini del libro moderno. Libri da banco, libri da bisaccia, libretti da mano," in *Libri, scrittori e pubblico nell'Europa moderna*, ed. A. Petrucci (Bari-Roma: Laterza, 1979), 137–156. Giovanni Bardazzi has pointed out that Ovid, who is second in Machiavelli's list, actually occupies a position of great importance, for example, in terms of recognizing one's own love torments in those read, as in *Amores*, II, I, 5–10. Giovanni Bardazzi, introduction to Machiavelli, *Dieci lettere private*, 19. On Machiavelli as a reader of Xenophon as well as on Machiavelli's ways of reading, see Lucio Biasiori, *Nello scrittoio di Machiavelli. Il* Principe *e la* Ciropedia *di Senofonte* (Roma: Carocci, 2017).

17. For all the preceding, see Machiavelli, *The Letters of Machiavelli*, 141–142.

18. *BF*, 215 (with minimal changes).

19. The metaphor of card play returns in a letter by Vettori dated 3 December 1514: "it is true," Vettori says, "that I have not helped you, but this is because I have not even been in a position to help myself"; he then invites Machiavelli once

more to play, quoting Horace: "although you are 'spectatus satis, et donatus iam rude, quaeram iterum te antiquo includere ludo,' I seek to enlist you in the old game, even though you have made enough appearances and have already been appointed the foil" (*BF,* 296) Once again literary memory underpins the code used by the two friends, this time with a theatrical inversion of their roles. Vettori readapts the opening of Horace's *Epistles* (I, 1, 2–3), "Prima dicte mihi, summa dicende Camena, / spectatum satis et donatum, iam rude quaeris, / Mecenas, iterum antiquo me includere ludo?" Maecenas's invitation was evidently that Horace should return to writing poetry; a little later, the game (*ludus*) is figuratively linked to the sport of the gladiators. We see therefore Vettori / Maecenas once again inviting his friend Machiavelli to return to a game that is in this context primarily that of writing (he asks for his opinion on the political situation, stating that he intends to show this to the pope), but there is also, very probably, an underlying reference to the game of politics.

20. Machiavelli, *Lettere,* 420; translation SG.

21. Ibid., 424; translation SG.

22. *BF,* 217.

23. *BF,* 217.

24. Machiavelli, *The Letters of Machiavelli,* 143.

25. Machiavelli, *Lettere,* 368.

26. Inglese points out the contrast between the "solemn and linear" language of the dialogue with the ancients; however, as soon as the theme becomes political, "the language ripples with irony, creating a certain distance": "Et se vi piacque mai alcuno mio ghiribizo." Introduction to Machiavelli, *Lettere a Francesco Vettori,* 5–55 (27).

27. *BF,* 220n8; the quote is generally linked to Seneca, *Epist. Ad Luc.,* CVII, 16. Larosa has suggested it is a quotation from *Carmen* I, 22 (Ad Bernardum Carapham de malis atque calamitate Neapolis) by the Florentine humanist Pietro Crinito (1474–1507), whose works Vettori says he had read and where the exact sentence is to be found. Stella Larosa, *Una 'metamorfosi ridicola.' Studi e schede sulle lettere comiche di Nicolò Machiavelli* (Manziana: Vecchiarelli, 2008), 192; see also the chapter on *Le fonti,* 87–161, on literary sources and their use in Machiavelli's letters.

28. Giulio Ferroni, describes it as "una disillusione signorilmente *blasée*" ("Le 'cose vane' nelle Lettere di Machiavelli," 236).

29. Among the models of "the narration of one's day" that Machiavelli may have in mind, Bausi suggests there may be a text we have already discussed, Boccaccio's *Consolatoria a Pino de' Rossi,* which was, he observes, much known in fifteenth-century Florence, as a letter of comfort in exile. Machiavelli carries out a sort of "reversal of the point of view and upending of the parts, revisiting, as it were, Boccaccio's idyllic portrayal of country life through the dark and bitter vision of the exile Pino de' Rossi." Francesco Bausi, *Machiavelli* (Roma: Salerno Editrice, 2005), 336.

30. Machiavelli, *The Letters of Machiavelli,* 107.

31. Ibid., 104.

32. *BF,* 105–106. "Because of such deficiencies, and for no other crime, / we are lost, and, injured only in this way, / we live without hope in desire."

33. The translation of this passage in *The Letters,* 142, is misleading: the Italian is "e poiché Dante dice che non fa scienza sanza lo ritenere lo avere inteso"; the translation here is by SG.

34. Machiavelli, *The Letters of Machiavelli,*140.

35. *Geta e Birria,* in *Novelle italiane. Il Quattrocento,* ed. G. Chiarini (Milano: Garzanti, 1982), 31–85; see xi–xiv of the introduction.

36. *BF,* 227; see also John M. Najemy, "Machiavelli and Geta. Men of Letters," in *Machiavelli and the Discourse of Literature,* ed. A. Ascoli and V. Kahn (Ithaca, NY: Cornell University Press, 1993), 53–79, where, among other things, the author stresses how the reference to Geta transforms the dialogue with Vettori into a confusion of voices, thereby helping Machiavelli to distance himself from his own self and from the solemn story he has told in the letter. "The purpose of that distance was that it allowed him to see all three—self, book, and story—as inevitably implicated in those textual migrations and transformations, in the indeterminacy and mutability to which 'uomini literati' are specially vulnerable" (79).

37. "Geta's person was disfigured, / black as the Ethiopian or the Indian, / he smelled like he had the ringworm, and on top of that he had a crown / of thin hair of a very strange colour; / his cheeks and nose, if truth be told, / came down to his nose, and with a rogueish mien / he eyed people with his red and liquid eyes / which seemed to roll back into his head, satiated with wine" (*Geta e Birria,* 12). In other words, "Giotto would have forsaken his own art before he had succeeded in painting his true form. / Full of vice he was, and with ardent frenzy / like the swine gave in to his lust" (13, 5–8). He had "a striking member / endowed with more power than any planet in the sky / to excite love for his ugly shape" (14, 5–8; translations SG).

38. Ezio Raimondi, "Il sasso del politico," in *Politica e commedia* (Bologna: Il Mulino 1972), 37–43; Machiavelli, *The Letters of Machiavelli,* 143.

39. Ezio Raimondi, "Il sasso del politico," 42–43.

40. Machiavelli, *The Letters of Machiavelli,* 133.

41. See Najemy's interpretation of this passage, which refers to Hanna Fenichel Pitkin, *Fortune Is a Woman: Gender and Politics in the Thought of Niccolò Machiavelli* (Berkeley: University of California Press, 1984), 2–51, and discusses Machiavelli's identification with the fox, a jittery, volatile animal, while the lion is strong, stable, and fearsome but somehow also vulnerable: "There is a sense in which these images encapsulate the underlying dynamic of the correspondence up to this point" (*BF,* 169). But the use of the tale also suggests, as Najemy argues, that Machiavelli has tired of the stance he has hitherto assumed and wishes to have a more authoritative voice.

42. *BF,* 166.

43. *BF,* 136.

44. Giorgio Inglese, *Per Machiavelli. L'arte dello stato, la cognizione delle storie* (Roma: Carocci, 2006), 38.

45. See Gennaro Sasso, *Niccolò Machiavelli* (Bologna: Il Mulino, 1993), vol. 1, 341–349.

46. Machiavelli, *Lettere,* 419; translation SG.

47. Letters dated 24 December 1513 and 18 January 1514 (ibid., 432–435, 438–440). See the comments by Bardazzi in his introduction to Machiavelli, *Dieci lettere private,* 18–36; and Stella Larosa, *Una 'metamorfosi ridicola,'* 44–65.

48. Machiavelli, *Lettere,* 488; translated in James B. Atkinson and Davis Sices, *Machiavelli and His Friends: Their Personal Correspondence* (DeKalb: Northern Illinois University Press, 1996), 311.

49. Machiavelli, *The Letters of Machiavelli,* 185.

50. *BF,* 117.

51. Writing from a critical perspective that engages in the "emotional turn," Nicole Hochner suggests that a strong emotional dimension is also present in Machiavelli's political writings and that "the crucial emotion in Machiavelli's political world is not necessarily fear, but rather love"; she distinguishes, however, between this form of love and erotic love. Nicole Hochner, "Machiavelli: Love and the Economy of Emotions," *Italian Culture* 32, 2 (2014): 122–137 (124).

52. Machiavelli, *The Letters of Machiavelli,* 105, with some integrations.

53. Ibid., 164.

54. Ibid.,165.

55. *BF,* 123, 237.

6. Montaigne's Tower

Epigraph: Francisco de Quevedo, *Selected Poetry of Francisco de Quevedo,* ed. and trans. Christopher Johnson (Chicago: University of Chicago Press, 2009), 57.

1. The inscriptions are usually published in the appendix to the *Essais:* see "Sentences peintes et autres inscriptions de la bibliothèque de Montaigne," text prepared by Alain Legros, in Montaigne, *Les Essais,* ed. J. Balsamo, M. Magnien, C. Magnien Simonin (Paris: Gallimard, 2007), 1309–1316, in particular 1315–1316. The English translation is from Jean Starobinski, *Montaigne in Motion,* trans. Arthur Goldhammer (Chicago: University of Chicago Press, 1985), 311n28. On the inscriptions and paintings that decorated the tower, see Alain Legros, *Essais sur poutres. Peintures et inscriptions chez Montaigne* (Paris: Klincksick, 2003); and, on some newly acquired material, see Alain Legros, "Buchanan et Cicéron chez Montaigne. Deux sentences inédites de sa 'librairie,'" in *Montaigne Studies/Montaigne écrivain* 26 (2014): 171–175. See also Barbara Pistilli, Marco Sgattoni, *La biblioteca di Montaigne,* foreword by Nicola Panichi (Pisa: Edizioni della Normale, 2014); N. Panichi,

"La Librairie," in *'Ecce homo.' Studi su Montaigne* (Pisa: Edizioni della Normale, 2017), 267–289.

2. Jean Starobinski, *Montaigne in Motion*, 7.

3. "Cum mutui amoris gratique animi sui nec immemoris singulare aliquod extare cuperet monumentum quando id facere significanter potuit eruditam hanc et praecipuam suppellectilem suas delicias consecravit" (in Montaigne, *Les Essais,* 1316).

4. See ibid., 1894; and J. Céard, "Montaigne et l'Ecclesiaste. Recherches sur quelques sentences de la 'librairie,'" in *Bibliothèque d'Humanisme et Renaissance* 33 (1971): 367–374, R. Ragghianti, "Montaigne lecteur sceptique de l' 'Ecclesiaste,'" *Montaigne Studies, Montaigne et les philosophes* 21 (2009): 137–154.

5. "Cognoscendi studium homini dedit Deus eius torquendi gratia." See A. Torno, "Presentazione," in M. de Montaigne, *La torre di Montaigne. Le sentenze iscritte sulle travi della biblioteca* (Milano: La Vita Felice, 2013), 13. The inscription echoes Ecclesiastes 1 (I, 13), which, however, is less violent: "Et proposui in animo meo quaerere et investigare sapienter de omnibus, quae sunt sub sole. Hanc occupationem pessimam dedit Deus filiis hominum, ut occuparentur in ea." There would appear to be, on Montaigne's part, a contamination with a passage from Eccles. III, 10; see Legros, *Essais sur poutres,* 283–284.

6. A. Torno, "Presentazione," 6–7.

7. Torno comments, "Like a sharp awl, his [Sextus Empiricus's] words carve the philosophy beloved by Montaigne: 'I suspend,' 'I cannot understand,' and similar phrases" (ibid., 7).

8. Michel de Montaigne, *The Complete Works of Montaigne: Essays, Travel Journals, Letters* (henceforth *CWM,* followed by book: chapter numbers and page number), trans. Donald M. Frame (Stanford, CA: Stanford University Press, [1948] 1957), I: 26, 115. See also Michel de Montaigne, *Saggi,* ed. F. Garavini, A. Tournon (Milano: Bompiani, 2012). The first two books of the *Essays* were published in 1580 and reprinted, with some additions, in 1582. The year 1588 saw the publication of an edition that included Book III and numerous additions. In the following years, Montaigne filled the margins with corrections and additions, with the aim of preparing a new edition; this exemplar is in the municipal library of Bordeaux.

9. See Alain Legros, *Essais sur poutres,* 105–118.

10. *CWM,* III: 3, 629.

11. Alain Legros, in his introduction to *Essais sur poutres,* cites Erasmus's *The Godly Feast,* in addition to *De pueris statim ac liberaliter instituendis* and *De ratione studii.*

12. Erasmus, *Collected Works,* vol. 1, *Colloquia,* trans. and ed. Craig R. Thompson (Toronto: University of Toronto Press, 1997), 178.

13. Jean Starobinski, *Montaigne in Motion,* x.

14. On the different way in which ancient texts feature in the various editions of the *Essays,* see Fausta Garavini, "La 'formula' di Montaigne," in *Itinerari a Montaigne* (Firenze: Sansoni, 1983), 3–33.

15. See Jean Starobinski, *Montaigne in Motion*, ch. 3, "The Relation to Others," 89–137.

16. The phrase is Starobinski's: *Montaigne en mouvement.*

17. *CWM,* I: 25, 97–98.

18. Ibid., 97, 100.

19. Plutarch, *Moralia, Quomodo quis suos in virtute sentiat profectus,* VIII, 80 A, which quotes the *Iliad,* IX, 324.

20. *CWM,* I: 25, 100.

21. "On the Education of Children: To Madame Diane de Foix, Comtesse de Gurson," *CWM,* I: 26, 107.

22. Ibid.

23. Ibid., 115. A strong polemic against education and more generally against contemporary customs is clearly perceivable in such positions. On the ethical value of the *Essays,* and in particular on their firm condemnation of the cruelty of the customs of contemporary aristocracy and of the wars of religion, see David Quint, *Montaigne and the Quality of Mercy: Ethical and Political Themes in the "Essais"* (Princeton, NJ: Princeton University Press, 1998).

24. *CWM,* I: 26, 115.

25. An elegant analysis of Montaigne's relationship with the great authors of the past may be found in Terence Cave, *The Cornucopian Text: Problems of Writing in the French Renaissance* (Oxford, UK: Clarendon Press, 1979), 271–321.

26. *CWM,* III: 5, 666.

27. Ibid., 667.

28. Fausta Garavini, "Prefazione. Il palazzo degli specchi," in Montaigne, *Saggi,* x. On Montaigne's complex relationship with memory, see Michel Beaujour, "Les 'Essais' de Montaigne," in *Miroirs d'encre. Rhétorique de l'autoportrait* (Paris: Seuil, 1980), 113–126.

29. *CWM,* II: 17, 495.

30. Ibid., 494.

31. Pierre Bayard, *How to Talk about Books You Haven't Read* (New York: Bloomsbury, 2007), 53, 55. I should like to thank Giorgio Pinotti for having pointed out this book to me.

32. Kathy Eden, "Reading and Writing Intimately in Montaigne's 'Essais,'" in *The Renaissance Rediscovery of Intimacy* (Chicago: University of Chicago Press, 2012), 96–118. The *Essays* themselves are presented as an alternative to letter writing, as their ideal addressee had died: "On the subject of letter writing, I want to say this: that it is a kind of work in which my friends think I have some ability. And I would have preferred to adopt this form to publish my sallies, if I had had someone to talk to. I needed what once I had, a certain relationship to lead me on, sustain me, and raise me up" (*CWM,* I: 40, 2).

33. *CWM,* I: 40, 2.

34. Ibid.

35. On the impact on Montaigne of the news that reached him on the way of life of the people of the New World, it is sufficient to quote the famous chapter "On Cannibals" (I: 31); see also the issue of *Montaigne Studies* 22 (2010): "Montaigne et le Nouveau Monde."

36. *CWM*, I: 40, 2.

37. Terence Cave highlights the tension between the two models (the book and the portrait): "The writer reflects on writing, it seems, in order better to reflect the total self; the book of *essais* separates itself like a mirror so that it may represent a living being. Yet, on the other hand, this duality is unstable because it can never be fully resolved either in unity or in antithesis; also because it is generated wholly by the writing process itself' (*The Cornucopian Text*, 273). See also Nicola Panichi, "Il libro fatto uomo. Passando per Erasmo," in *I vincoli del disinganno. Per una nuova interpretazione di Montaigne* (Firenze: Olschki, 2004), 301–322.

38. Lucan, *Pharsalia*, IV, 704.

39. *CWM*, I: 8, 21. See Fausta Garavini, *Mostri e chimere. Montaigne, il testo, il fantasma* (Bologna: Il Mulino, 1991).

40. *CWM*, I: 26, 108–109.

41. In a chapter from Book III, datable therefore to 1588, Montaigne (who was then fifty-five years old) sees death in the distance between how he looked then and his youthful portraits: "Death mingles and fuses with our life throughout. Decline anticipates death's hour and intrudes even into the course of our progress. I have portraits of myself at twenty-five and thirty-five; I compare them with one of the present: how irrevocably it is no longer myself! How much farther is my present picture from that of my death!" (*CWM*, III: 13, 848).

42. *CWM*, III: 2, 610–611.

43. Ibid., 611–612.

44. *CWM*, III: 5, 677.

45. Ibid., 644.

46. *CWM*, I: 24, 93.

47. See Michel Charles, "Épilogue. Sur une phrase de Montaigne," in *Rhétorique de la lecture* (Paris: Seuil, 1977), 289–298, connecting the "sidelong glance" (for which, see following note) to anamorphosis.

48. *CWM*, III: 9, 761.

49. *CWM*, I: 40, 184–185.

50. *CWM*, I: 28, 135. See Karlheinz Stierle, "Le cadre vide. Montaigne peintre," in *La conscience de soi de la poésie*, ed. Yves Bonnefoy (Paris: Seuil, 2008), 45–56.

51. Fausta Garavini, "Postilla," in Montaigne, *Saggi*, 2331–2332.

52. See also, for the further bibliography it contains, Renzo Ragghianti, *Rétablir un texte. Le 'Discours de la servitude volontaire' d'Étienne de la Boétie* (Firenze: Olschki, 2010).

53. *CWM*, I: 29, 145.

54. It is starting from this passage that Michel Butor has put forward his hypothesis on the structure of the *Essays*. Michel Butor, *Essais sur Les Essais* (Paris: Gallimard, 1988).

55. *CWM*, II: 6, 273.

56. Ibid., 274.

57. Antoine Compagnon connects these statements to the theme of Montaigne's lack of a male heir who might continue his line of descent; the book thus becomes a substitute for the missing son. The "production ouvragère," which had earlier been negated to the aereal body of the voice, therefore, "est ici pleinement reconnue dans l'engagement à l'écriture, étude, ouvrage et métier, en revanche de la langue et de la fantaisie, de la voix." Compagnon, *Nous, Michel de Montaigne* (Paris: Éditions du Seuil, 1980), 228. By the same author, see also *A Summer with Montaigne* (New York: Europa Editions 2019).

58. *CWM*, II: 18, 503.

59. Ibid.

60. Ibid.

61. Ibid., 504.

62. *CWM*, III: 3, 628.

63. *CWM*, III: 9, 736.

64. Ibid., 749–50. See Eden, "Reading and Writing Intimately in Montaigne's 'Essais,'" 112; Terence Cave, "Problems of Reading in the 'Essais,'" in *Montaigne: Essays in Memory of Richard Sayce*, ed. I. D. McFarlane, I. Maclean (Oxford, UK: Clarendon Press, 1982), 133–166, 155–156, 159–160.

7. Tasso and the Dangers of Reading

1. Torquato Tasso, *Il Malpiglio secondo overo del fuggir la moltitudine*, written in 1585, first published in 1666. The text I am using is in Torquato Tasso, *Dialoghi*, ed. G. Baffetti, introduction by E. Raimondi (Milano: Rizzoli, 1998), vol. 2, 623–663. All translations from *Dialoghi* are by SG.

2. In 1584, he founded the Accademia degli Oscuri in Lucca (from which the Accademia Lucchese di Scienze, Lettere ed Arti derives), taking inspiration from the Accademia degli Intronati di Siena; see Marcello Marcucci, "Accademia Lucchese di Scienze Lettere e Arti," in *Accademie e istituzioni culturali in Toscana*, ed. F. Adorno (Firenze: Olschki, 1988), 209.

3. Torquato Tasso, *Il Malpiglio secondo*, 623.

4. "I now dedicate to you this short dialogue, in which, copying Plato, who hid his own self under the name of the Athenian Guest, I introduce . . . myself as the Neapolitan Stranger" (Torquato Tasso, epistle dedicatory for *Il Conte overo de l'imprese*, in *Dialoghi*, vol. 2, 1111). See Ezio Raimondi, "La prigione della letteratura," in Torquato

Tasso, *Dialoghi,* 9–56: the character of the Neapolitan Stranger "becomes on almost every occasion the main character in a new dialogue setting. . . . The Stranger is a double of Tasso himself, who projects into the fiction the truth of his own history and at the same time succeeds in distancing himself from it, to the point that he is able to speak of himself in the third person almost as if he were a cool and punctilious witness" (22). "As for the mask, the body-double, as it were, of the Neapolitan Stranger, everything seems to indicate that it does not merely allude to a place of origin, a lost homeland, but that the phrase also signals an extraneousness, a condition defined by difference, a state of 'déracinée' wondering" (27). On the *Malpiglio secondo,* see 30–37.

5. Torquato Tasso, *Il Malpiglio secondo,* 623–624.

6. Galileo Galilei, "Considerazioni al Tasso," in *Scritti letterari,* ed. A. Chiari (Firenze: Le Monnier, 1943), 96: "When I consider the knights with their actions and the adventures that befall them, as well as all the other fables in this poem, it seems almost as if I am entering the study of some little man with a taste for the bizarre, who has delighted in decorating it with objects that have something strange about them, either because they are old or rare or for some other reason, but are, in fact, nothing but bric-a-brac" (translation SG). The development of the dialogue shows how such order and such an ideal of unitary recomposition are but fragile, ever on the brink of disgregation. Giovanna Scianatico looks at this idea from a different perspective in "Dallo studio di Giovanlorenzo Malpiglio," in *Studi in onore di Bortolo Tommaso Sozzi* (Bergamo: Centro di studi Tassiani, 1991), 59–70; Matteo Residori, "'Del fuggir la moltitudine.' Néoplatonisme et scepticisme dans le 'Malpiglio secondo' du Tasse," *Italique* 5 (2002): 95–105; Massimo Rossi, "Lontano dal frastuono della solitudine. Il 'Malpiglio secondo,'" in *'Io come filosofo era stato dubbio.' La retorica dei 'Dialoghi' di Tasso* (Bologna: Il Mulino, 2007), 95–135. On the "studio" and the library in Tasso's ouvre, see Guido Baldassarri, "La prosa del Tasso e l'universo del sapere," in *Torquato Tasso e la cultura estense,* ed. G. Venturi (Firenze: Olschki, 1999), 361–409 (361–366).

7. Torquato Tasso, *Il Malpiglio secondo,* 624.

8. The elder Scipio Africanus was fond of saying "numquam se minus otiosum esse quam cum otiosus, nec minus solus, quam cum solus esset" (Cicero, *De officiis,* III, 1, 1).

9. Torquato Tasso, *Il Malpiglio secondo,* 624–625.

10. On the role that Tasso believed should be assigned to the imagination, see Antonio Corsaro, "Il pensiero incredulo," in *Percorsi dell'incredulità. Religione, amore, natura nel primo Tasso* (Roma: Salerno, 2003), 49–96.

11. Torquato Tasso, *Il Malpiglio secondo,* 626.

12. Ibid., 627.

13. Ibid., 629.

14. As Matteo Residori ("Del fuggir la moltitudine") has shown, Tasso picks up, and occasionally translates, passages from Proclus's commentary on Plato's *Life of Alcibiades,* which was included in the collection of Neoplatonic writings published by Aldo Manuzio in 1497. The commentary sets out the four necessary steps to escape

the press of inner multitudes: the multitude of affections, of emotions, of the senses, of the imagination, and of opinions.

15. Torquato Tasso, *Il Malpiglio secondo*, 663.

16. The reference is to the closing lines of the *Enneads* by Plotinus: "This is the life of gods and of the godlike and blessed among men, liberation from the alien that besets us here, a life taking no pleasure in the things of the earth, the passing of solitary to solitary" (translation SG). See Massimo Rossi, "Lontano dal frastuono della solitudine,'" 133–135.

17. Torquato Tasso, *Il Malpiglio secondo*, 663.

18. Ibid.

19. Baldassare Castiglione, *The Book of the Courtier*, trans. and introduction by George Bull (London: Penguin, 2004), 32; Torquato Tasso, *Il Malpiglio overo de la corte*, in *Dialoghi*, vol. 2, 599–618 (613).

20. Torquato Tasso, *Il Malpiglio overo de la corte*, 610.

21. Torquato Tasso, *Le lettere di Torquato Tasso*, ed. Cesare Guasti (Firenze: Le Monnier, 1854), vol. 2, no. 341 (to Don Angelo Grillo), 22 February 1585, 327.

22. Torquato Tasso, *Le lettere*, vol. 2, 1854, p. 475.

23. Ibid., 479–480.

24. Torquato Tasso, *Rime*, ed. B. Basile (Roma: Salerno, 1994), vol. 1, part 3, no. 871, 865.

25. Ezio Raimondi, "La prigione della letteratura," 32.

26. Torquato Tasso, *Le lettere*, vol. 4, 1854, no. 937, 20–22 (21–22).

27. Torquato Tasso, *Le lettere*, vol. 5, 1855, no. 1348, 61–63 (62).

28. Torquato Tasso, *Il Cataneo overo de le conclusioni amorose*, in *Dialoghi*, vol. 2, 861–899 (865).

29. See Giovanni Boccaccio, *Decameron*, ed. V. Branca (Milano: Mondadori, 1985), III, vii, 275: Tedaldo degli Elisei, an unrequited lover, "entrò in fiera malinconia e ispiacevole."

30. Torquato Tasso, *Costante, overo de la clemenza*, in *Dialoghi*, vol. 2, 827–856 (829–830).

31. "Sempre è infinita la maninconia che mi tormenta"; Torquato Tasso, *Le lettere*, vol. 2, 1854, no. 122, 6. See Bruno Basile, "Poëta melancholicus," in *Poëta melancholicus. Tradizione classica e follia nell'ultimo Tasso* (Pisa: Pacini, 1984), 11–64.

32. Michel de Montaigne, *The Complete Works of Montaigne: Essays, Travel Journals, Letters*, trans. Donald M. Frame (Stanford, CA: Stanford University Press, [1948] 1957), Book II, chapter 12, 363.

33. Torquato Tasso, *Il Cataneo overo de gli idoli*, in *Dialoghi*, vol. 2, 747–781 (772, 773).

34. Ibid., 773, 774.

35. San Girolamo, "Letter XXI, 13," in *Le Lettere*, ed. S. Cola (Roma: Città Nuova editrice, 1996), vol. 1, 163–164, quoted in Tiziana Plebani, *Il "genere" dei libri. Storie*

e rappresentazioni della lettura al femminile e al maschile tra Medioevo e età moderna (Milano: Franco Angeli, 2001), 73; translation SG.

Epilogue

1. John Ruskin, *Sesame and Lilies: Three Lectures by John Ruskin* (London: Smith, Elder, 1871), 8–9. Marcel Proust's translation of Ruskin, which will be the subject of this epilogue, is *Sésame et les Lys précédé de Sur la lecture,* introduction by Antoine Compagnon (Bruxelles: Éditions Complexe, 1987) (henceforth *SL*): "Il y a une société qui nous est continuellement ouverte, de gens qui nous parleraient aussi longtemps que nous le souhaiterions, quels que soient notre rang et notre métier; nous parleraient dans les termes les meilleurs qu'ils puissent choisir, et des choses les plus proches de leur coeur. Et cette société, parce qu'elle est si nombreuse et si douce et que nous pouvons la faire attendre près de nous toute une journée (rois et hommes d'État attendant patiemment non pour accorder une audience, mai pour l'obtenir) dans ces antichambres étroites et simplement meublées, les rayons de nos bibliothèques, nous ne tenons aucun compte d'eux; peut-être dans toute la journée 'écoutons-nous un seul mot de ce qu'elle aurait à nous dire!" (115–116).

2. Ruskin, *Sesame and Lilies,* 13–14. "Vous flattez- vous de garder quelque dignité et conscience de vos propres droits au respect, quand jouez des coudes avec la foule affairée et vulgaire, ici pour une "entrée" et là pour une audience, quand pendant tout ce temps-là cette cour éternelle vous est ouverte où vous trouveriez une compagnie vaste comme le monde, nombreuse comme ses jours, la puissante, la choisie, de tous les lieux et de tous les temps. Dans celle-là vous pouvez toujours pénétrer, vous y choisirez vos amitiés, votre place, selon qu'il vous plaira; de celle-là, une fois que vous y avez pénétré, vous ne pouvez jamais être rejété que par votre propre faute; là, par la noblesse de vos fréquentations, sera mise à une épreuve certaine votre noblesse véritable, et les motifs qui vous poussent à lutter pour prendre une place élévée dans la société des vivants, verront toute la vérité et la sincérité qui est en eux mésurée par la place que vous désirez occuper dans la société des morts. . . . Elle [cette cour] est ouverte au travail et au mérite, mais à rien d'autre. Aucune richesse ne corrompra, aucun nom n'intimidera, aucun artifice ne trompera les gardiens de ces portes Elyséennes" (*SL,* 125–132).

3. Ruskin, *Sesame and Lilies,* 37. "Nous recherchons donc cette grande assemblée des morts, non pas seulement pour apprendre d'eux ce qui est vrai, mais surtout pour sentir avec eux ce qui est juste" (*SL,* 178).

4. Ruskin, *Sesame and Lilies,* 67. "Que nous conduisions nos paysans à l'exercice du livrea au lieu de l'exercice de la baïonnette! Que nos recrutions, instrisions, entretenions en leur assurant leur solde, sous un haut commandement capable, des armées de penseurs, au lieu d'armées de meurtriers!" (*SL,* 233).

5. Ruskin, *Sesame and Lilies,* 69. "Pain fait avec cette vieille graine arabe magique, le Sésame, qui ouvre les portes;—les portes non des trésors des voleurs, mais des trésors des Rois" (*SL,* 238–239).

6. See Donata Feroldi, "Proust e la traduzione," in Marcel Proust, *Il piacere della lettura,* foreword by E. Trevi (Milano: Feltrinelli, 2016), 77–83.

7. Antoine Compagnon, introduction to *SL,* 9–24 (17).

8. Marcel Proust, *Sesame and Lilies: Proust by Way of Ruskin* (henceforth *PR*), trans. R. A. Goodlake Lowen (Bell & Clews, 2014), 128. "Par là ces quelques pages où il n'est guère question de Ruskin constituent cependant, si l'on veut, une sorte de critique indirecte de sa doctrine. En exposant mes idées, je me trouve involontairement les opposer d'avance aux siennes" (*SL,* 37).

9. *PR,* 135n31; *SL,* 112n10.

10. *PR,* 9. "Et rien que pour répondre: 'Non, merci bien,' il fallait arrêter net et ramener de loin sa voix qui, en dedans des lèvres, répétait sans bruit, en courant, tous les mots quel es yeux avaient lus" (*SL,* 41).

11. *PR,* 17. "Puis la dernière page était lue, le livre était fini. Il fallait arrêter la course éperdue des yeux et de la voix qui suivait sans bruit, s'arrêtant seulement pour reprendre haleine, dans un soupir profond" (*SL,* 55).

12. *PR,* 138. "Notre mode de communication avec les personnes implique une déperdition des forces actives de l'âme que concentre et exalte au contraire ce merveilleux miracle de la lecture qui est la communication au sein de la solitude" (*SL,* 113n10).

13. *PR,* 138. "On est cet autre et pourtant on ne fait que développer son moi avec plus de variété que si on pensait seul, on est poussé par autrui sur ses propres voies"; "le choc spirituel est affaibli, l'inspiration, la pensée profonde, impossibile" (*SL,* 114).

14. *PR,* 138. "La valeur des choses écoutés ou lues étant de moindre importance que l'état spirituel qu'elles peuvent créer en nous et qui ne peut être profond que dans cette solitude peuplée qu'est la lecture" (*SL,* 115).

15. *PR,* 20. "La lecture de tous les bons livres est comme une conversation avec les plus honnêtes gens des siècles passés qui en ont été les auteurs"; "c'est elle en réalité qu'on retrouve partout dans sa conférence, enveloppée seulement dans un or apollinien où fondent des brumes anglaises, pareil à celui dont la gloire illumine les paysages de son peintre préféré" (*SL,* 60–61). The quotation from Descartes is from *Discours de la méthode,* I, 6.

16. *PR,* 21. "C'est-à-dire en continuant à jouir de la puissance intellectuelle qu'on a dans la solitude et que la conversation dissipe immédiatement, en continuant à pouvoir être inspiré, à rester en plein travail fécond de l'esprit sur lui- même" (*SL,* 62).

17. *PR,* 26–27. "Tant que la lecture est pour nous l'initiatrice dont les clefs magiques nous ouvrent au fond de nous-mêmes la porte des demeures où nous n'aurions pas su pénétrer, son rôle dans notre vie est salutaire. Il devient dangereux au contraire quand, au lieu de nous éveiller à la vie personnelle de l'esprit, la lecture tend à se substituer

à elle, quand la vérité ne nous apparaît plus comme un idéal que nous ne pouvons réaliser que par le progrès intime de notre pensée et par l'effort de notre coeur, mais comme une chose matérielle, déposée entre les feuillets des livres" (*SL,* 73).

18. Sainte-Beuve is, now overtly now implicitly, among his polemical targets; indeed, in *Contre Sainte Beuve,* on which Proust was working a few years later, in 1908, some of the themes that we have examined, such as a certain disregard for conversation, return: "In actual fact what one gives to the public is what one has written when alone, for oneself. . . . What one gives to sociability, that is to conversation . . . is the work of a far more external self, not of the deep self which is only to be found by disregarding other people, the self that has been waiting while one was with others, which one feels clearly to be the only real self, for which alone artists end by living like a god whom they leave less and less and to whom they have sacrificed a life that serves only to do him honour." Marcel Proust, *Against Sainte-Beuve and Other Essays,* trans. and introduction and notes by John Sturrock (London: Penguin, 1998), 15.

19. *PR,* 148n57. "A si bien et si souvent montré que l'artiste, dans ce qu'il écrit ou dans ce qu'il peint, révèle infailliblement ses faiblesses, ses affectations, ses défauts (et en effet l'oeuvre d'art n'est-elle pas pour le rythme caché—d'autant plus vital que nous ne le percevons pas nous-mêmes- de notre âme, semblable à ces tracés sphygmographiques où s'inscrivent automatiquement les pulsations de notre sang?)" (*SL,* 146n35).

20. Emanuele Trevi, *"Il nostro cuore cambia." Proust e le rivelazioni della lettura,* in Proust, *Il piacere della lettura,* 8.

21. *PR,* 31–32. "Sans doute, l'amitié, l'amitié qui a égard aux individus, est une chose frivole, et la lecture est une amitité. Mais du moins c'est une amitié sincère, et le fait qu'elle s'adresse à un mort, à un absent, lui donne quelque chose de désintéressé, de presque touchant. C'est de plus une amitié débarassée de tout ce qui fait la laideur des autres. Comme nous ne nous sommes tous, nous les vivants, que des morts qui ne sont pas encore entrés en fonctions, toutes ces politesses, toutes ces salutations dans le vestibule que nous appelons déférence, gratitude, dévouement et où nous mêlons tant de mensonges, sont stériles et fatigantes. . . . Dans la lecture, l'amitié est soudain ramenée à sa pureté première. Avec les livres, pas d'amabilité. Ces amis-là, si nous passons la soirée avec eux, c'est vraiment que nous en avons envie. Eux, du moins, nous ne les quittons souvent qu'à regret. . . . Toutes ces agitations de l'amitié expirent au seuil de cette amitié pure et calme qu'est la lecture. Pas de déférence non plus: nous ne rions de ce que dit Molière que dans la mesure exacte où nous le trouvons drôle . . . et quand nous avons décidément assez d'être avec lui, nous le remettons à sa place aussi brusquement que s'il n'avait ni génie ni célébrité" (*SL,* 82–83).

22. *PR,* 32–33. "L'atmosphère de cette pure amitié est le silence, plus pur que la parole. Car nous parlons pour les autres, mais nous nous taisons pour nous -mêmes. Aussi le silence ne porte pas, comme la parole, la trace de nos défauts, de nos grimaces.

Il est pur, il est vraiment une atmosphère. Entre la pensée de l'auteur et la nôtre il n'interpose pas ces éléments irréductibles, réfractaires à la pensée, de nos égoïsmes différents. Le langage même du livre est pur (si le livre mérite ce nom), rendu transparent par la pensée de l'auteur qui en a retiré tout ce qui n'était pas elle-même jusqu'à le rendre son image fidèle; chaque phrase, au fond, ressemblant aux autres, car toutes sont dites par l'inflexion unique d'une personnalité; de là une sorte di continuité, que les rapports de la vie et ce qu'il mêlent à la pensée d'éléments qui lui sont étrangers excluent et qui permet très vite de suivre la ligne même de la pensée de l'auteur, les traits de sa physionomie qui se reflètent dans ce calme miroir" (*SL,* 84).

23. *PR,* 34. "Si les mots sont choisis, non par notre pensée selon les affinités de son essence, mais par notre désir de nous peindre, il représente ce désir et ne nous représente pas. . . . De sorte que quand un livre n'est pas le miroir d'une individualité puissante, il est encore le miroir des défauts curieux de l'esprit" (*SL,* 86).

Index

Aeneas, 43, 45
Aesculapius, 38, 40, 41, 48–52, 60, 61
Aesop, 156, 157
Agesilaus, 65
Alberti, Leon Battista, 57, 59, 60, 75, 181
Albertus Magnus, Saint, 83, 87, 88, 93, 96
Alexander VII, 80
Alexander the Great, 176
Alfonso d'Este, 185
Al-Jâdiz Habu Hayyan, 1
Ambrose, Saint, 57, 69, 83, 87, 89, 96, 111
Ammanatini, Manetto (il Grasso), 154
Ammianus Marcellinus, 151
Amphytrion, 154
Androgeos, 50
Antony, Marc, 52
Apelles, 132, 149, 150
Apollo, 136
Apuleius, 58, 134, 137
Ariosto, Ludovico, 124, 125
Aristotle, 56, 90, 96, 101–104, 109, 157
Atticus Titus Pomponius, 19, 20, 68
Augustine Aurelius, Saint, 18, 20, 57, 83, 87, 88, 99
Augustus Gaius Iulius Caesar Ottavianus, 70, 176
Averroes, 108

Babboni, Irene, 12
Babeuf, François Noël, 7
Bacchae, 43
Baldi, Camillo, 66
Barbaro, Daniele, 124
Barbaro, Ermolao, 60
Barbaro, Francesco, 48, 49
Barberini, Antonio, 82
Baricci, Federico, 147
Bartolo da Sassoferrato, 89, 96, 101, 103
Battiferri, Laura, 3, 5

Bausi, Francesco, 50
Bayard, Pierre, 169
Beatrice, 62, 63
Beckett, Samuel, 128
Bembo, Pietro, 60, 62, 63, 127, 130–132
Benassi, Alessandro, 12
Benjamin, Walter, 6
Berenson, Bernard, 11
Bernardine da Siena, Saint, 57
Berruguete, Pedro, 75, 76, 86, 88–90, 92, 93, 95, 98–100, 102, 105–107, 109, 111
Bessarion, 83, 89, 96, 112, 113
Bettini, Maurizio, 69
Birria, 154
Boccaccio, Giovanni, 5, 13, 15, 17, 19, 33, 35–42, 49, 106, 130, 154
Boccaccio, Iacopo, 37
Bodley, Thomas, 9, 10, 78
Boethius Anicius Manlius Torquatus Severinus, 17, 55, 56, 92, 96
Bollioud-Mermet, Louis, 6
Borsselen, Anna van, 139
Bovary, Emma, 192
Bracciolini, Poggio, 43–49, 52–54, 71, 72, 127
Brancaccio, Giuliano, 158
Bronzino, Agnolo Tori, 3, 5
Brunelleschi, Filippo, 154
Bruni, Leonardo, 46, 47
Brutus Marcus Iunius, 20, 176
Buonarroti, Filippo, 7
Butades, 64

Caesar Iulius, 147, 176
Caloiro, Tommaso, 33
Calvino, Italo, 128
Camillo Giulio, 123, 132, 133, 142, 143, 145
Camillus Marcus Furius, 48

Index

Campbell, Stephen J., 73
Canettti, Elias, 10
Capra, Enrico, 69
Casavecchia, Filippo, 157
Castiglione, Baldassarre, 61, 74, 183
Catiline Lucius Sergius, 64
Cato Marcus, 59, 65, 68, 176
Cattaneo, Maurizio, 184, 186, 187, 190
Charles IV, 70
Cheles, Luciano, 84
Chines, Loredana, 24
Christina of Sweden, 126
Cicero Marcus Tullius, 16–21, 28, 38, 52, 54, 56, 59, 64, 65, 68, 81, 84, 88, 94, 96, 101, 110, 114–116, 129–131, 134–138, 181
Cicero Marcus Tullius (son), 21
Cicero Quintus Tullius, 21
Cleanthes, 65
Colonna, Giacomo, 22, 26, 29
Colonna, Giovanni, 29
Compagnon, Antoine, 196
Corno, Donato del, 147
Correggio, Azzo da, 30
Cortese, Paolo, 130
Cosimo de' Medici, 50
Costante, Antonino, 188
Crassus Lucius Licinius, 136
Croesus, 50
Curtius, Ernst Robert, 16

D'Abanus Petrus, 91, 96, 107
Daedalus, 40, 41
Danaïds, 166
Dante Alighieri, 2, 3, 41, 56, 83, 91, 100, 109, 112, 144, 149, 153, 154
Dantés, Edmond, 41
Darthé, Augustin, 7
Decembrio, Angelo Camillo, 71
Decembrio, Pier Candido, 53
Deiphobus, 43, 48, 49
De Lignamine, Francesco, 54
Della Seta, Lombardo, 26, 70, 71
Descartes, René, 197
Dolet, Étienne, 137, 138
Donato, Maria Monica, 69
Doni, Anton Francesco, 123
Donnino da Parma, 39
Duns Scoto, 83, 91, 92, 96, 110
Dürer, Albrecht, 116, 117

Eden, Kathy H., 169
Epicurus, 21
Erasmus Desiderius Roterodamus, 5, 73, 113–120, 122, 127, 129, 131, 132, 135–142, 145, 164, 171, 178
Erodianus, 151
Étienne de la Boétie, 162, 174
Euclid, 85, 91, 96, 105
Eusebius, 73, 164

Farnese, Alessandro, 123
Federico da Montefeltro, 5, 26, 47, 51, 74–80, 82, 83, 91, 93–97, 100–103, 108, 110, 112, 113
Ferroni, Giulio, 145
Ficino, Marsilio, 50, 51
Filarete, Antonio Averlino, 72, 73
Floriani, Piero, 21
Florus Lucius, 151
Foix-Candale, Charlotte Diane de, 167
Fonzio, Bartolomeo, 39, 49
Foxe, John, 46
Francesca da Rimini, 192
Francesco il Vecchio da Carrara, 70
Francis of Assisi, Saint, 19
Franco, Ernesto, 12
Froben, Johann, 121, 140
Fumaroli, Marc, 11, 71

Galilei, Galileo, 180
Garavini, Fausta, 168
Gardini, Nicola, 11, 38
Garin, Eugenio, 56
Gaurico, Pomponio, 60, 67
Geta, 154, 155
Ghirlandaio, Davide, 73
Ghirlandaio, Domenico, 73
Giamatti, A. Bartlett, 38, 43, 48
Gilles, Peter, 117–120, 127–132
Giovanni dell'Incisa, 15
Giovio, Paolo, 122–124, 132–134
Giuliano da Maiano (Giuliano di Leonardo d'Antonio), 81
Giuliano de' Medici, 151
Goethe, Johann Wolfgang, 66
Gonzaga, Francesco, 51
Grafton, Anthony T., 149
Gramont, Marguerite d'Aure, 175
Grasso. *See* Ammanatini, Manetto
Greenblatt, Stephen J., 45
Greene, Thomas M., 2
Greenup, Sylvia, 12
Gregory the Great, Saint, 57, 83, 84, 98, 111
Gruber, Thomas, 12
Guanto, Girolamo del, 147
Guarinus Veronensis, 43
Guidubaldo da Montefeltro, 75, 76

Hannibal, 147, 148
Hector, 45
Helen of Troy, 43, 114, 115, 136
Herennius Gaius, 21
Hippocrates, 91, 96, 98, 104, 107, 108
Hippolytus, 38, 40, 49, 50, 52, 61, 127, 184
Holbein Hans the Younger, 116
Homer, 21, 50, 67, 68, 81, 90, 98, 104, 111
Horace Flaccus Quintus, 17, 61, 67, 136, 174
Hortensius Ortalus Quintus, 21
Hugh IV King of Cyprus, 39
Hustvedt, Siri, 11

Index

Inghirami, Tommaso, 60
Inglese, Giorgio, 147, 167
Ixion, 114, 136

Jacobi, Friedrich Heinrich, 66
Jardine, Lisa, 116
Jeanneret, Michel, 141
Jerome, Saint, 57, 71, 83, 88, 90, 96, 111, 119, 191
Jerome of Prague (Jeronym Prazsky), 45, 46, 47
John XXIII, Antipope, 43
Jove, 154
Juno, 115
Justus van Ghent (Joos van Wassenhove), 75, 76, 84–111
Juvenal Decimus Iunius, 127

Kempen, Ludwig van, 16
Kien, Peter, 10

Laelius, 65
Lampridius Aelius, 151
Landriani, Gerardo, 53
Lapo da Castiglionchio the Elder, 20, 21, 41
Laura, 181, 189
Laurana, Luciano, 74
Lavater, Johann Kaspar, 66
Legros, Alain, 164
Leo X, 61, 130, 140
Leonzio, Pilato, 21
Leto, Pomponio, 60
Licht, Mike, 3
Licino, Giovan Battista, 186
Lionello d'Este, 57, 71
Lorenzo de' Medici, 49, 54, 72
Lucan Marcus Annaeus, 134, 170
Lucceius Lucius, 64
Lucian, 58, 119, 137
Lucilius, 66, 132
Lucretius Titus Caro, 155, 156, 163

Machiavelli, Niccolò, 5, 49, 59, 143–160, 183
Malpiglio, Giovanlorenzo, 179, 180, 182
Malpiglio, Vincenzo, 179, 180, 183, 187, 189, 190
Manguel, Alberto, 6, 9
Mantegna, Andrea, 90
Marcolini, Francesco, 13
Maréchal, Sylvain, 7
Mari, Michele, 145
Marrione, 146
Martial Marcus Valerius, 58
Matsys, Quentin, 116–119
Mattia Corvino (Matyas Hunyad), 51
Mazarin, Giulio Raimondo, 126
Mc Laughlin, Martin, 11, 58, 59
Menander, 163
Menelaus, 43
Merula, Giorgio, 52
Minos, 50
Molière (Jean Baptiste Poquelin *kwon as*), 199

Montaigne, Michel de, 5, 161–177, 179, 190
More, Thomas, 118, 119–121
Morelli, Giovanni di Paolo, 55, 56
Moro, Cristoforo, 113
Moses, 86, 97, 99

Najemy, John M., 147, 153, 154, 160
Napoleon III, 82
Naudé, Gabriel, 122, 126, 127
Nelli, Francesco, 27, 69
Neri, Morando, 18
Nero Claudio Caesar Augustus Germanicus, 28
Niccoli, Niccolò, 54, 72

Orpheus, 43, 49, 51, 52
Osiris, 38
Ossola, Carlo, 11
Ovid Naso Publius, 36, 149

Panzano, 150
Paris, 115, 136
Parmigianino (Francesco Mazzola), 188, 189
Patin, Guy, 127
Paul, Saint, 57, 118, 139, 141, 163
Payne, Alina, 11
Pericoli, Tullio, 128
Perna, Petrus, 124
Pertile, Lino, 11
Pesante, Sandra, 11
Petoletti, Marco, 210
Petrarch, Francis, 1–3, 5, 11, 13–23, 25–33, 37, 41, 43, 45, 49, 56, 59, 66, 68–71, 83, 92, 99, 112, 127, 129, 130, 147, 149, 152, 154, 163, 168, 181, 189, 191
Phidias, 16
Pico della Mirandola, Giovanfrancesco, 130, 131, 135
Pico della Mirandola, Giovanni, 11
Piero della Francesca, 75, 77
Pietro da Siena, 13, 37
Pinotti, Giorgio, 12
Pirckeimer, Willibald, 116
Pius II, 83, 85, 89
Plato, 8, 15, 51, 65, 86, 95, 98, 101, 103, 104, 109, 112, 131, 167, 187, 190, 197
Plautus Titus Maccius, 17, 58, 154
Pliny the Elder, 11, 64, 67, 68, 123, 134, 163
Plutarch, 151, 164, 166–168
Poliziano, Agnolo, 49–52, 130, 135
Pollio Caius Asinius, 68
Pompey Magnus Gnaeus, 147
Procopius, 151
Propertius Sextus Aurelius, 50
Proust, Marcel, 5, 193, 195–198
Ptolemy, 85, 95, 96, 105, 106

Querini, Vincenzo, 60
Quevedo, Francisco de, 161
Quint, David, 12
Quintilian Marcus Fabius, 41, 43–49, 57, 60, 134

Index

Rabelais, François, 127
Raimondi, Ezio, 155, 185
Ramusio, Giovanni Battista, 16
Raphael, Sanzio, 60, 61, 78
Ravasi, Gianfranco, 18
Richelieu, Armand-Jean Du Plessis de, 126
Romulus, 48, 50
Rossi, Pino de', 37
Rousseau, Jean-Jacques, 165
Ruskin, John, 5, 193–198

Sainte-Beuve, Charles Augustin, 127
Sallust Gaius Crispus, 151
Santi, Giovanni, 78
Schrader Laurentius, 82
Scipio Cornelius, 59, 181
Seneca Lucius Anneus, 11, 28, 32, 55, 65, 66, 88, 96, 99, 112, 132, 166
Sextus Empiricus, 163
Sforza, Battista, 75–78
Silk, Emily, 12
Silla Lucius Cornelius, 176
Sisyphus, 155
Sixtus IV, 73, 83, 86, 96, 112
Socrates, 16, 65
Solomon, 90, 96, 103
Solon, 68, 89, 96, 100, 102
Sophocles, 163
Sosia, 154
Spartianus Aelius, 151
Starobinski, Jean, 161, 165
Statius Publius Papinius, 134
Steiner, George, 9
Stimmer, Tobias, 124
Suetonius Tranquillus Gaius, 68, 151

Tasso, Torquato, 5, 79, 179–181, 183–191
Tebaldeo, Antonio, 60

Terence Publius, 58, 60
Thomas Aquinas, Saint, 83, 92, 96, 109, 110
Tibullus, 149
Tissoni Benvenuti, Antonia, 213
Titian Vecellio, 124
Tommaso da Messina. *See* Caloiro, Tommaso
Torno, Armando, 163
Torre, Andrea, 17, 19
Tosetti, Angelo, 70
Trask, Willard R., 20
Trevi, Emanuele, 198
Tulliola, 38
Turner, William, 197
Tylus, Jane, 12

Urban VIII, 82

Varro Marcus Terentius, 54, 68
Vecchi Galli, Paola, 20
Venus, 51, 159
Vespasiano da Bisticci, 50, 51, 75, 79, 94, 110
Vettori, Francesco, 49, 143, 145–160
Vigevani, Marco, 12
Virgil Maron Publius, 3, 17, 27, 43, 48, 49, 55, 56, 60, 61, 63, 81, 90, 96, 105, 111, 130, 134, 153, 168
Visconti, Giovanni, 69
Vitalis of Blois, 154
Vitelli, Alessandro, 191
Vittorino da Feltre, 91, 96, 106, 112, 113

Wolf, Teodoro, 3, 4
Woolf, Virginia, 8

Xenophon, 44, 65, 176

Zanobi da Strada, 24, 27
Zeno, 65
Zeuxis, 114, 116